Christian Attitudes to Marriage

Christian Attitudes to Marriage

*From Ancient Times
to the Third Millennium*

Peter Coleman

Edited by
Michael Langford

scm press

Scripture quotations are from the New Revised Standard
Version of the Bible, copyright 1989 by the Division of
Christian Education of the National Council of the Churches
in Christ in the USA. Used by permission.
All rights reserved.

British Library Cataloguing in Publication data

A catalogue record for this book is available
from the British Library

Extracts from *Marriage in the Early Church*,
edited by David G. Hunter © 1992, Augsburg Fortress,
are used by permission

0 334 02956 2

First published in 2004 by SCM Press
9–17 St Albans Place, London N1 0NX

www.scm-canterburypress.co.uk

SCM Press is a division of
SCM-Canterbury Press Ltd

Printed and bound in Great Britain by
Biddles Ltd, www.biddles.co.uk

Contents

Editor's Preface

Peter Everard Coleman was born in August 1928 and was killed in a tragic car accident on 27 December, 2001, at the age of 73. Originally he was set for a career in law, graduating with an LLB from King's College London and passing his final bar examinations as a member of the Middle Temple. However, at the end of his undergraduate courses he decided to seek entrance to the Anglican ministry. After postgraduate training at Westcott House, Cambridge, and ordination in 1955, he worked in a number of church positions, both pastoral and academic, finishing his full-time career as Bishop of Crediton, from 1984 to 1996. (Following an ancient tradition, clergy were not allowed actually to be called to the bar, so he took that formal step only in 1965, after the rules had been changed.)

This is not the place to detail the many personal and intellectual qualities that Bishop Coleman possessed – some of which were articulated in obituaries and funeral orations – but an indication of the breadth of his activities has relevance for this book because it helps to explain his grasp of the issues that relate to Christian marriage. In addition to his official, full-time appointments, he was at different times much involved in the work of the World Council of Churches. He was also an active member of General Synod; a fellow of the Woodard Corporation (and Provost of its Western Division – involving the governance of six schools); chairman of the British Trust for the Tantur Ecumenical Institute in Jerusalem; Anglican co-chairman in the official discussions on Anglican–Moravian Church relations; a full member of the 1988 Lambeth Conference; Religious Adviser to HTV Bristol for many years; and – as if these things were not enough – joint editor of *Theology* from 1982 to 1991, and from 1960 until his retirement a lecturer in Christian Ethics, first at King's College London and then at the Universities of Bristol and Exeter. In terms of background for a book on marriage, it is also worth noting that he was married for 41 years, and the father of four.

Bishop Coleman produced a number of useful books in which there was a rare combination of scholarship and practical wisdom. His publications include:

Experiments in Prayer, London: SCM Press, 1961

A Christian Approach to Television, London: Church Information Office, 1968

Christian Attitudes to Homosexuality, London: SPCK, 1980 (based on a 1976 M. Litt. thesis at Bristol University)

The Ordination of Women to the Priesthood, London: Church House Publishing, 1990 (A Digest of the Second Report by the House of Bishops. 70–80,000 copies were distributed)

Gay Christians, London: SCM Press, 1989

At the time of his death Bishop Coleman was in the process of finishing the book that follows. Eight chapters were virtually complete, although they needed some correcting and filling out of references, but much of the ninth and final chapter existed only in the form of notes and indications of the likely section headings. Some of the notes were substantial and have only needed slight reworking; some existed only in the form of enigmatic sentences, which I have had to try and fill out; and some consisted merely of headings, indicating topics to be included. At the request of Donata Coleman, and with the agreement of the SCM Press, I have edited the entire book for the press.

The reasons for the task being given to me are in part personal and in part a matter of our joint interests. Bishop Coleman and I had been close friends since January 1955 (when I joined him at Westcott House). I became godfather to his elder son, and while I taught in Canada he twice came to stay with me, and along with my wife and children I used to stay in his medieval house in Exeter and at his cottage in Somerset. Further, we had many long conversations on matters of mutual interest. We were both Anglican priests who shared pastoral and academic responsibilities. More particularly, we had a common interest in the interface between law, ethics and theology. He studied law and then theology, and kept up a life-long interest in their relationship, making important contributions in print. I was a pupil of H. L. A. Hart (Professor of Jurisprudence at Oxford), did my doctoral work on Grotius, and taught jurisprudence in a Philosophy Department in Canada. Our mutual interests in Christian ethics helped to strengthen our friendship over the years.

However, once into the task of editing this book I faced significant problems when it came to Chapter 9. In particular, I had to decide how far it was wise to write a complete and polished chapter, attempting to guess what Bishop Coleman's final product would have been. In the end I decided not to attempt such a task, in part because of what I conceive the purpose and value of this book to be. The achievement of an adequate understanding of Christian marriage is not a task that can ever be completed, once and for all – it is rather (like both philosophy and theology in general) an ongoing, eternal task, as one tries to understand certain eternal truths in the context of the shifting patterns of human life – with each generation needing to find new ways of articulating meaning. Congruently, near the end of his notes for Chapter 9, Bishop Coleman wrote: 'Individualism has a social cost, and the search is on to find an acceptable overview of morality, with a set of abiding values, to succeed older formulations of Natural Law, the Old Christian tradition, and Human Rights. For Christian marriage, is it perhaps a case of trying to put old wine in new bottles?'

The upshot is that this book is not seen by me, and I am sure it was not intended by Bishop Coleman, to be a definitive statement of a Christian doctrine of marriage. It is much more a contribution to 'work in progress'. Nevertheless, I think it may provide a significant contribution. One reason for this is because the contemporary issues outlined in the final chapter are placed in a more general context, historical and theological, going back to ancient Egypt and Sumeria, which informed discussion needs. Another reason is because Bishop Coleman identifies what are the central issues to be addressed in the development of a Christian philosophy of marriage. One of the most important of these is understanding the proper relation of church or canon law on marriage to civil law and civil custom. Thus, to ask a question that reflects two rather extreme positions: should the church accept the general, civil view of marriage, claiming that its ceremonies and teaching enrich a basic understanding of what marriage is about that is shared by most members of society; or does Christian teaching have something so distinctive to say about marriage that what 'marriage' means to the ordinary citizen is just not the same as what 'Christian marriage' means? Intimately related to these questions are issues relating to when, if ever, divorce, nullity and remarriage should be accepted by the church, and to what extent it should be actively involved in these matters.

Behind these questions lie others, concerning how the church should view sexual activity, both heterosexual and homosexual, that is outside traditional marriage relationships. This is one of many issues where there is considerable tension between those loosely called 'conservatives' and those called 'liberals' – not only within the Anglican Church, but throughout the religious world (with equivalent divisions within all the major religions).

Despite reservations concerning the words 'conservative' and 'liberal', putting the matter very crudely, conservatives wish to maintain the essential sinfulness of all sexual relationships outside marriage; liberals – while strongly condemning those relationships that are unloving or expoitative – tend to think that the rules that applied when most people got married shortly after puberty have to be rethought in line with biblical *principles* rather than absolute biblical *rules*.[1]

Given this usage, there is much to be said for the view that Christian ethics is a matter of discerning and applying principles rather than rules, and this conclusion may have many implications for Christian attitudes to sexual behaviour in general, and to the appropriate rules for marriage. The suggestion is that one should move away from a 'literalist' view in which the issues are to be settled by identifying absolute rules, either from Scripture (biblical, Qur'anic, or other) or from a Magisterium emanating from an authority that is not to be questioned. Instead one should seek to identify moral 'principles'. This, it should be stressed, is in no way a denial of either the rationality or the 'objectivity' of moral judgements, and I will close with a brief comment on these two matters.

In ethics, rationality involves many overlapping abilities, including the application of general rules to specific cases (casuistry), a search for consistency, and the ability to make appropriate distinctions. Among these abilities, and possibly foremost among them, is the ability to make 'judgements' – as when a judge balances different relevant principles in order to decide how long a prison sentence to give someone already found guilty of a criminal offence. Corrrespondingly, in the field of medical ethics, those seeking to decide how long to keep a neonate on life-support systems try to balance moral principles that are in tension (especially benevolence – seeking the best for the patient, and justice – seeking to be fair to others in need).

Such dilemmas, I suggest, are typical of many of the issues that face serious-minded people when they are in disagreement – and the fact that there is disagreement does not imply that there is no rationality involved, only that, as in all cases of judgement, even when there is agreement on what the relevant moral principles are, there may not be agreement on exactly how to balance them. Nevertheless, the rationality of the judgement lies in the fact that the range of reasonable decisions will be increasingly evident to those familiar with the principles and the issues.

With respect to 'moral objectivity' a similar point can be made. Moral objectivity does not have to entail that there is one and only one right answer to every moral issue. It does entail that intelligent people should (i) be able to identify certain moral principles that they agree to be important and relevant; (ii) that these shared moral principles rule out certain actions, x, y, z etc. as being morally wrong because they conflict with all the agreed principles; (iii) that when there is no precise agreement between the parties, because the balancing of the principles is not agreed, nevertheless, the possible lines of right action fall within the range a, b, c etc. The fact that x, y, z etc. are distinguished from a, b, c etc. distances this approach from what most people mean by 'moral relativism'.

One of the values of the Natural Law approach is that it allows for the kind of rationality and objectivity just described, without having to insist that people share the same religious or non-religious philosophy. There may well be some occasions when having a particular religious philosophy has a direct effect on the way the balancing of principles is made. Nevertheless, most of the time, and for most issues, one will expect convergence on moral issues, as suggested by St Paul in Romans 2. The Christian, Muslim, Jew, etc. may have different reasons for holding the shared moral principles than most secular thinkers, and may very likely see them as having a different, perhaps metaphysical status, but this does not prevent a rational discussion between religious and non-religious people on the implications of the moral principles that are shared. In the case of developing a philosophy of marriage, this suggests that there will be at least some overlap between what a Christian sees marriage to be all about and what civil society sees it to be.

Michael J. Langford

Note

1 The distinction between 'principles' and 'rules' is not always clear, and English
  language is not always consistent with respect to the matter. I have in mind the
  distinction made by Ronald Dworkin in his famous article 'Is Law a System of
  Rules?' (reprinted in *The Philosophy of Law*, ed. R. M. Dworkin, Oxford:
  Oxford University Press, 1977). Here the word 'rule' is used to apply to a
  precept that is alleged to have no exceptions, such as, 'In no circumstances may
  a deliberate lie be told'. They apply, says Dworkin, 'in an all-or-nothing
  fashion', while 'principle' is used for a precept that always 'carries weight', but
  which does not tell one exactly what to do. 'Rather, it states a reason that
  argues in one direction.'

I

Israel's Inheritance from its Near Eastern Neighbours

Introduction

For much of Christian history, it was assumed that the most reliable accounts of the origin of the world and of mankind's primeval history were to be found in the early chapters of Genesis. While ample information about the classical world was available from Greek and Roman literature, relatively little was known of the ancient and powerful Near Eastern states which surrounded Israel in the Fertile Crescent. The Old Testament authors depicted them as the neighbours from hell, pagan oppressors who threatened their security, destroyed their temple and took them into captivity. Nevertheless, trade and intermarriage meant that there was bound to be some intermingling, and God's people were themselves immigrants into Egypt and Canaan, so some impression of the laws and culture of these neighbours could be gleaned from the Old Testament. The references, however, are sparse and often derogatory. It was obvious from Genesis, however, that marriage was a universal custom, and all the Patriarchs were married as a matter of course. So what were the rules for marriage in the Near Eastern lands from which Abraham and his first descendants came, and did the early Israelites copy them, modify them or replace them with something different?

Answers to these questions began to appear in the sixteenth century onwards from merchants and explorers who travelled through the Near Eastern countries. Then, the Napoleonic conquest of Egypt at the end of the eighteenth century initiated an enormous enthusiasm for archaeology. At first, the search was on for Egyptian artefacts, destined for the museums of Europe, but interest gradually switched towards Mesopotamia, now Iraq, in the hope of discovering what remained of the oldest cities mentioned in the Bible, such as Ur,

Babylon and Nineveh. These sites began to yield data about the domestic lifestyles and marriage customs of prehistoric and ancient peoples. Archaeologists explored both the cultural and sociological aspects, while the anthropologists traced the stages in mankind's evolutionary development. The discovery of legal codes from the Mesopotamian city-states showed that there were quite detailed and systematic regulations about marriage in force when Terah and Abraham lived in Ur, some centuries before Moses led the Israelites out of Egypt. In fact, the Covenant Codes in Exodus and Deuteronomy contain rules about marriage that bear some obvious resemblance to those of their Near Eastern neighbours.[1] By comparing the sources it became clear that Mesopotamia provided much of the raw material for Israel's family law. Marital arrangements in Genesis reflected the common domestic pattern of Near Eastern life, but with a special emphasis. Israel's ancestors understood marriage as the God-given way of ensuring that their faith was passed on to the next generation and a trustworthy leadership provided for them, hence the emphasis on religious and ethnic genealogy.[2]

Neither the Pentateuch nor the ancient secular legal codes contain much information about family life and sexual relationships. On issues such as the meaning of love and gender equality that preoccupy us in the twenty-first century, these old records are almost silent; the ancient world had a different agenda in their system for arranging marriages. Men's work was defence and protection, women's work was reproduction and family rearing, and both worked together to provide for the family, but these normal roles were assumed, rather than described in these documents. Further, legal precedents only dealt with difficulties that needed resolving outside the normal arena of domestic life. Ordinary arrangements for getting married or divorced followed local custom, under the supervision of the patriarchal father of the extended family, or were referred to the elders of the local community who applied their own sanctions as needed. Our knowledge of those arrangements is scant, but the written marriage contracts from richer families are a useful supplementary source. These were drawn up between the parents of the couple before their betrothal. Originally simple, to ensure a dowry for a divorced woman, they became more complex in Hellenistic times and included prohibitions of behaviour likely to lead to divorce.

Primitive social organization

Archaeological evidence from many primitive settlements and communities shows ordered patterns of domestic and family life for several millennia before the Old Testament history of the people of Israel begins. There is a long-standing debate among scholars about the primacy of a monogamous system. Clearly this was a preferred choice in many primitive communities, while others were clearly polygamous, polyandrous, or matriarchal in structure. As the basic system of food supply changed from hunting and gathering to farming and simple craft work, the pattern of life became less mobile and provided the conditions for a more stable family life, including at least embryonic forms of marriage. By the time written records become available, from *c.* 3300 BC onwards, the institution of marriage has clearly become a basic element of human domestic life. A simple and often serial form of monogamy was the norm, but polygamy was acceptable for those who could afford it or, more often, used it for political or dynastic reasons.

Social life was conducted within a threefold structure. The primary unit was the household, an extended family of parents, grandparents and widows, with the eldest son and wife and their children. Unmarried adult siblings might be included. Households adjoined each other in the kinship group and together formed a village or clan community. The clans were linked by affiliation to their tribe. Marriages were arranged between families within the clan or tribe, strangers being excluded, and sexual activity between members of the household group were taboo. Incest was always condemned.

During the Bronze Age, *c.* 3000 BC onwards, new skills in agrarian management led to a gradual change in patterns of work. For example, in Mesopotamia (the land of the two rivers, Tigris and Euphrates), where fertility depended on regular river flooding rather than intermittent rain, the entrepreneurs developed better production methods. They grew richer and gained control of the labour force, while the women withdrew from the fields and became more confined to domestic and parental activities. The consequence for a society that was becoming increasingly urbanized was a sharper division of class and status, within which women and labourers were disadvantaged. Similarly, tribal wars and clan feuds provided a source of cheap labour for the victors as the captives became slaves. While the whole community benefited from the efficiency and wealth-producing capacity of better-used resources, the price was a dependency culture and, to modern eyes, some denial of basic human rights.[3]

Ancient Near Eastern law codes – general characteristics

The law codes of Mesopotamia and the Babylonian and Hittite Empires from pre-biblical times were royal decrees, laying down the basic principles local judges should observe in deciding difficult cases. They were often specific about fines and punishments, setting a common tariff to be applied throughout the kingdom. A final appeal for pardon could be made to the ruler. The codes have a common pattern and reflect the structural and class division of their time, but they were not merely a means of enforcing the cultural status quo. In limited ways they served to ameliorate its harshness by affording the *Untermenschen* some protection. They supported serial monogamy rather than polygamy, though rich men might have both chief and subsidiary wives, together with concubines. The overriding consideration was male progeny, and this justified the divorce of barren women, who were however still to be cared for, usually by returning to their families with a parting payment. Long-term support was to be given to surrogate wives if the principal wife proved barren. The custom of betrothal before marriage was already established at this early date and took the form of a contract, with compensation required for its breach by a prospective father-in-law. A wife who seduced another man by 'employing her charms' was given short shrift, because it was assumed she had taken the initiative and betrayed her husband (Ur-Nammu). Virgins and pregnant women were protected from assault; respect for parents was important and primogeniture guaranteed inheritance, though adopted children could also inherit.

The Sumerian codes

Sumer is the collective name for a group of city-states that flourished around the river estuaries of Southern Mesopotamia between the fourth and second millennia BC. Only fragments of the early Sumerian codes have been found, but their precepts about marriage are adapted and expanded in Hammurabi's more comprehensive code.[4] The earliest known Sumerian law code was promulgated by Ur-Nammu, who ruled in Ur *c.* 2100 BC. Some two centuries later, the second Sumerian Code, authorized by Lipit-Ishtar, ruler of the city of Isin in Southern

Mesopotamia, contains similar provisions. The Code of Eshnunna comes from a small kingdom in northern Sumer, *c.* 1900 BC.[5]

Babylon – the Code of Hammurabi

The Code of the Babylonian ruler Hammurabi, dating from mid eighteenth century BC, was written on a stone column, and later taken off to the Elamite capital, Susa, where it was discovered by French archaeologists in 1902. It is now in the Louvre. The text is nearly complete, and deals *inter alia* with a wide range of domestic and marital issues. This code was intended to improve justice, especially for the weak, and to act as a general guide for the group of city-states gathered under Hammurabi's rule, while not replacing all their individual legislative practices. The Sumerian codes only knew two classes, citizens and slaves, while in Babylon at this time there was a threefold distinction of status, between free citizens, vassals and slaves. Hammurabi's Code had to legislate differently for each class and offences against citizens more often incurred capital punishment.[6]

The Hittite Code

The Hittites were a warrior people who controlled Anatolia (Turkey) from *c.* 1800 BC onwards, and their empire dominated much of Mesopotamia and Canaan intermittently until they were themselves invaded by the so-called Sea Peoples, raiders from the Eastern Mediterranean *c.* 1200 BC. Abraham knew the Hittites, and when his wife died, he had to ask their permission to bury her in Hebron. The Hittite Code dates from the sixteenth century BC, probably contemporary with the oldest sources of the Pentateuch; it has the usual subjects, betrothal, bride price, marriage, adultery and divorce. Untypically, marriage between citizens and unfree persons was permitted, and Hittite women held responsible positions in their own right, several of them becoming queens regnant of their extensive empire. They were a religious people, with set prayers for stressful moments, including one for women in labour.[7]

Marriage rules in the Pentateuch

The five books of the Pentateuch as we know them are a collection of ancient oral traditions, early written sources and later material woven together by a series of editors or redactors. Their purpose was to set down a religious record of God's dealings with his chosen people, not merely a national history. So they recorded both the benefits of obeying God's will and the consequences of ignoring it in Israel's often troubled life. Although the redaction in its final form was completed much later than the Mesopotamian codes, the Pentateuch contains in its Covenant Codes several precepts about marriage which are both similar to and developed from the earlier common pattern. Since human relationships in every era tend to produce the same kinds of conflicts and evils, judicial processes applied to them will have many common features, irrespective of the immediate context, race or religion. There is however one obvious difference. In Israel, breaches of God's Covenant law led to exclusion from the community. In the secular codes, religious sanctions were not a component of the laws, though the ruler who promulgated them claimed to be speaking as the representative of the gods, and veracity was often tested by religious omens.

The three Israelite codes are the Covenant Code in Exodus, a much revised and expanded edition in Deuteronomy, and the Holiness Code in Leviticus. These are not generally much studied by Christians, who pay more attention to the Decalogue, which is of a different character and requires separate assessment. All these codes are attributed to Moses, but this cannot be literally true. The final editors of the Pentateuch completed their work after the Exile, that is, not earlier than the fifth century BC, after Ezra returned from exile in 458 BC and the Temple was rebuilt. Starting with the original sources (Yahwist, Elohist and Deuteronomist), the editors assembled the epic story of Israel, albeit with much repetition, and then inserted the Jerusalem Priestly tradition at appropriate points. The largest insertion is in Leviticus.[8]

The Book of the Covenant within the Book of Exodus (20.23—23.19), in origin a separate law book, addresses an agricultural rather than a desert lifestyle. It fits best the period when the Israelites occupied Canaan as a confederation of tribes, before the monarchy was established in the ninth century BC. Among its provisions, it refers to the position of married slaves (21.2–11), compensation for pregnant women who miscarry from violence (21.22–5) and the seduction of virgins (22.16–17). Deuteronomy is also a composite work, probably not completed until after the Temple in Jerusalem was destroyed and most of its inhabitants taken into captivity in Babylon in 587 BC. It is said to mark the watershed between Israel and Judaism. The law code, which forms the central section (12.1—26.15), is a revised and updated version of the Exodus Covenant code. At one time this code was identified with the book discovered in the Temple during Josiah's reign (*c.* 623 BC) but it is now thought more likely to have been a copy of a document originating earlier in the history of the Monarchy.[9] Much of the Book of Leviticus must have been composed after the return from exile (587–538 BC) and is largely concerned with cultic and religious matters. Within it, the Holiness Code (17.1—26.46) is a reworked version of an older pre-exilic source. It includes a special section of twelve prohibitions, the so-called Sexual Duodecalogue (Lev. 18.1–30). These are directed against incest within the extended family or kinship group, or offences against modesty. They repeat the precepts of Deuteronomy 27, but re-set them in the context of opposition to the orgiastic fertility rites of the Canaanite cults.

Getting married – betrothal and marriage

Near Eastern custom understood marriage as family business; in principle girls of marriageable age expected to have their partners found for them, and they were informed rather than consulted. Men were free to make suggestions, but courting was frowned upon. All marriages were arranged between the two families involved, and the crucial step was the financial contract made between the fathers of the prospective partners. This settled the bride price, a payment to the girl's father notionally intended to compensate him for the loss of her services, either at the going rate in the community, or at a price agreed between the parties. Also agreed was an endowment for the new bride with some possessions of her own for use in the new household, together with a dowry as a provision for the future should she be divorced or widowed. If the endowment was in cash, the husband could benefit from the interest but his wife retained the capital. Once the details of the marriage contract had been settled, recorded by the scribe and signed by witnesses, the couple were betrothed and declared their commitment verbally with the formula 'you are my wife, you are my husband'.

The marriage proper began when the new wife moved into her husband's house, and was marked by a family feast. A betrothed woman was given a legally protected status, though it was assumed that she remained a virgin until cohabitation began. Eshnunna held that if either of the betrothed couple died before marriage, the bride price was returned to her father, but if the girl died after the marriage it was not. This code also made clear that without parental permission and a marriage contract living together did not create a marriage. Hammurabi repeated this prohibition.[10]

In Genesis, the Patriarchs are described as simply taking the woman they chose into their households without formality, and their authority was such that they presumably did not need to bother with contracts and consents. But for ordinary people the usual rules were applied. In early Israel it was normally sufficient that the husband pay an agreed bride price to her father, and a scribe would record the deal. Later, in Judaism, the bridegroom was required to give his wife a *keturbah*, a written document pledging that she will receive a sum of money on his death, or if he divorces her.

The use of a slave as surrogate mother was customary if the wife proved barren. The Lipit-Ishtar code provides that when a man's wife is barren, and he has a child with a prostitute, he must provide for her, and her children will become his heirs, but she may not live in his house with his wife while she lives.[11] Abraham's need of an heir reflected this custom. The status of female slaves was considered in the Exodus and Deuteronomic codes, the general purpose being to allow them to leave with their husband when he was freed under the six-year Jubilee rules. If they were not married, they could remain as a wife to their master or leave with a cash payment. Abraham treated Hagar less generously (Genesis 21.14) but God provided for her.

Examples of marriage contracts

The four contracts summarized here show the gradual development of a more relational equality between the spouses and a shift from parental to personal choice between partners. The first two contracts come from apparently rich families in Assyria and Babylon in the nineteenth century BC, where the culture tended to treat women as chattels, but expected divorced women to be provided for. Family property was involved and marriage contracts were carefully preserved. More than a thousand years later, a marriage contract from the Jewish community on Elephantine Island is perhaps surprisingly somewhat similar. Elephantine, opposite Aswan, was a Southern Egyptian frontier post manned by Jewish mercenaries. The last example, also from Egypt, is for a Greek couple living under Roman rule. Here, the consent between the partners is paramount, and offences justifying divorce are spelled out.

An Assyrian marriage contract from Kultepe, ancient Turkey, nineteenth century BC, between Laqipum and Hatala:

Laqipum has married Hatala, daughter of Inishru in the country. Laqipum may not marry another woman, but in the city he may marry a heirodule. If within two years Hatala does not provide him with offspring, she herself will purchase a slave-woman. After she will have produced a child by him, he may dispose of her by sale. Should Laqipum choose to divorce Hatala he must pay her five minas of silver and should she choose to divorce him, she must pay him five minas of silver.[12]

An old Babylonian contract of similar date; the marriage of Sabitum to Warad-kubi:

Ibbatum delivered his daughter Sabitum into the house of Ilushu-ibni, her father-in-law as wife to Warad-kubi, his son, with 2 beds, 2 chairs, 1 table, 1 millstone, etc. Sabitum brought all these items into her father in law's house. Having received her bride price of ten shekels of silver, Ibbatum kissed her and bound up the money in the hem of Sabitum's skirt. Should Sabitum ever say to her husband Warad-kubi: 'you are not my husband' they shall bind her and cast her into the water. And should Warad-kubi ever say to his wife Sabitum: 'you are not my wife', he shall weigh out her divorce money of one-third mina of silver. Emuq-Adad, her brother shall be responsible for her word.[13]

These two contracts show some common features. They are formal written documents, with named witnesses, between relatively wealthy families where property rights on divorce mattered. A heirodule was usually a temple prostitute. In the Assyrian contract both partners have an equal right to choose divorce and the compensation was identical. In the Babylon contract, a wife who proposed divorce might risk drowning, a husband who divorced his wife merely had to pay her compensation. In general terms, Babylonian domestic law is more humane than Assyrian, so the harsh penalty here may be no more than a family rule. Ibbatum, Sabitum's father, seems to have been generous, setting her up with basic furniture and allowing her to keep the bride price as future security.

A Jewish contract from Elephantine 420 BC, the marriage of Annaniah to Yehoyishma:

Annaniah asks Zakkur if he can marry his sister Yehoyishma, a freed slave. Zakkur agrees, and Annaniah takes Yehoyishma into his house. 'She is my wife and I am her husband from this day to eternity.' Annaniah has paid the bride price to Zakkur, and Yehoyishma has taken plenty of household goods and some cash with her into her new home. 'If at some future date, Annaniah goes to the Assembly and declares "I divorce my wife Yehoyishma; she shall not be a wife to me" he becomes liable for divorce money, and must return to her the cash dowry and all her goods.' However, if Yehoyishma divorces Annaniah, she must pay him divorce money, and is then free to go to her father's house, taking her own goods with her.

The contract concludes with arrangements for the property when either spouse dies. If there were male or female children from the marriage, they would inherit, but provision for the surviving parent would be made. If they were childless, the survivor takes all. The contract also requires that Annaniah should treat his wife as well as if she had been a free woman before marriage. If he fails, she has grounds for divorce.[14]

The Elephantine Jews had their own Temple and kept contact by letter with the religious and civic authorities in Jerusalem, but as this contract shows, they were much influenced by Egyptian attitudes to equality for women. Divorce was open to both parties on equal terms and had to be registered by local authority. The phrase 'her father's house' is a standard term that meant in effect the family home.

In both the Babylonian and in the Egyptian contracts marriage and divorce are effected by a precise form of words, and the phrase 'I am her husband for eternity' in the latter is interesting, but difficult to interpret. It may mean no more than 'till death us do part, unless divorce intervenes'.

A contract in Roman form for a Greek couple in Egypt, 92 BC, Philiscus and Apollonia:

Her dowry having been paid to Philiscus, Apollonia shall live with him, obeying him as a wife should her husband. They own their property in common and he will provide her with clothing etc. While she lives, he may not bring another wife, concubine or male lover into the house nor have a child by another woman, nor may he live in another house of which she is not the mistress. Equally, she may not live outside the matrimonial home without his consent or consort with another man. If she chooses to divorce her husband, her dowry must be returned.[15]

The contract reflects Roman marriage customs of the time and is made between Philiscus and Apollonia, not their parents. The home is sacrosanct and the wife may not have escapades outside it, but the double standard applies to the husband. What he does away from home is his own business. First-century Judaism and Christianity abandoned the double standard, as the Romans did later.

Divorce

As the contracts show, marriage was taken seriously in the Mesopotamian states, but divorce was a common experience. Apart from adultery and barrenness, a man could change his partner more or less at will, though he might find resistance from her family on financial grounds. The laws tried to ensure that women were not pushed out of their homes to starve. The Ur-Nammu Code requires that on divorce a man must pay his chief wife a silver mina, or half that for a former widow.[16] If he failed to provide for her, his own property might be forfeit.[17] Hammurabi's code deals at length with a wide range of divorce arrangements, varying with the class of the wife. If a citizen wishes to divorce a barren wife, he has to return her dowry. If a commoner wishes to divorce his barren wife, he has to pay her one third of a mina.[18] If a citizen's wife falls ill, he may marry another wife without divorcing his sick wife, but she is entitled to retain accommodation and support from him while she lives.[19] The Hittite laws are somewhat more humane, especially in allowing marriages between free and unfree persons. After divorce, a Hittite mother was allowed to keep one of her children.[20]

Somewhat unexpectedly we might think, the problem of working wives was included in Hammurabi's Code. If she decides to leave him to start up her own business, 'neglecting her house and humiliating her husband', he may agree to divorce her but she cannot claim any divorce settlement. If he decides not to agree to a divorce, he can marry another woman, while the working wife has to remain living in his house as a maidservant. However, if the wife asked for a divorce because she 'hated' him and the city council decided the fault was his not hers, she was free to go back to her father's house without blame, taking her dowry with her. It was however a chancy business, because if the council decided she was at fault, she was thrown into the river; that is to say, drowned.[21]

The Pentateuch is equally silent about reasons for divorce, except obliquely in Deuteronomy in the somewhat complicated case of the duty of a first husband to a twice-divorced woman:

> Suppose a man enters into marriage with a woman, but she does not please him because he finds something objectionable about her, and so he writes her a certificate of divorce, puts it in her hand, and sends her out of his house; she then leaves his house and goes off to become another man's wife. Then suppose the second man dislikes her, writes her a bill of divorce, puts it in her hand, and sends her out of his house (or the second man who married her dies); her first husband who sent her away is not permitted to take her again to be his wife after she has been defiled; for that would be abhorrent to the LORD, and you shall not bring guilt on the land that the LORD your God is giving you as a possession. (Deut. 24.1–4)

This old case law shows that a first husband loses any obligation to his wife after she remarries; she becomes the responsibility of her second husband. The divorce procedure requires a simple certificate,[22] but in later Judaism there was a stricter procedure of assessment by elders or rabbis. Originally it seems that anything 'objectionable' would suffice, but after the exile there was much debate between rabbinic schools about what 'objectionable' implied. The correct interpretation of this phrase became a major issue between Jesus and the Pharisees.

Adultery

Adultery by the wife of a citizen is strictly condemned in Hammurabi's Code. The wife is to be killed if she entices the man, and if they are caught in the act, both the man and the woman shall be drowned, unless the husband spares his wife. If he does, the king may pardon the adulterer.[23] The situation is different if the husband is absent from home. If he leaves voluntarily but has left his wife enough to live on, she must manage her resources properly and remain faithful to him. If her husband deserts her without providing for her maintenance, she is free to remarry and if he then returns he has no claim on her. However if he is taken away as a prisoner of war, on return he can claim her back, even if she has had children with her second husband.[24] Unless there are witnesses, adultery is difficult to prove. If a husband accuses his wife without evidence, Hammurabi orders that she must 'appeal to the god', and if exonerated go home, but if the omen finds her guilty, she must commit suicide.[25]

In Israel, the simplest form of the rule against adultery was that a woman could violate only her own marriage, while a man could violate only that of another. If caught in the act, the punishment is death; it is an offence against the Covenant community.

> If a man is caught lying with the wife of another man, both of them shall die, the man who lay with the woman, and the woman. So you shall purge the evil from Israel. (Deut. 22.22, repeated in Lev. 18.20 and 20.10.)

The case of suspected adultery, where there is no direct evidence, is referred to in the Book of Numbers. A priest is asked to adjudicate, which he does by invoking a religious procedure. The ritual test of innocence requires the accused woman to drink 'the waters of bitterness', and if she survives the test without pain or swelling of her body she is declared innocent (Num. 5.11–31). The rabbis later based their procedure on this text.

The protection of women

The protection of women was taken seriously in the ancient world and the codes are realistic about the risks they are exposed to from their vulnerability in a male-dominated society. Unmarried young women were the responsibility of their families. In the country they worked in the fields with other women, but if anything happened to a girl while out of earshot, she was assumed to have cried out unsuccessfully. However, in towns, the parents were held responsible unless they did not know their daughter was out in the streets. In Israel's codes, a man who seduces a virgin has to pay her bride price and marry her.

> When a man seduces a virgin who is not engaged to be married, and lies with her, he shall give the bride-price for her and make her his wife. But if her father refuses to give her to him, he shall pay an amount equal to the bride-price for virgins. (Ex. 22.16–17)

But if he had raped her he had to pay higher compensation to her father, marry her, and not subsequently divorce her (Deut. 22.28–9).

In Mesopotamian law, a betrothed woman was regarded as bespoke, in effect already married, and both her old and her new family wanted to keep her safe from rape or seduction. If she was found to be pregnant, the marriage contract would be dissolved and the bride price repaid. A more difficult situation might arise if a man immediately after his marriage alleged his new wife was not a virgin. She or her parents might have deceived him, or he might be using the allegation to escape from a marriage he regretted without having to pay for the consequences of divorce. There would be a problem of proof either way, and it was seriously considered in Deuteronomy (22.13–21). In short the elders had to determine the matter as best they could. If they decided the girl was a virgin at the time of the marriage ceremony, and had not cohabited with her husband-to-be, he was guilty of slander and would have to pay the girl's father one hundred shekels. But if their decision went against the girl she was to be stoned outside her father's house because she had brought disgrace on him (Deut. 22.20–21). Since the proof of virginity would be unreliable in any case, and the apparent loss of it might have been by accident, the risk of gross injustice to the girl must have been high. The text may have come from a very old law, and been included in Deuteronomy not because it was to be followed in practice, but because it lent weight to the prophetic teaching that unchastity was a metaphor for Israel's unfaithfulness to God, a major theme of Hosea. The problem of proof was frequently discussed by the rabbis at the time of Jesus.

In the Mishnah, as part of a survey of rules concerning marriage contracts, R. Gamaliel and R. Eliezer hold that if the woman claims rape or accident she is to be believed. But R. Joshua maintains the traditional view that she must bring proof to support her words.[26]

Pregnant wives need to be protected from violence lest they miscarry, so if an assault causes them to lose a foetus, that is a criminal offence. Hammurabi provides that if a citizen strikes another citizen's daughter accidentally and she miscarries, he must pay ten shekels, but if it was a deliberate blow he must pay one third of a mina, but if the daughter dies, the attacker's daughter must be put to death. The penalties are reduced if the daughter's father is a commoner or she is a female slave.[27] The Exodus Covenant is broadly the same:

> When people who are fighting injure a pregnant woman so that there is a miscarriage, and yet no further harm follows, the one responsible shall be fined what the woman's husband demands, paying as much as the judges determine. If any harm follows, then you shall give life for life, eye for eye, tooth for tooth . . . (Ex. 21.22–4)

The wording in Exodus specifies harm to the woman rather than death as the justification for reciprocal punishment. This makes one kind of sense if harm to the daughter is a synonym for her death, but it might mean other injuries to her, perhaps leading to an inability to have children. Another possible interpretation can be made in the light of a similar Hittite rule which distinguishes between foetuses who are too young to be born viable, in practice less than six months *in utero*, and those who, but for the assault, could be expected to have been born normally. The Septuagint version of the Old Testament in Greek adopts this interpretation to distinguish between injuries to viable and non-viable foetuses, an early example of the recognition of the rights of an unborn child.[28]

Incest

The prohibition of sexual activity between blood relations, members of the same household and the wider family was clearly important in Near Eastern culture generally, and also in Early Israel. Hammurabi's Code punishes incest by a father on his daughter by expulsion from the city, on his daughter-in-law by death, on his son's fiancée by the return of her dowry to her father, and payment to her. She is also released from the betrothal and is free to marry elsewhere. If a man commits incest with his mother after his father's death, both the mother and son are to be burned.[29]

Prohibitions of incest are found in Deuteronomy and Leviticus as part of a wide-ranging list of offences. The Deuteronomic list of ten offences was recited at the Shechem ceremony of blessing and cursing which dramatized Israel's covenant responsibilities. Sexual relations with one's mother, mother-in-law and sisters are accursed (Deut. 27.20–3). A more extensive list of sexual prohibitions, the so-called Sexual Duodecalogue, is found in Leviticus (18.6–18) with an introductory verse: 'None of you shall approach anyone near of kin to uncover nakedness. I am the LORD' (Lev. 18.6). The twelve prohibitions of the Duodecalogue are directed against incest within the extended family or kinship group, and offences against modesty. They expand the precepts of Deuteronomy and re-set them in the context of opposition to the orgiastic fertility rites of the Canaanite cults. They also serve as a list of the prohibited degrees for marriage, though not all the persons mentioned are strictly consanguineous.[30]

The account of incest by Lot's daughters can be noted in parenthesis. Lot, a nephew of Abraham, escaped from the devastation of Sodom, but his wife looked back and was turned into a pillar of salt. Lot's daughters thought they should preserve the family line by making their father drunk and sleeping with him. They each had a child, said to be the ancestors of the neighbouring tribes of Moab and Ammon. It was a nice insult to say they were born of incest (Gen. 19.30–8)!

Respect for parents

Given the Patriarchal system, it is not surprising that the ancient codes stress respect towards parents. The rule from the Decalogue, 'to honour your father and your mother' (Ex. 20.12) reflects ancient tradition, but it has a wider scope than the slogan 'Father knows best'. If a son repudiates his sonship, he loses his inheritance rights and his parents may sell him as a slave. Conversely, parents may not deny his right to inheritance by declaring falsely that he is not their child. Hammurabi's Code warns that a son who strikes his father should have his hand cut off,[31] and this severity is repeated in Exodus 21.15. Criticism of one's parents was, however, allowed, as a letter from this period shows. A schoolboy, Iddin-Sin, writes to his father Shamash-hazir, a high official in Hammurabi's administration, with this message for his mother:

May Shamash, Marduk and Ilabrat for my sake forever keep you well. Gentlemen's clothes improve year by year. By cheapening and scrimping my clothes, you have become rich. While wool was being consumed in our house like bread, you were the one making my clothes cheaper. The son of Adad-iddinam, whose father is only an underling of my father, has received two garments, but you keep getting upset over just one garment for me. Whereas you gave birth to me, his mother acquired him by adoption, but whereas his mother loves him, you do not love me.[32]

Marriage in Egypt

Egypt is well known for its monuments, its Pharaohs and their Queens, not least Nefertiti, wife of Akhenaten. He introduced a form of monotheism, worshipping only Aten, the sun god, at their new capital Tell el-Armana *c.* 1350 BC. Nefertiti had six daughters but no son, and the next but one Pharaoh was Tutankhamun, whose mother was probably Kiya, Akhenaten's favourite minor wife. Akhenaten's prayer to the sun god is preserved and has some parallels with the Psalms. It begins with an account of the sun's rise and people starting to go to work and then has this account of Aten's role in conception and birth:

> You make the seed grow in a woman, make fluid into mankind; you keep the child alive in its mother's womb and soothe it so it does not weep, you are the nurse even in the mother's womb. You are the one who gives breath to all that is made, to preserve life. When the child descends from the womb to breathe on the day of his birth, you open his mouth completely to speak and supply his needs.[33]

In Egyptian civilization, marriage and family life were highly valued, and women had a respected place as mistress of their households, especially if they had children. Men were required to hold their mothers in special regard; they were the matriarchs of an extended family that often lived together in single households. Life was short, marriage took place in the early teens and many wives died in their twenties. Polygamy was frowned upon except among rulers who used it for dynastic or political ends. Women were allowed to own and administer property in their own right, had equality before the law and could present their own cases in court, even to the point of suing their own husbands on property matters. On death, her husband's heir was normally the eldest son, but she was entitled to a legacy.

No ancient Egyptian legal codes concerning marriage have been discovered; those we have come from the third century BC and reflect Greek or Roman legal practice. Divorce was easy, made by a private agreement between the couple, and could be initiated by either the husband or the wife. The sufficient cause for a break-up was that the partner was no longer pleasing, as in Deuteronomy. Egyptians took a stern view of adultery by a wife; both she and her lover might be fed to the crocodiles or burnt, but by the deceived husband, not the State – it was regarded as a private matter.[34] Egypt had a rich literature of love poetry, eroticism and pornography. For example, a young man remembers how he braved a lurking crocodile to cross the river and reach his beloved, and a girl lures her lover to the water's edge with the promise that she will let him see her bathe. *Plus ça change!*[35]

A very popular Egyptian folk story of the thirteenth century BC, 'The tale of the two brothers', tells at length how the wife of the elder brother attempts unsuccessfully to seduce the younger brother. He denies her charge of rape, and her husband kills her. The younger man mutilates himself and goes into exile, but eventually obtains a high position in Egyptian administration. The story of Joseph and Potiphar's wife (Gen. 39) is similar. 'With God's help' Joseph becomes interpreter of dreams to Pharaoh. These are entertaining stories with a moral ending, but the problem of verifying accusations of rape is perennial.

Marriage among the Patriarchs

It mattered enormously to Jewish people that they were able to say 'Abraham is our Father' (John 8.39). One of the challenges to the authority of Jesus as Teacher was that his parentage was uncertain or irregular. To meet that challenge, St Matthew began his Gospel with a careful genealogy, tracing the ancestry of Jesus back through the royal lineage of David to the original appointment of Abraham, from whom Jesus is said to be directly descended (Matt. 1.1–16). After Abraham, Matthew lists the Patriarchs from Genesis, Isaac, Jacob, Judah and Perez, and continues the line from the periods of the Judges and Monarchy. The stories of the Patriarchs in the Book of Genesis 12—37 serve as a link between the origins of mankind in the Creative Acts, Eden, the Fall, Noah and Babel, and the start of Israel's redemptive history with the arrival of Joseph in Egypt. They are not the kind of records a modern genealogist would use to trace a family tree. They are stories so old that no one knows whether or not they are true, but they give supposedly accurate details of all the relevant marriages and the birth of sons, crucial to the belief that all the Israelites are legitimate heirs of Abraham.

The lifestyle of the Patriarchs was similar to that of any minor Near Eastern potentate. They were reasonably prosperous, with slaves to do the chores. They were not always honest, monogamous or chaste, but that did not matter because they lived long before covenant codes were given. Their wives were probably cosseted, with time on their hands, while nannies looked after the children. Their aim in life was to provide male heirs, not always a simple matter. In contrast to Patriarchal opulence, ordinary families lived in small one-roomed houses with mud walls, brushwood roofs and little furniture. Life was congested, and goats were everywhere.

Abraham and Sarai

Abraham's first wife Sarai was barren and followed custom by offering her Egyptian bondwoman Hagar as a surrogate. She gave birth to Ishmael, adopted as Abraham's son. Eventually, Sarah, as she was later called, had a child of her own, Isaac, who became Abraham's heir. Jealousy led to Hagar and Ishmael's banishment and they wandered off into the desert, but God provided for them. The story illustrates the normal rule that slave women used as surrogates should be cared for. Isaac and Ishmael were traditionally regarded as respectively the ancestors of the Jews and the Arabs (Gen. 16—18, 21).

God's intention to provide a legitimate heir for Abraham was promised twice, first at the institution of the Covenant between God and Abraham, of which the sign was circumcision (Gen. 17.15–21), and secondly when Abraham and Sarah received the angelic visitors at the oaks of Mamre (Gen. 18). One of the visitors, or perhaps all three, represented the divine presence at this discreet encounter, and the scene has been depicted in one of the most famous Russian icons, by Rublev. This serene icon is often associated in Christian devotion with the communion of the Blessed Trinity.

In reality Abraham and Sarah's lives were never serene. A puzzling and repeated tale in Genesis is the attempt Abraham makes to pass off his wife as his sister on his journeys to Egypt. In the 'J' version

(Gen. 12.10–20), Abraham had moved from Haran in Syria to Canaan, but the onset of famine there obliged him to move on to Egypt. Sarah was a beautiful girl and Abraham feared he would be killed and his wife would then be taken into Pharaoh's harem. If he told the Egyptians that she was his sister, they would still take her but his life would be spared, and so it worked out. But God intervened with a plague on Pharaoh and his household, and when Pharaoh discovered the truth he returned Sarah to her husband.

A more ethically sensitive version of this tale, from the 'E' source (Gen. 20.1–18), is set at Gerar in the southern coastal plain of Canaan, occupied by the Philistines. Abimelech, the Philistine king, takes Sarah, but is warned by God in a dream not to have sex with her. Challenged by Abimelech, Abraham explains that he thought there was no fear of God in the Negeb, but has found there obviously is; he was only being slightly economical with the truth because Sarah was Abraham's half-sister, with the same father but a different mother. Anyway, she agreed to the deceit. Abimelech lets them go. In the third and later version of the story, probably from the 'P' source (Gen. 26.1–33), the main characters are changed. Isaac and his wife Rebekah have settled in Gerar as aliens, having been forbidden by God to go into Egypt. When asked, Isaac says Rebekah is his sister, but Abimelech spots him 'fondling' her, complains at the deceit, and warns his people 'whoever touches this man or his wife shall be put to death' (verse 11). Isaac and Rebekah stay in Gerar; they prosper, a sign of God's blessing, and eventually after a conflict over wells agree a peace covenant with Abimelech at Beersheba.

It is not accidental that the final editors of the Pentateuch use this story three times; each has a distinct didactic purpose. All three versions stress God's providence and ability to intervene to protect the mothers of Israel. Both Sarah and Rebekah were originally barren but eventually God enabled them to have children. Neither Abraham nor Isaac was able to frustrate God's purpose by callous behaviour to his wife. The third version confirms that God's promise to Abraham (that his descendants should possess the land of Canaan), now applies through Isaac, and hence to Jacob and Joseph. There is a subsidiary theme that God's will is universalizable and can be perceived by secular rulers. Pharaoh is forced into submission by the plagues, Abimelech is warned to obey in a dream and subsequently requires his people to respect the marriage of Isaac and Rebekah. The story reappears in various modified forms in some of the intertestamental Jewish literature and in an allegoric form by Philo. Josephus recounts it twice and adds the intriguing suggestion that Abraham went to Egypt not only to escape the famine, but to see if the religion there was better than his own. God's rescue of Sarah proved it was not.[36]

Isaac and Rebekah

The choice of a suitable wife for Isaac is clearly an important matter for Abraham, and she must be from his kindred, not a Canaanite woman. So Abraham sends off his senior servant, Eliezer, to his old family home at Nahor, near Haran, where he finds Rebekah, a grandchild of Abraham's brother, who appears eminently suitable. He puts a heavy gold ring on her nose, bracelets on her arms and goes off to meet her family. They welcome the proposed match, suggesting a ten-day pause for Rebekah to reflect, but she wants to go at once. Since her father was dead, her consent is needed. After present-giving all round she sets off with the servant and meets Isaac who falls in love with her and takes her into his house (Gen. 24). Eliezer, a prayerful man, has asked for God's help throughout this somewhat hazardous mission, and the narrative suggests that God has stage-managed the whole affair. The idea that God should choose a partner for Isaac makes some sense in the particular context, but later became an idea of more general application, with the obvious difficulty that what God had apparently joined together might still work out badly.[37] Rebekah is sadly barren, but Isaac prays for her and she bears twins, first Esau, and then Jacob. Jacob persuades Esau to surrender his birthright for a meal (Gen. 25.27–34).

Jacob and Rachel

To escape Esau's vengeance, Jacob flees to Laban's house, the old family base at Haran. Laban is Isaac's uncle, a somewhat crafty character. Jacob falls in love with Rachel, Laban's younger daughter, and promises to work for Laban for seven years. Having done this, a deceitful marriage takes place. The veiled woman is not Rachel but Laban's elder daughter Leah, whom he thinks ought to be married first. Jacob marries Rachel a week later and continues to work for Laban. The Lord disapproves of this arrangement, pitying the despised Leah, so he 'opens her womb', while Rachel remains barren. Desperate, Rachel takes the usual step of providing her slave Bilhah to Jacob, and Leah, being past child-bearing, replies with her slave Zilpah. Rachel herself then conceives a son, Joseph, and subsequently dies in childbirth. A complicated story of jealousy and intrigue between Jacob's twelve sons follows, and the saga ends with Joseph becoming established as an important person at Pharaoh's court, and that sets the scene for the Exodus.

Judah and Tamar

Although the story of Joseph, Moses and the Exodus predominates in Israel's history, Abraham's family line is continued through Judah, another son of Jacob and Leah. Judah married Shua, a Canaanite woman, and has three sons by her, Er, Onan and Shelah. Judah chose Tamar as wife to his eldest son Er, 'but he was wicked and the Lord slew him'. Onan was told to follow the Levirate rule and marry Tamar, to continue the line of Er, but he refused and also died. Tamar was told she would have to return to her father's house and remain a widow until the youngest son became old enough to marry her. That did not happen, perhaps because Judah suspected she had something to do with the death of his other sons. Tamar therefore disguised herself as a prostitute and lured her father-in-law, now widowed, to have sex with her, taking a pledge *pro tem* in lieu of a kid as payment. When Judah sent the kid, no trace of the prostitute could be found, but he is told his daughter-in-law has behaved like a prostitute and is pregnant. Judah orders her to be burned, but she produces the pledge and Judah acknowledges his fault. He admits he should have let her marry Shelah. Later she has twins. The first born, Perez, is an ancestor of King David (Gen. 38). This story of deceit which nevertheless fulfils God's purpose has much to do with the ancient history of the tribe of Judah. Tamar's course of action is to be understood as heroic in that context.[38]

In our world, sensitive to the equal status of men and women, these tales of married life among the Patriarchs have several jarring notes. It was not a good time for women and we would think Sarah, Rebekah and Rachel were trapped in unreasonable situations, but there is an extra factor that needs attention: they were all barren. Knowledge of the processes of human fertilization in the primitive world supposed women were no more than incubators of their husband's seed. God was presumed to have power to open their wombs. But even so, the tales of three barren women seem a coincidence too far, unless the barrenness is an important element of the teaching. These women are the mothers of the great ancestors of Israel and therefore their sons are to be conceived in special ways. It is not suggested that God impregnated these mothers himself in the style of Greek mythology, where heroes have a divine and a human parent. Since Isaac, Jacob and Joseph are crucial participants in God's plan, these stories tell us that God directed both when and to whom they were born.[39] The accounts in Genesis may seem to us somewhat contrived, but clearly their purpose is to stress God's intention to found the dynasty, not tell us about human biology.

Some of the issues emerging from these codes are still important for the present day, though the sanctions are very different. We still have laws about inheritance and trusts to preserve family property. The informal agreement of engagement has replaced legal betrothal, though still with joint family celebrations. After a long period in which the Christian attitude to the permanence of marriage predominated in the Western world, divorce by consent is now as standard as it was in Mesopotamia four millennia ago, and the same need of maintenance for divorced wives who do not remarry is recognized. Protection for women is much the same, but loss of virginity and single parenting are no longer penalized. The double standard is largely abandoned. Polygamy and slavery still survive in some parts of the world, but are increasingly criticized. In sum, marriage, families and sexual relationships in the twenty-first century are not so remote from the concerns of the Near Eastern and Mosaic legislators as might be expected. Between them and the Christian attitudes of the New Testament stood the classical civilizations of Greece and Rome.

2

The Old Testament

Introduction

In the previous chapter, the covenant codes from the Pentateuch were considered in the historical context of other ancient codes from the Near Eastern lands; in some ways the attitudes to marriage and sexual behaviour were similar, in others distinct. The Patriarchs, driven by their obligation to produce appropriate heirs, lived before the covenants so they were not bound by its rules. They had fathered their nation, and their story set the scene for the next great stage in Israel's history, the Exodus from Egypt and the occupation of Canaan. But of course the Pentateuch did not start with Abraham. It looks back to the original creation of Adam and Eve, which defines the man–woman relationship, and it includes two editions of the Ten Commandments or Decalogue. These have served ever since in Jewish and Christian history as a basic guide to human behaviour. The seventh commandment forbade adultery.

The immigration into Canaan did not establish a coherent state of Israel. The twelve tribes were dispersed into different areas and loosely linked as a confederacy, struggling to maintain their own ethnic and religious identity against the syncretistic pressures of the indigenous population. The solution seemed to be the establishment of a monarchy, based on the royal capital of Jerusalem, and the centralization of worship in the holy sanctuary of the Temple. For a time this kingdom flourished, commercially and politically, because there was a power vacuum among Israel's neighbours, but that did not last long. In retrospect, the prophets from the eighth century regarded the monarchy as a mistake – Israel was meant to be a theocracy. Saul, David and Solomon served their purpose, but their successors were seldom commendable, and their sexual morality was deplorable. Hosea likened Israel to an unfaithful wife.

The Babylonian captivity clarified Israel's vocation. While the people wept beside the river, the priests were busy writing. They believed the tragedy of Israel was its failure to keep the Law of Moses, which they now edited into one comprehensive book, the Pentateuch, which Ezra brought back to Jerusalem. This was the core teaching, or Torah, and to aid its interpretation the prophetic books were added as sources of authentic interpretation. Once back in Israel, further writings were gradually recognized as authentic, known to the rabbis as the Writings, and these three (Torah, Prophets and Writings) eventually comprised the Hebrew Bible.[1]

This threefold division of the Jewish sacred scriptures seems confusing to modern Christian readers of what we now call the Old Testament.[2] We are interested in the development of religious and moral ideas chronologically and how these different types of literature show this development. The post-exilic priests were concerned to protect the unique authority of the Mosaic corpus, but by the time of Jesus the Writings were gaining wide acceptance. In the Gospels he often refers to the Law and the Prophets, and in Luke mentions the Psalms, part of the Writings (Luke 24.44). Extracts of them were read in the synagogue as supplements to the Pentateuch. Jesus reads from Isaiah and refers to Jonah, and there are many quotations from the Writings in New Testament books other than the Gospels. In practice therefore nearly all the biblical books later incorporated into the Hebrew Bible were already available to the Jews and Christians in Palestine in the first century AD, and the Septuagint was equally available to the Diaspora.

Adam and Eve

The familiar story of Adam and Eve describes the fundamental relationship between God and humankind and between men and women in a sequence of simple archetypal narratives. This account of origins in the Book of Genesis in its final form is usually assigned to the post-exilic period. Aetiological legends and didactic stories long known in Israel are assembled by an editor or redactor to make one story and his main sources are readily identifiable. Thus, there are two accounts of the creation, Priestly and Jahwistic; they are significantly different, but complementary, coming from separate periods and contexts in Israel's history. Their juxtaposition is obviously crucial to the editor's purpose and taken together they provide prototypes for the man–woman relationship, and have always been for both Judaism and

Christianity the key texts for their understanding of marriage. Although their setting looks back through the mists of time to the start of history as it was understood in early Hebrew thought, the perceptions they offer relate directly to ordinary human experience through all ages. We are all caught up in the paradoxes of creation and fall.

The Priestly vision of the original good creation (Gen. 1—2.3) presents a somewhat idealized picture of what human life is meant to be and serves as a theological introduction to all that follows. It records in concise form the place of human beings in the natural order as this was understood in the mature thought of post-exilic Israel, in some ways correcting in advance the more limited perspective of the Jahwist account. God has created the cosmos in six careful stages, demonstrating his supreme power and control over all things. In particular, he has placed humankind at the summit of his creation, made in his own image as his representative with a unique mandate to be his managing agent on earth. Man and woman are created together, not one from the other, and share responsibility. 'Then God said, "Let us make humankind in our image, according to our likeness"' (1.26). 'So God created humankind in his image, in the image of God he created them; male and female he created them' (1.27). The New Revised Standard Version uses inclusive language, and therefore in the priestly narrative has 'humankind' where the older English versions had 'man' to render the Hebrew word *adam* (1.26–7). In Hebrew, *adam* usually refers to the human race corporately, and that is the intended meaning here. In the Jahwist account, the same generic meaning may be intended when God formed man (*adam*) from the dust (2.7), but from then on, a particular man is envisaged.

The story continues with a blessing of the man and the woman who are to exercise dominion over the already present fish, birds and every living thing that moves upon the earth (1.28), and are commanded to be fruitful and multiply. The seventh day is to be hallowed as a day of rest (2.3).

In contrast, the longer Jahwist account of creation (2.4b onwards), depicts the realities of existence in a more sombre way, but it represents God as directly concerned with the human predicament. This account is not much concerned with the origins of the cosmos and focuses immediately on the creation of the man, from the earth, but designated to take the centre of the stage. The woman is created out of the man's flesh, in an apparently subservient role as his 'helper' in the Garden of Eden. But they seek to know good and evil, and after the

Fall human relationships become complex, leading to strife and Cain's murder of Abel. 'Then the Lord God formed man from the dust of the ground, and breathed into his nostrils the breath of life; and the man became a living being' (Gen. 2.7). After a short interlude, God planted a garden in Eden and put the man there to look after it, but he feels isolated, so God says: 'It is not good that man should be alone; I will make him a helper as his partner' (Gen. 2.18). (The priestly narrative resumes in chapter 5 with a list of Adam's descendants and moves on to the story of Noah.)

So God creates animals and birds, and then watches over the man with tenderness and concern as he names the various beasts, thus expressing his authority over them, but without finding any who can offer him a sufficient relationship. Naming the animals has been described as man's 'act of appropriative ordering, by which he brings conceptual order to his sphere of life'.[3] Some modern commentators detect a certain hilarity in the story as if Adam prefigures Noah's Ark – 'I really love the elephants but . . .'[4] In fact, some rabbis suggested that God paraded the animals two by two before Adam. However, it is unlikely that the Jahwist is being light-hearted about the naming of the animals. From his pastoral situation, he is aware of the affection a farmer may have for his beasts. There may even be an implied warning against bestiality, regarded as a serious offence in Israel's law, but the main point here must be to prepare the scene for Eve's arrival. Since neither animals nor birds provide the man with an adequate partner,

> the LORD God caused a deep sleep to fall upon the man, and he slept; then he took one of his ribs and closed up its place with flesh. And the rib that the LORD God had taken from the man he made into a woman and brought her to the man. Then the man said,
> 'This at last is bone of my bones
>   and flesh of my flesh;
> this one shall be called Woman,
>   for out of Man this one was taken.' (Gen. 2.21–3)

When the woman is made from the man's rib, flesh of his flesh (2.23), their unity is stressed by the Hebrew words *ishshah* (woman), and *ish* (man), used to describe woman and man generically as species of the human race, but not particular people. The NRSV here prints 'Woman' and 'Man' with capital letters to clarify this meaning. As the story moves on the 'woman' has no capital, since the man's companion is meant, but she is not named until after the Fall, when the man calls her 'Eve, because she was the mother of all living' (3.20). Adam retains the name 'the man' until the end of the Jahwist narrative (4.25). English is able to convey this meaning directly because it has a similar verbal link, 'man–woman' from the early English *wyfman*. To make the same point, Luther invented a special feminine word to give *Männe–Männin*, and this is still printed in modern German Bibles, with an explanatory footnote, since *Männin* is not otherwise used in German.

The physical details of the woman's creation are of interest. Anatomically, a man can do without a rib, hence the expression that a woman is a spare rib. The rabbis suggested a number of reasons for the choice of a rib, symbolic or literal in terms of equality or otherwise, and there is a charming Quaker reflection about this: 'God did not take Eve out of Adam's head, that she might lord it over him, nor from his heel, that he might trample on her, but out of his rib, nearest his heart, that he might cherish her.'[5]

The original story makes clear that the man and the woman shared a common flesh which gave them a unique 'I–Thou relationship' which the man could not find with the animals. The editor then adds his own comment that in the sexual relationship of marriage the once divided flesh of a man and a woman is reunited (Genesis 2.24–5). Apart from Adam and Eve, and the marriage of siblings, this cannot be understood literally, for obvious genetic reasons. Nevertheless, this sense that the sexual union between Adam and Eve healed the original wound of creation has proved to be a powerful metaphor in Judaism and Christianity. But the original Jahwist narrative was intending a wider meaning. Human beings achieve their potential not merely through sexual conjunction with their own kind, but through fellowship with God and each other. Both men and women need partners, but the paradigm of their relationship is the covenant with God himself; their relationship is not only for breeding. The Swiss theologian Karl Barth wrote at length about this, drawing attention to the divine likeness of man revealed in Genesis 1.27. God created human beings male and female, corresponding to the fact that God Himself exists in relationship and not in isolation. 'God is no *Deus solitarius*, but *Deus triunus*.'[6]

Eve as helper

Notwithstanding the stress in the Jahwist narrative that the man and woman are of the same substance, bones and flesh, and together distinct from other living things, the reference to the woman as 'helper' (2.20) has caused some difficulties in interpretation. Since the animals have not been able to assuage the man's sense of isolation, he is provided with a better helper, a woman who shares his human nature. In Hebrew the phrase appears quite simple, almost laconic; she is to be his 'helper like him' (Hebrew *ezer k'negdo*).

The Hebrew word *ezer* often refers to God as the only trustworthy helper, particularly in the Psalms. 'I am poor and needy; hasten to me, O God! You are my help and my deliverer' (Ps. 70.5).[7] In human terms *ezer* is sometimes used in a military context, where extra forces come to the rescue, but it also means help in the domestic sense, which suggests an assistant, and this meaning has often been assumed for Genesis 2.20. It seems the woman is allotted this secondary status, brought to the man by God to help him out of his loneliness. This was of course the standard view of the place of women in early Israel's culture, though it was qualified by the equally important recognition that her motherhood provides the essential means of perpetuating the race. Given the emphasis in the priestly account that both share the divine image, that they are like each other in that as well as in flesh, it is perhaps unnecessary to look for a definition of gender role in the original use of the word *ezer*. Sexual politics were not part of the agenda when these stories were written.

Similarly, *k'negdo* is an unusual Hebrew expression, difficult to translate, and its meaning is best discerned from its context. Literally, it probably meant 'opposite him, in front of him, or corresponding to him', and clearly it is legitimate to interpret it as simply 'Eve was like Adam but distinct', a commonplace truism everyone knew. By using this expression the Jahwist is emphasizing that since Adam is neither God nor animal, a true companion for him has to come from his own body. Eve is to share his uniqueness; only she can be an adequate or suitable fit corresponding to his nature. Men and women are *sui generis*, and their place in the cosmos is neatly summed up in Psalm 8: 'What are human beings that you are mindful of them, mortals that you care for them? Yet you have made them a little lower than God (or divine beings, i.e. angels) and crowned them with glory and honour.'

The Jewish people of the Diaspora were largely Greek-speaking with scant knowledge of Hebrew so they used the Septuagint, a Greek translation made in Alexandria, *c.* 200 BC. Its authors took care to distinguish the kind of helper the woman was. When an animal was in mind, it should be *boethon kat' auton* (v. 18), that is, 'an assistant in accord with' the man, but when, instead, a woman was formed, she was to be *boethos homoios auto*, that is, 'an assistant in all respects like him' (v. 20).[8]

The Apocryphal Book of Ecclesiasticus (ben Sirach), contemporaneous with the Septuagint, was composed in Hebrew, but only fragments of the original have been discovered, and the complete text is only known in Greek translation. There are many references to women, generally not very complimentary, and in particular one comment on Genesis 2.18:

> He who acquires a wife gets his best possession, a helper fit for him and a pillar of support. Where there is no fence, the property will be plundered, and where there is no wife, a man will become a fugitive and a wanderer. (Ecclus. 36.29–30)

The Greek text in ben Sirach is the same as in the Septuagint for Genesis 2.18, *boethon kat' auton*. Within Judaism itself at this time there was a similar debate among rabbinic thinkers, some of whom were sensitive to the need to balance the theoretical equality of men and women against their own practices of subordination. They picture Adam as bewailing his partnerless state as the animals march past, but that sympathy did not necessarily imply any repudiation of the traditional view that Eve was the helper rather than the co-partner of Adam. However, in the Mishnah there are some passages discussing the duties of marriage where it is clear that the more liberal rabbis are quoted as pressing for 'equal right', echoing the Priestly rather than the Jahwist tradition.

English translations of Genesis 2.18–20

The Septuagint was the primary source for the Latin Vulgate, and for many later translations of the Old Testament. As other ancient manuscripts have come to light, modern translators have had to reconsider how to render accurately the different nuances given to Eve's status in the Priestly and Jahwist narratives. Their choices are sometimes influenced by the tendency to look for answers to their own questions about the difference between men and women in ancient texts whose authors had different issues in mind.

It is suggested above that the difficult Hebrew phrase *ezer k'negdo* was originally intended to express the truism that Eve was like Adam but distinct, without specifying her particular role or status in relation to him. English translations of the Bible from the sixteenth to the nineteenth century were usually content to aim for literal accuracy, but twentieth-century translations have included extra phrases and additional footnotes to suggest that the original meaning was more favourable to a doctrine of equality.

William Tyndale was the first translator of the Hebrew Text of the Pentateuch into English, in 1534. He introduces the extra idea of companionship to verse 18: 'The Lord God said: "it is not good that man should be alone. I will make him an helper to bear him company."'[9] The King James Authorized Version (1611) and the Revised Version (1885) use 'help meet for him', sometimes mistakenly read as 'help-*mate*'. The archaic 'meet' means appropriate, suitable, a good fit. Although both these versions were generally dependent on Tyndale's translation of both the Pentateuch and the New Testament, their concern with literalism led them to reject his paraphrase, and they give slightly different marginal notes on the meaning of the Hebrew words. The Revised Standard Version (1952) has 'a helper fit for him', with the footnote to v. 18: 'To be alone is not good, for man is social by nature. A helper fit for him means a partner who is suitable for him, who completes his being.' The English version of the Roman Catholic Jerusalem Bible (1966) has for v. 21: 'no helpmate suitable for man was found for him' from the original French *une qui lui soit assortie*, changed to 'no helper suitable for the man was found' in the 1985 New Jerusalem Bible. The Jerome Biblical Commentary (1968), a guide to Catholic biblical scholarship for general readers, has an extensive comment on vs. 18–24 which carefully retains the dependent status of women.

> 'A helper like himself' expresses two profound ideas: Woman complements man, a social being by nature, but she is not a mere service appendage; *she corresponds to him*, i.e. has a similar nature . . . The description of woman's formation is, like that of man, etiological. All the expressions [rib, bone, woman] indicate the unity of nature of man and wife . . . But woman's existence, psychologically and in the social order, is dependent on man.[10]

Among more recent translations, the Good News Bible (1976) uses a paraphrase 'a suitable companion to help him' and the New International Version, 1979, has 'a helper suitable for him'. The concept of partnership is introduced in the New English Bible (1970): 'It is not good for the man to be alone, I will provide a partner for him.' The New Revised Standard Version (1989) has 'a helper as his partner' for both verse 18 and 20. A footnote to the annotated version adds this explanation: 'vs.18–21. To be fully human one needs to be in relation to others who correspond to oneself. *Helper*, not in a relationship of subordination, but of mutuality and interdependence.'

Twenty-two years divide the Jerome commentary from the NRSV, and the latter was criticized on publication for reflecting modern feminist theology overmuch. Although both versions claim with some justice to reflect ecumenical consultation it seems clear that they also illustrate somewhat different theological premises, Catholic and Protestant. It has also been argued that it is high time the process of patriarchal censorship of the place of women in society, shown in the earlier translations but not so clear in the original 'P' and 'J' sources, should be abandoned.

To sum up this rather convoluted analysis of recent translations of *ezer k'negdo*, it may be helpful to apply Nicholas Lash's observation that 'words take their meaning from the company they keep'. For the twentieth century, the idea of an interdependent partnership was a less misleading description of the Christian understanding of the relationship between men and women than such words as helper, or suitable companion. However the ordinary use of 'partnership' between men and women is now changing; it no longer necessarily describes a committed long-term relationship. Colloquially, it serves as a tactful or camouflage word that inhibits further enquiry, a deliberately nebulous label for a couple who may be friends for the evening, short or long-term cohabitees, or actually married. Given this ambiguity, it may be that for the twenty-first century we will have to look for another synonym for *ezer k'negdo*. Certainly both the snapshots of man–woman relationships in the 'P' and 'J' sources come from a culture which had no place for the wide range of partner relationships now so familiar. Perhaps what the redactor wanted to tell us was simply 'Adam, alone you are helpless, but you don't need a pet, you need a wife!'

Marriage and the Fall

Having set the scene ideally with the 'P' account of a good creation, and from the 'J' source having explained the place of man and woman in the order of God's world, the narrator moves on to the realities of human life. The Jahwist narrative of the Fall is an attempt to solve the problem of evil; it explains how the man and the woman, lords of the created world and intimately belonging to each other, lost their paradisal privileges. This corresponds with the standard awareness of early Israel that the frustration and disappointment of human aspiration are the direct result of disobedience to God's command. The serpent that initiates this disaster is recognized as being part of creation, and the awkward question 'who put it there' is left unanswered. The consequences of disobedience are spelled out in the tragedy of Cain and Abel, but all is not lost. Eve has a final son, Seth, to replace Abel, and the line is continued through Enoch and his descendants who learn to 'invoke the name of the LORD' (Gen. 4.26).

Taken together, these first four chapters of Genesis provide a series of explanatory stories that are clearly meant to be pondered together, but not understood as an explanatory sequence of a chronological kind. Obviously the redactor knew his stories overlapped and were sometimes inconsistent. For example the animals arrive before or after Adam, who is himself made with Eve or before her, but that is not a problem. What the redactor offers is a set of pictures, each already well known in Israel, and the message of each picture is clear enough. Humankind is centre stage in the image of God, Adam and Eve are intimately related, human disobedience explains evil, but God's purpose is not defeated. To use a modern computer analogy, there are four 'windows' on the screen, to be seen separately, and then assessed together. So the enthusiasm of Adam that he now has a proper partner, from his own flesh, is followed by the sad discovery of their joint vulnerability to temptation. Adam finds himself in a no-win situation. If his excuse is that Eve led him astray, then he is not her master; if they are equal then he shares the responsibility. Once they collude in tasting good and evil, they lose the freedom of unrestricted access to God, and their future depends on his forbearance.

Before the narrative of the Fall begins, there is an editorial interpolation that sums up in two short sentences some crucial beliefs about the nature of marriage. 'Therefore a man leaves his father and mother and clings to his wife, and they become one flesh. And the man and his wife were both naked, and were not ashamed' (Gen. 2.24–5).

The suggestion that loyalty between the spouses is to take precedence over obligation to parents has to be understood in the context of
the customary pattern of early Israelite family life, where the new wife
was usually drawn into her husband's home. It is a clear assertion that
a new commitment is being undertaken, and its priorities have to be
protected from parental interference. This does not abrogate the fifth
commandment, honouring one's parents, and in fact the new wife is
regarded as joining their family; she becomes one of their kin. The
husband only leaves his parents in the sense that the newly married
couple are entitled to a measure of respect for their personal commitment in what was in practice usually the crowded environment of
small rooms around a communal courtyard or a group of tents. The
Jahwist did not envisage a nuclear family unit in its own separate
dwelling as we understand it.

The man is said to cling to his wife, not the other way round. He
wants to recover his missing part. The woman is now called wife for
the first time, before the Fall, and this is obviously important. In both
Jewish and Christian thought, God's bringing together of Adam and
Eve was said to be the first wedding ceremony, and was thus depicted
in medieval art.[11] Strictly speaking Adam and Eve are not married in
the usual sense of that word. There was no choice, no consent, but
Adam recognizes his other half, and the fact that God brings Eve to
him validates their reunion. In the priestly account, God not only
makes them, he also blesses them and commands them to be fruitful
and multiply (Gen. 1.28). If they had been merely cohabitees, their
children would have been illegitimate. Luther recognizes this text as a
sign that marriage is good in itself, part of God's natural dispensation
in Paradise before the Fall, and as such not needing to be redeemed.
Cranmer echoes this thought in the 1549 Prayer Book preface to his
'Forme of solemnization of Matrimonie': 'Matrimonie is an honorable
estate instituted of God in paradise, in the time of mannes innocencie.'

The one-flesh biological link of the ancestral pair is metaphorically
adopted to define married relationship generally. This is an imaginative leap, extending the one-flesh concept beyond the original creation
to include all subsequent unions, but it is not unique to Israel. The
androgynous myth was widely used in Near Eastern culture to explain
the original splitting and reunion of humankind.[12] It is used here with
a unique theological spin. Rejoining one's other half establishes a
new type of bonding, a God-willed replacement for the parent–child
relationship. Although the practice in patriarchal times of marrying

cousins or members of the wider family or clan provided some genetic links, the prohibition of incest kept direct siblings apart. Unlike Adam and Eve, their descendants were not of one flesh in a physiological sense, so the metaphor is being used to stress the intimacy of the marriage bond, taking priority over previous family obligations.

This one-flesh relationship is often interpreted sexually, as if the act of sexual intercourse is being referred to here, but the metaphor's meaning is wider than that. In Jahwist thought, the identity of flesh and bone that Adam recognizes in Eve is used to express family kinship.[13] The new wife becomes a daughter to her husband's father, under his patriarchy, and she is recognized as a sister to her husband's brothers, entitled to their protection. Since chastity in marriage in early Hebrew law was obligatory only for the wife, the Jahwist uses the metaphor to establish the special status of marriage, not to define the role of sex within it. By marriage the wife is brought into her husband's family, as if she had been born into it, and the process of family agreement leading to the betrothal affirms that she is now of one flesh with them. The Hebrew word *basar* usually means 'flesh' in the direct sense of meat or muscle, but is also used in the Old Testament either in a kinship sense or as the frail aspect of humanity in comparison to the soul.[14] The Church of England Report of 1978 makes this kinship meaning very clear:

> To avoid misunderstanding, it must be pointed out that 'flesh' in this verse, as often in this context, refers to kinship. What Gen. 2.24 means is that, in marriage, a man leaves the family home and creates a new kinship unit. It is the conclusion of the story of the creation.[15]

Sexual desire and children

The purpose of sexual intercourse was to obey the command to be fruitful and provide children. Although the means of doing so involved a particularly intimate act, copulation as such was a standard feature of animal and human reproduction, and not in Hebrew thought the predominant meaning of the one-flesh metaphor. A man having sex with his slaves did not become one flesh with them. The initial sexual coupling between married partners was nevertheless given a special importance. This was not only because the woman was bestowing her virginity on her man, and therefore guaranteeing the legitimacy of a subsequent child, but also because in the rupture of her hymen, the blood on both bodies symbolized the mingling of two married persons into one flesh. Distasteful as this seems to modern minds, it was consonant with the legal procedure that a blood-stained cloth was regarded as proof that a wife had married *virgo intacta*. She could thus provide her token of virginity and, as noted above, some rabbis thought the test should still be used. In medieval Europe it survived as a customary sign that newly-weds had consummated their marriage.

Similarly, the comment that Adam and Eve in the Garden were 'naked and not ashamed' is mistakenly understood as a euphemism suggesting that Adam and Eve enjoyed sex without embarrassment. The Hebrew word for 'naked' here, *erom*, refers to their innocency, their unselfconscious openness to God and to each other, there are no private secrets to drive them apart. The same word is used by Job to proclaim his uprightness before God: 'Naked I came from my mother's womb, and naked shall I return there; the LORD gave, and the LORD has taken away, blessed be the name of the LORD' (Job 1.21).

This spiritual openness, *erom*, is different from the nakedness of the body (Hebrew *ervah*), which often refers to the modesty of covering genitalia. Noah's son Ham discovers his father naked in this sense, and his other sons, Shem and Japheth, take care to cover him up. They are blessed but Ham is cursed and his descendants become Egypt and Canaan (Gen. 9.20–7). *Ervah* is also used more specifically in the Holiness Code of Leviticus to prohibit sexual relationships within the family (Lev. 18.6–23).

After the forbidden fruit is eaten, the man and woman's perception of themselves, of each other and of God is marred. In hubris they have hoped to gain the capacity to be like God, knowing good and evil, that is, to share his 'entirety of knowledge' (NRSV), but in fact this is beyond them. Knowledge is power, and to seek the knowledge that only God has, 'to whom all hearts are open, and from whom no secrets are hid', is a demand to be equal with him in power. They now perceive that their knowledge will always be limited, they cannot emulate his power, and their nakedness (Hebrew *erom*, not *ervah*) now becomes a symbol of their inadequacy. Becoming self-conscious in this way, they lose their innocence and in fear seek to hide from the presence of God. 'Then the eyes of both were opened, and they knew that they were naked; and they sewed fig leaves together and made loincloths for themselves' (Gen. 3.7).

Knowing they were naked means withdrawing into privacy from God and each other. The loincloths are the sign that modesty and privacy are now important, of which the artistic device of medieval painters covering the genitalia with a single leaf is symbolic. This area of the body is vulnerable, but its protection did not in Hebrew thought suggest that sex in itself was sinful. Denied the power of knowledge, the fig leaf represents the human need for privacy and restricted communication. It is a means of retaining some personal space and autonomy, some power to control events in one's own interests. Secrets are shared between people who trust each other, but with the expulsion from Paradise, that trust is impaired.

The catastrophe of the Fall affects the relationship of Adam and Eve as well as their relationship with God. The serpent is cursed as the cause of all the misery, since a good God could not be such a cause, and Adam and Eve are warned of the tough life ahead of them. God said to the woman: 'I will greatly increase your pangs in childbearing; in pain you shall bring forth children, yet your desire shall be for your husband, and he shall rule over you' (Gen. 3.16). And to the man God said: 'Because you have listened to the voice of your wife . . . By the sweat of your face you shall eat bread until you return to the ground, for out of it you were taken; you are dust and to dust you shall return' (Gen. 3.17–19).

At this point in the narrative the Jahwist has to reconcile human vocation and human experience and his solution is that humankind has chosen alienation. The blame is apportioned equally. Eve listened to the serpent and Adam listened to Eve, so both are responsible. The examples chosen are apparently those where what should have been agreeable activities have become arduous. In Eden, it is supposed, childbearing would be simply a happy event, tilling the ground an easy and rewarding experience, and Adam and Eve could live together as equals. Out of Eden, Eve would long for a husband and children, even though it meant her subjugation to him, while Adam would wrestle a living from a grudging earth. And so it turns out, for them and for all their descendants. Adam and Eve are destined to long for each other despite the toil of the fields and the pain of childbirth. The man wants to recover what was taken from him, the woman wants to get back where she belongs – they have to find their other half before death overcomes them both. All humankind returns to the dust of the earth, from which Adam came.

Only after their act of disobedience and God's judgement on it, does Adam name his wife Eve, the mother of all living (Gen. 3.20), and the Jahwist story concludes with the birth of the first children: 'Now the man knew his wife Eve, and she conceived and bore Cain, saying, "I have produced a man with the help of the LORD"' (Gen. 4.1).[16]

The Ten Commandments (the Decalogue)

In some Anglican churches, the Ten Commandments are still to be seen painted up on the Eastern wall behind or at the side of the altar, a visual reminder of their importance in the Christian tradition. From the time of Augustine, the Decalogue has been regarded as an important part of the corpus of instruction given to catechumens, being continued in the new dispensation because it had been endorsed and supplemented in Christ's Sermon on the Mount. In the eucharistic liturgies of the medieval church the penitential section often contained the Decalogue or an Old Testament lesson followed by the Kyries. In most of the Orders of Service and the Catechisms that stem from the Reformation, though not in the Catholic Mass, the Decalogue is given similar emphasis. Martin Luther regarded these Commandments as the kernel of the Old Testament and included them in his Short Catechism, the only reference he makes there to the Old Testament. Subsequent catechisms usually refer to them as 'my duty towards God and my neighbour', and at one time confirmation candidates had to tell the bishop that they had learned them.

In the Anglican Communion services, the Commandments were introduced into the penitential section of the Prayer Book of 1552, immediately after the collect for purity, reflecting the influences of Bucer, Luther and Calvin, and they were retained in that position in the revision of 1662. In the 1928 Prayer Book, Christ's Summary of the Law was added as an alternative, and soon became popular, as it was in the 1980 ASB. In *Common Worship* (2000) the summary is the first choice, while the Commandments, the Beatitudes and the Comfortable Words are all described as supplementary 'penitential material'. This shift in emphasis from the old law to the new probably recognizes that modern worshippers in all-age congregations are not well attuned to the propitiatory character of these old tersely expressed precepts. For marriage, the old warning against adultery is transmuted into 'you shall live with your partner in love and trust'.

So what function did the Decalogue fulfil in the world of the Old Testament? Much scholarly attention has been directed to its original provenance and meaning, but it has proved difficult to determine how it came into its prominent positions in Exodus (20.1–17) and

Deuteronomy (5.6–21). It may have existed as a simple guide to the basic beliefs of Israel, dating back to the tribal period, when the judges ruled, or even to Moses himself as an oral tradition. It could be a very late post-exilic compilation of ordinary precepts of universal criminal law, prohibiting murder, theft and adultery, with a fully developed description of duty towards God, which suggests a late priestly theology. A more widely accepted theory is that the Decalogue was originally compiled as an exhortation to be used in the cultic worship of Ancient Israel as a summary of the people's commitment and duty towards God and their fellow Israelites as this was understood in the Deuteronomic Covenant. It would have been recited clause by clause during sanctuary worship with a congregational response, in much the same way as the traditional Anglican custom has been to respond to each precept with 'Lord, have mercy upon us, and incline our hearts to keep this law'.

There is an obvious difficulty in describing the Decalogue as law, because of its limited scope. Only some forms of human misbehaviour are mentioned, and the terse expressions leave ample room for interpreters to decide what is and what is not to be included. The prohibition of killing and/or murder is an obvious example. Further, if Decalogue law is understood as like other laws, then the controversy of law versus grace comes into play. It is one thing to say, following St Paul, that the laws of Judaism as such no longer apply to the Christians, the people of the New Covenant, but it is another to dismiss the precepts of the Decalogue as such as equally redundant. Jesus fulfils that which is not done away with. So rather than use the familiar expression 'summary of the law' we should understand that the function of the Decalogue was (and is) to show by its selection of fundamental characteristics what differentiates God's people from other nations and cultures. The Decalogue then is not a list of particular laws but a set of parameters within which the People of God should live.

The final editors of the Pentateuch incorporated this familiar text at appropriate points in their narrative as a summary of the Covenant laws, entirely consonant with the teaching of the Major Prophets. No actual documentary evidence of the text as a separate entity has so far been discovered, but it is also noted that the literary form of the Decalogue has some similarity with the vassal treaties of the Near Eastern states.[17] For those who hold that the Decalogue predates the codes as an independent tradition, the later teaching on the same subjects in the prophetic books and the covenant codes amounts to a detailed exposition of these basic rules. In either case most of the commandments relating to human conduct are identical with those found in the older codes of the Near Eastern states. Murder, theft, adultery and false witness are universally prohibited in ancient human cultures; the Decalogue is unique in incorporating these duties into one entity with belief in God, all part of the deal as we might say.

Although there are some differences of emphasis between the Exodus and Deuteronomy versions of the Decalogue, the prohibition of adultery is equally succinct in both of them: 'You shall not commit adultery' (Ex. 20.14) and 'Neither shall you commit adultery (Deut. 5.18). This prohibition was understood, as we have seen, to prevent a man's adultery with a fellow Israelite's wife. Neither polygamy nor fornication as such were forbidden to him, but there were provisions in the covenant codes for the care of first wives, and for female slaves who were usually treated as concubines. The double standard allowed women no sexual transgression; if detected, her only defence was to claim rape. The original purpose of the prohibition was to assure the husband that his children were his own and his name protected. Adultery was a theft of his assurance.[18]

A more discursive version of the Decalogue is given in Exodus (34.11–28). Adultery as such is not mentioned, but there is a typical polemic against consorting with the inhabitants of the land, Canaanites, Hittites, etc. They will lure the Israelites to eat of their sacrifices; and 'you will take wives from among their daughters for your sons, and their daughters who prostitute themselves to their gods will make your sons also prostitute themselves to their gods' (Ex. 34.16). The pre-exilic prophets denounced Israelite participation in Canaanite cult prostitution as a breaking of their bond of faithfulness to Jahweh. This led to a gradual extension of the human adultery rule to include males. Eventually some rabbinic teaching forbade fornication and all forms of extra-marital sex as species of adultery.[19]

The tenth Commandment in Exodus reinforces the seventh under the general heading of covetousness, and at first sight seems to continue the normal attitude of treating wives as the property of the husband, along with his house and other possessions. Male and female slaves are equally protected, but in the Deuteronomic version there is a hint of amelioration of a wife's inferior status; she is mentioned separately.

You shall not covet your neighbour's house; you shall not covet your neighbour's wife, or male or female slave, or ox, or donkey, or anything that belongs to your neighbour. (Ex. 20.17)

Neither shall you covet your neighbour's wife. Neither shall you desire your neighbour's house, or field, or male or female slave, or ox, or donkey. (Deut. 5.21)

Compared with previous English translations, the NRSV changes 'covet' to 'desire', reflecting a change in the Hebrew text from Exodus to Deuteronomy. To 'covet' often implies also to take, while to 'desire' introduces the mental attitude involved, the intention and motivation, not otherwise considered in the Decalogue but a key theme of the prophets. In English Bibles the word 'desire' is used to translate several Hebrew words and can be ambiguous. Thus, Eve is said to 'desire' her husband, but the Hebrew might be better rendered as to 'long for', implying legitimate sexual desire between married partners. It may seem an insignificant point to make here, but motivation does became a serious issue in later Jewish thought, and Jesus stresses the importance of it in this context during his Sermon on the Mount, when he observes: 'You have heard that it was said, "You shall not commit adultery." But I say to you that everyone who looks at a woman with lust has already committed adultery with her in his heart' (Matt. 5.27–8).

Our equivalent modern phrase is 'Don't even think about it'. There is a more positive rabbinic saying: 'If you see a beautiful woman across the street, you should pray Blessed be she, and Blessed be he who shall be her husband!'

Judges and Kings

After considering the timeless importance of the Decalogue, we need to refocus on the narrative of Israel's life in the Promised Land. The 'history of Israel' from Joshua to Esther is permeated by the theological insights characteristic of Deuteronomy. The initial success of crossing the Jordan and beginning the conquest of the Promised Land is seen as a sign that Joshua is being 'careful to do all the law which Moses commanded you' (Josh. 1.7), and the promise of the Shechem Covenant is therefore being fulfilled (Deut. 28.14). He received unexpected help from Rahab, a prostitute in Jericho, the crucial frontier town. Joshua sends two spies across the river to check for opposition, and they spend the night at Rahab's house on the walls of the city. The

King of Jericho tries to find the spies, but Rahab hides them in her attic. She is no simple harlot, but well informed about the miraculous crossing of the Red Sea, and Joshua's campaigns, and she has decided where the future of her family lies. She wants the Lord to deal kindly with them, as he does (Josh. 2). An agreeable tale then, not least because her occupation is no bar to her acceptance.[20]

In the ensuing confrontation between the Israelites and the indigenous people, the Canaanites and Philistines, temptations abound, and human frailty reasserts itself in the tale of Samson and Delilah. Samson was a (possibly legendary) hero in Israel's struggle with the Philistines, who came from Crete and occupied Gaza and the Western coastal strip about the same time as the Israelites came into Palestine from the East. Samson's life story personifies their ethnic and religious clash. His father, Manoah, had a barren wife who was promised a son by an 'angel of the Lord'. Samson was to be brought up as a Nazirite, to keep him well clear of Canaanite customs, but he actually married a Philistine woman. She deceived him and he then fell in love with Delilah, who may have been a sacred prostitute. The Philistines offered her a large bribe if she would entice him into revealing the true source of his strength. Once the secret of the Nazirite vow, symbolized by his uncut hair, was given away, the Lord temporarily withdrew Samson's strength, but he eventually destroyed both Philistines and himself. The moral is simple enough. Beware of female enticement, especially from foreigners with their false religions; it will only lead to apostasy (Judg. 13–16).

The story of Ruth is interpolated between Judges and Samuel in the Septuagint Old Testament as a counterpoint to the ferocity towards foreigners shown in Judges, Samuel and Kings. Naomi, widow of Elimelech, originally from Bethlehem but now in Moab, has two sons who marry Moabite women, Orpah and Ruth. The sons die, Naomi decides to return to Judah, but advises her daughters to stay in their own country and re-marry. Orpah agrees, but Ruth insists on going with her mother: 'Where you go, I will go; where you lodge, I will lodge; your people shall be my people, and your God my God' (Ruth 1.16). They return to Bethlehem and as the warm-hearted story continues Ruth gleans in the field of Boaz, a rich farmer, who turns out to be a kinsman of Elimelech. After all the proprieties of courtship are observed, they marry and have a son, Obed, who becomes the grandfather of King David.

The monarchy

As we move into the short period of the monarchy, one might expect that Israel's leaders would be appointed because of their holiness and commitment to Jahweh and his laws, but this was clearly not the case. With hindsight, the biblical writers tended to regard the period from Saul to Josiah as in many ways not a success because human kingship was contrary to the theocratic principle. But at least in its early stages, the united monarchy ruled during an economically prosperous and politically relatively powerful period in Israel's history. Israel's territory was never as large again until the reoccupation of the West Bank in our times.[21]

In their personal lives the first kings of Israel behaved much like the Patriarchs, but the narratives show that now even kings are not above the covenant laws. They are no longer free to do as they like, even for dynastic reasons, and foreign wives are unacceptable. Saul, the first king of Israel, soon proved himself unsuitable, and the next choice, David, used various dubious means to demonstrate his qualifications for kingship. David married Abigail, eventually succeeding Saul as king. The well-known story of David's obsession with Bathsheba follows. She was the wife of Uriah, a senior mercenary in the palace guard. She became pregnant, and Uriah had to be disposed of with the connivance of Joab, the commander of Israel's army, at war with the Ammonites in Trans-Jordan. After Uriah was killed in battle, David married Bathsheba and they had a son, but the Lord was displeased. The prophet Nathan is sent to reveal God's judgement: the son will die. However, David repents and Bathsheba bears him another son, Solomon, who in due course becomes king.[22] Solomon amasses wealth, marries the daughter of Pharaoh, and has many other wives and concubines. They persuade him to honour their gods, and all this is contrary to the specification for kingship in Israel set down in Deuteronomy 17.14. When Solomon dies the kingdom is split.

In the North, Ahab is king and wishes to buy a vineyard for a vegetable garden. Naboth refuses, but Ahab's wife, Jezebel, a Phoenician princess and worshipper of Baal, arranges for Naboth to be falsely accused of blasphemy, and he is stoned. Like Nathan to David, Elijah brings God's sentence to Ahab: 'Thus says the LORD: In the place where dogs licked up the blood of Naboth, dogs will also lick up your blood' (1 Kings 21.19).

The same fate is promised for Jezebel, and it is clear that she is not only the initiator of the crime, but a powerful person in her own right, perhaps acting as viceregent to Ahab. Ahab repents and survives, but Jezebel is later killed by Jehu (2 Kings 9.30–7).

The final story in the history of the monarchy, Esther, has no proper place there. It is a fable, composed not earlier than 200 BC, about the deliverance of the Jews resident in the Persian Empire from a pogrom to exterminate them, and explains the origin of the Jewish Festival of Purim, celebrated in early spring. Ahasuerus is looking for a replacement for his queen Vashti, who has refused to attend him. A skilful Jew, Mordecai, manages to arrange for his niece to be appointed, concealing her race. The pogrom is being planned by Haman, the king's chief minister, but Esther, advised by Mordecai, manipulates events so that the pogrom is cancelled, Haman is hanged, and the king appoints Mordecai in his place. Esther has no actual rights to appear before the king or advise him on policy but she succeeds because she makes a fuss of him, and invites him to a dinner party, where she reveals her nationality and the threat facing her. She is a brave lady, and the story assumes that God may have discreetly influenced events. The characters in these stories, Rahab and Bathsheba, Jezebel and Esther, Samson and David, Solomon and Ahab, lived as they could, capable of making choices for good or ill, both for themselves and their peoples. The women were able to influence events despite their legally subservient status.

The prophets

Israel's prophets were not much concerned with foretelling the distant future. Their task was to study the contemporary situation in Israel and discern God's will for it, and it is those perceptions that have been preserved. Who they were and when they lived is usually irrelevant except in the sense that one needs to know the context to make sense of their comments.[23] The groups of professional prophets around the royal courts were soothsayers to the king, and are sharply distinguished from the tough men from the desert like Elijah who spoke the word of Jahweh and then fled for their lives.[24] For pre-exilic prophets in the mould of Amos and Hosea, the main cause of the failure of Israel's monarchy was not its feeble and vacillating kings, but the national apostasy, of which their leaders were merely the up-front exemplars. When the kings and their people failed the test of righteousness before God, the warnings of Deuteronomy were fulfilled. By their disobedience to God's commands, not least in their syncretism and sexual licence, they have forfeited his blessings and incurred his curse.[25] Hosea's account of his wretched marriage to Gomer is an allegory of God's fury and forbearance with Israel. He is told by the Lord: 'Take for yourself a wife of whoredom, and have children of whoredom, for the land commits great whoredom by forsaking the LORD' (Hos. 1.2).

Although the basic point being made is clear enough – however bad Israel is, God is determined to redeem her – the actual text is somewhat disjointed and may be a series of oracles rather than one straight narrative. In human terms, it is somewhat discouraging. If Hosea really loved Gomer, the vigour of his denunciation could not aid their reconciliation.[26] Allegorically, those who worshipped Baal were sometimes called whores, unfaithful to Jahweh, which may have been Gomer's real offence, rather than anything sexual. Some scholars see the allegory, a popular one in prophetic texts, as suggesting a mutation in Israel's understanding of covenant. It is no longer a vassal treaty imposed by a superior on an inferior; it now has some sense of mutual agreement and obligation. Hosea strikes a more positive note in chapter 11:

> When Israel was a child, I loved him,
>   and out of Egypt I called my son . . .
> I led them with cords of human kindness,
>   with bands of love.
> I was to them like those
>   who lift infants to their cheeks.
>   I bent down to them and fed them . . .
> How can I give you up, Ephraim?
>   How can I hand you over, O Israel? . . .
> I will not execute my fierce anger;
>   will not again destroy Ephraim;
>   m God and no mortal,
>   ly One in your midst,
>   not come in wrath.
>   (Hos. 11.1, 4, 8, 9)

verses ameliorate the vigour of Hosea's denunciation, and size the loving steadfastness of God (Hebrew *chesed*), ultimately ral truth for both Jews and Christians. Similar teaching is given by Deutero-Isaiah. Both Hosea and Jeremiah, and in most extravagant terms Ezekiel, use the analogy of the frailty of human marriage to condemn Israel's apostasy.[27]

Among post-exilic prophets, the marriage analogy as a symbol of faithfulness to God recurs. Malachi, *c.* 500 BC, stresses the love of God for Israel (1.2) but also for other nations (2.11) and then appears to repeat the familiar analogy, but he subtly inverts its meaning to press men to be faithful to their wives.

> You cover the LORD's altar with tears, with weeping and groaning because he no longer regards the offering or accepts it with favour at your hand. You ask, 'Why does he not?' Because the LORD was a witness between you and the wife of your youth, to whom you have been faithless, though she is your companion and your wife by covenant. Did not one God make her? Both flesh and spirit are his. And what does the one God desire? Godly offspring. So look to yourselves, and do not let anyone be faithless to the wife of his youth. For I hate divorce, says the LORD, the God of Israel. (Mal. 2.13–16)

There is, however, an additional reason for this preoccupation with faithful marriage in the writings of the post-exilic period, and that is the concern for racial purity. The Books of Ezra and Nehemiah are supplementary to the alternative version of Israel's history in the Chronicles. They describe the situation in Jerusalem immediately after the return from Babylon. The city is not an unoccupied ruin, only the walls and the temple have been destroyed. Those still living there seem to have been a mixture, Jewish families who stayed behind and Canaanites who moved in, and there has been some intermarrying, so among their descendants who are to be counted as proper Jews within the Covenant?[28] The problem is of course bound to occur among all the Diaspora communities, including Babylon itself, where many Jews remain to form eventually an important centre. But Jerusalem, it is argued, must be the centre of orthodoxy, and the priestly caste in particular must be kept racially pure. Ezra discovers that some of the priests and Levites have married the daughters of non-Jewish people, Hittites, Egyptians, Ammonites, etc:

> 'They have taken some of their daughters as wives for themselves and for their sons. Thus the holy seed has mixed itself with the

peoples of the lands, and in this faithlessness the officials and leaders have led the way.' When I heard this, I tore my garments and my mantle, and pulled hair from my head and beard, and sat appalled . . . until the evening sacrifice. (Ezra 9.2–4)

The upshot of this discovery is an investigation of those who had intermarried, and their wives and children are sent away.[29]

The Wisdom literature in the Old Testament, Proverbs and Ecclesiastes, is a genre of its own, certainly post-exilic. Proverbs, as its name implies, is a collection of words of the Wise, addressed to young people. Popular aphorisms still quoted from it are: 'the fear of the Lord is the beginning of wisdom' (1.7); 'Go to the ant, you sluggard' (6.6); and 'Wisdom has built her house, she has hewn her seven pillars' (9.1). On sexual relationships, Proverbs shows the trend in post-exilic Jewish thought to abandon the double standard in sexual morality and commends faithful marriage on prudential grounds. There is quite a vivid description of how a woman whose husband is away might entice 'a young man without sense' into her bed. He goes 'like an ox to the slaughter . . . but her house is the way of Sheol, going down to the chambers of death' (7.22–7). A somewhat parallel judgement is delivered on a prostitute sitting at the door of her house, inviting custom: 'Stolen water is sweet, and bread eaten in secret is pleasant . . . But they do not know that the dead are there, that her guests are in the depths of Sheol' (9.13–18).

Proverbs ends with a much more positive account of a capable wife, set out at some length in the advice of his mother to King Lemuel. This is the fullest description of a wife's role in the Old Testament.

> A capable wife who can find?
>   She is far more precious than jewels.
> The heart of her husband trusts in her,
>   and he will have no lack of gain.
> She does him good, and not harm,
>   all the days of her life . . .
> Charm is deceitful, and beauty is vain,
>   but a woman who fears the LORD is to be praised.[30]

The Old Testament's references to human love between men and women are sparse, except in the sense of loyalty and mutual support. The Song of Songs is the notable or notorious exception, and because of the emotional intensity of its love poetry its suitability as scripture has often been questioned. In both Jewish and Christian tradition it has been accepted as an allegory of God's love for his people, but modern views are that it should be taken literally as a collection of human love poems collected in the third century BC. Every culture has its love poetry so there is nothing very special about the Song of Songs, but it is valuable as a reminder that this was equally true of Judaism.

3

Marriage in the Classical World

Pagans, Jews and Christians

In our day, the great stories from the classical world are continually retold on television, in the theatre and in historical novels. The attitudes to marriage and sexual relationships depicted in this retelling often suggest a licentiousness and social disorder that owes more to our fantasies than the realities of domestic life in Greece and Rome. In fact the Christian doctrine of marriage was built on a model derived from later Roman law combined with fundamental precepts about human relationships set out in the Old and New Testaments. This might seem an unholy alliance, but given the dominance of the Greek and Roman empires it was inevitable. It was a time of great development and change for all the peoples of the Mediterranean and Near Eastern lands. The Jews in Palestine had never lived in isolation, but after the exile, in the Second Temple period, they had to learn to face West instead of East. The Jews of the Diaspora had no choice; they lived and worked among the pagans and spoke their language. Provided they obeyed the civic laws, their religious observances were tolerated. Although the first apostles were all Jewish, the next generation of Christian leaders were all, or nearly all, Greek or Roman and advised their converts to obey the laws of the governing authorities where they lived insofar as these did not directly conflict with the Christian ethos. For the legalities of marriage they did not, but for divorce they did.

There was of course a religious problem. Jewish awareness of a single and austere supreme deity directing events for the benefit of mankind was not replicated in the pagan myths. For Greece, the vast family of Zeus, gods and goddesses, interfered with human life in a somewhat arbitrary and intermittent fashion, concerned to demonstrate their distinct spheres of influence, and Zeus had to struggle to restrain their rivalry and ensure that in the end justice was done. Hera, primary wife of Zeus, was goddess of marriages, Aphrodite, daughter of Zeus by another consort, Dione, was goddess of love, beauty and fertility. Hera's and Aphrodite's interests often conflicted. Despite the complications of this Pantheon, humans had to demonstrate their loyalty to their godly patrons by careful maintenance of the appropriate sacrifices. Although the three great philosophers Socrates, Plato and Aristotle often made clear that their religious beliefs were centred on a supreme single deity[1] they were careful to attend some religious ceremonies in Athens, and accepted them as in a diffused sense witnesses to an ultimate reality beyond their representations.

The Roman attitude to religion was syncretistic; they adopted and renamed most of the Greek gods and goddesses. In their early history the Romans thought of the gods in less anthropomorphic ways than the Greeks, and only later had statues of them in their temples, as in Pompeii. The gods were believed to be partners with humankind in the enterprise of living, in a relationship built on mutual trust, and it was assumed that, unless proved otherwise, the gods were on the side of Rome. The Romans had family as well as community gods, and were careful to invoke their blessing before major events such as marriage. For Rome, Zeus became Jupiter, Hera became Juno, and Aphrodite was Venus, the mother of Eros, the god of sensual love whom neither gods nor humans could resist. One account of Aphrodite's origin was that she emerged from the sea off Paphos in Western Cyprus, having been formed from the seminal foam of the castrated Uranus. The famous picture 'The Birth of Venus', by the fifteenth-century Florentine, Botticelli, has her floating to the shore on a shell.

Attitudes to marriage in the classical world

The marriage customs of Greece and Rome were quite similar to those of Judaism. Just as there were many parallels between the Mesopotamian rules for marriage and those of early Israel, so there were between the classical world and the Near East. They shared the common pattern of an earlier stage in human history, probably inherited from the Caucasian peoples who moved south in the third millennium BC to occupy both Greece and Mesopotamia. Migration and commerce were continually fretting away at any attempts at isolationism. Greece itself took its early ideas of sculpture from Egypt, its mathematics from Babylon, and most enduringly its alphabet from Phoenicia *c.* 750 BC. The Phoenicians, based in Canaan, were great sailors and traders, as were the Greeks, and they both had many settlements around the Mediterranean. These links provide a possible explanation of similarities between some aspects of family law in the Athenian and Near Eastern codes.

Every woman in Greece and early Rome had a guardian, her *kurios* or *pater familias*, who would be either her father or another senior male relative, but at marriage guardianship transferred to her husband. These guardians chose partners for their children and negotiated the usual marriage contract and dowry at the time of betrothal. The marriage ceremony itself began with the procession of the bride to the bridegroom's home and there was prolonged feasting. Girls were carefully guarded at home and married soon after puberty. The double standard was allowed to men, who usually delayed marriage until their late twenties. Human biology at that time was largely guesswork and it was thought a man's semen achieved its maximum virility when he was twenty years old or after. A more commonplace reason was that women aged more quickly than men, so a young wife was preferable, and anyway she would be more malleable!

In pagan belief the gods on occasion arranged marriages or at least influenced events so that appropriate people met each other and fell in love, a romantic or hazardous notion depending on the outcome. Invoking the blessing of a god to guarantee the fertility of a union was standard practice, and in artistic representations of the ceremony, Hera or Juno was depicted as joining the couple's hands. In real life, infertility could be overcome by divorce and a new marriage, or by the use of a slave concubine. Sons were always wanted, daughters less so, and they risked being abandoned. Adoption, often of a suitable adult rather than of a child, could be used to provide an heir. Serial marriage was acceptable but polygamy was not. The Jewish preoccupation with preserving the blood-line was less important to the Greeks because the democratic system made citizenship of the *polis* more significant. For the Romans, Patrician ancestry mattered but most important was clan and family loyalty, as in Israel.

In sexual mores, women were expected to remain virgin until marriage, but young men were not. Adultery by a man was no great matter, except with another citizen's wife; a deceived husband could kill the interloper personally without penalty. Homosexual behaviour and pederasty were common in Greece and portrayed explicitly in paintings and pottery decoration. Among equals it could be an expression of friendship and mutual affection, not always involving physical sex, but as pederastia it could also involve the vicious exploitation of young males by their patrons. Homosexual relationships were considered inappropriate for married men, who risked ridicule from their peers. Rome had a law prohibiting homosexual relationships, but it was not much invoked except as an excuse for blackmail. Among sexual offences, rape was less severely punished than seduction, the reason (strange to modern minds) being that to entice a woman was a threat to the system while assault only damaged one person.

Marriage among the Greeks from Homer to Aristotle

Although the civilization of Ancient Greece seems familiar, we know far more about its art, aesthetics and literature than we do of ordinary life in Athens or Sparta. Greece was a loose federation of largely independent states linked by language, trade and some common interests when not fighting each other, so they have left us no universal set of laws. Early Greek attitudes to sex, personal relationships and marriage can be seen in the Homeric legends. The great dramatists of the classical period build on these legends to explore the emotional struggles of human relationships by imaginative reconstruction of the lives of the heroes and their women, their best and worst efforts overruled by the gods. In later literature, real history breaks through, but most records inevitably refer to VIPs. The philosophers reflect more profoundly on the meaning of life, Plato being especially critical of the institution of marriage as he observed it. In his *Republic* he proposed a drastically different system as the ideal, and in his last work, the *Laws*, he set out detailed regulations for marriage which were in practice a revised form of the civic codes of Crete and Sparta, pragmatic but still informed by his idealism. Plato's criticisms and proposals influenced both Roman and Hellenistic Judaism through Neo-Platonism, and were taken seriously by early Christian theologians.

Homer's epics

The *Iliad* and the *Odyssey*, epic poems attributed to Homer *c.* 800 BC but as legends much older, gave the early Greeks aetiological myths about their origins. To the Greek mind epic poems were to history as poetry is to prose. Human love, passion and jealousy are depicted with an intensity absent from Genesis, and the characters are more accessible. The heroes of the narratives are constantly embattled in the struggle for Troy, unrestrained in their violence and superhuman in strength, but in the end they are mortal, pawns of the gods. Thus Homer underscores the ultimate folly of war.

Women figure intermittently in the narratives, apparently at the mercy of both gods and men, but sometimes with highly significant roles. Helen, wife of Menelaus, King of Sparta, is abducted by Paris, a Trojan prince. This is the ostensible justification for the war, but the real cause was the Greeks' attempt to expand eastwards through the Dardenelles, which Troy protected. Helen is torn by divided loyalties and eventually returns to Sparta with Menelaus. Her tragic life is contrasted with that of the faithful patient Penelope, wife of Odysseus, who stays at home, fearing her husband is dead. After many trials Odysseus returns home to find his wife Penelope staunchly resisting other suitors. She has kept them waiting by saying she will decide when she has finished weaving a piece of cloth, which in fact she unravels every night. Odysseus kills all the suitors and is reunited with Penelope in a moving scene of middle-aged love.[2]

Traditionally Helen's character has been treated unsympathetically, but Homer actually portrays her as the victim of Aphrodite's jealousy and the obsession of Paris.[3] When Menelaus and Paris meet in single combat outside the walls of Troy, Aphrodite rescues Paris and tries by deceit to lure Helen to his bedroom. Helen is by now longing to return home to Sparta, her husband, family and children, but Aphrodite overcomes her resistance by threatening that if she does not submit, the war will go on and end in misery for them all. Helen appeals to Aphrodite: 'I refuse to go and share his bed again – I should never hear the end of it. There is not a woman in Troy who would not curse me if I did. I have enough to bear already.'[4] However, her appeal fails, and she submits again.

The dramatists

The great Greek dramatists of the sixth and fifth century BC, Aeschylus, Sophocles, Euripides and Aristophanes, recast Homer's legends. Among them, Euripides is especially concerned with disadvantaged people, slaves and women, and in *Alcestis* he deals with the problems of family loyalty. In *Medea*, he describes the dreadful power of a wronged woman, the perennial conflict between men's fear of strong independent women and their right to be treated fairly. As Congreve put it, 'Heaven has no rage like love to hatred turned, nor hell a fury like a woman scorned.'[5] Medea is an enchantress and protects Jason and the Argonauts in their search for the Golden Fleece. Later Jason tires of her and seeks to marry instead the daughter of Creon, King of Corinth. Jason thinks Medea is content with this, as she will be provided for, but her resentment builds up until she takes revenge by arranging in turn the murder of Creon, his daughter and her own children, and finally escapes to sanctuary in Athens. It is a grim tale but her speech depicting the despair of an abandoned woman is timeless. 'Of all things that are living and can form a judgement, we women are the most unfortunate creatures . . . I would very much rather stand three times in the front of battle than bear one child.'[6]

Aristophanes' comedy *Lysistrata* has a historical background. The women of Athens have grown tired of the war with Sparta (431–404 BC), and the inability of their men to make peace. So they agree with the women of Sparta to occupy the Parthenon treasury to cut off the money supply, and they resolve to deny sex to their husbands until the war is ended. Sparta makes peace and the play ends with a banquet for all involved on the Acropolis.[7] The skill with which wives and their lovers devise ways to cuckold their husbands is a frequent and very popular subject of Greek comedy, explicit about goings-on behind and sometimes in front of the curtain. This reflects the generally robust attitude in Greek culture to the physical aspects of human sexuality. Sex was a simple natural function, of no great interest to philosophers, written about and depicted humorously and without embarrassment in ways which later ages tend to regard as coarse or even pornographic.

An equally famous quotation on the status of women comes from a surviving fragment of a play, *Tereus*, a tragedy by Sophocles (496–406 BC). This retells the legend of Philomela and Procne, daughters of Tereus, a mythical king of Athens. He rapes Philomela and locks her up. Procne helps her escape, and they reap a terrible revenge on their father. Sophocles describes the predicament of women thus:

> Outside my father's house I am nothing; yes often I have looked on the nature of women thus, that we are nothing. Young girls, in my opinion, have the sweetest existence known to mortals in their fathers' homes, for innocence keeps children safe and happy always. But when we reach puberty and understanding, we are thrust out and sold away from our ancestral gods and from our parents. Some go to strangers' homes, others to foreigners', some to joyless homes, some to hostile. And all this, once the first night has yoked us to our husband, we are forced to praise and say that all is well.[8]

Real family life

The family structure was monogamous and nuclear; a household would include husband, wife and children, with dependent relatives and slaves. Their houses were built in long street-side blocks, each with its own courtyard. The interior layout provided a ground-floor dining room (for men only), a kitchen and the usual offices and storerooms, with a more secluded sitting room (for the women) and bedrooms upstairs.[9] In Athens citizenship was all-important, the qualification which admitted men to the Assembly, its debates and voting rights. Male children of Athenian citizen parents had this qualification, so marriage to foreigners was discouraged. Athenian wives were also nominally citizens, but they could not attend the Assembly, nor vote. If they left the home alone they were assumed to be inviting unsuitable attention, but they could go in company to the theatre and religious festivals.

Private entertainment at home was provided by dinner parties (*symposia*) to which the householder invited male guests. The women of his family prepared the meal but did not share in the party. Other women were present, the serving girls, the musicians, and the courtesans, *hetairai*, who were either mistresses or high-grade prostitutes. However, some of them were educated women, expected to contribute to the serious discussions at the *symposia*. Visiting Egypt, the Greek historian Herodotus was shocked at the relative freedom of Egyptian women. An Athenian advocate, Appolodoros, defined Greek marriage thus:

> For this is what living in marriage means: when a man sires children and introduces the sons to phratry and deme [roughly, family and neighbours] and gives the daughters to their husbands as their own. For we have courtesans for pleasure, and concubines for the daily service of our bodies, but wives for the production of legitimate offspring and to have reliable guardian of our household property.[10]

In some ways country wives fared better than urban ones. In peasant families they laboured in the fields and kept the home in order. Richer farms had slaves in the fields and cottage industries that gave the owner's wife considerable management responsibility. Xenophon wrote a 'good housekeeping' manual about this in the form of a dialogue between Socrates and a gentleman farmer, Ischomachus. Xenophon (428–354 BC) was an Athenian historian and disciple of

Socrates, but he admired country ways. Ischomachus was a retired army officer and has chosen a sensible young woman as his wife. He tells Xenophon how he has defined their roles within the marriage. In H. D. F. Kitto's description of the passage Ischomachus tells how his wife was not yet fifteen when he married her and had spent her early life in strict seclusion, so that she might not know too much. She knew how to make a garment out of wool, and how to supervise the servants at their spinning, but for the rest Ischomachus instructed her, first offering a sacrifice with prayers, in which the young wife piously joined. Ischomachus had chosen her and her parents him as the likeliest partner to manage the joint house and to beget children to be in every way excellent and to be the support of their old age. His part is to look after what is outside, choose the bailiff and the labourers, train them and keep them loyally at work and happy. Her part is to manage to the best advantage what he brings in; and God has carefully differentiated the natures of men and women accordingly; though in the moral virtues men and women are on the same footing. The wife is compared with the queen bee. It is her duty to manage so that what is intended for a year may not be used up in a month, that garments should be made for those who need them, that the dried foods may be in proper condition when they are wanted. Hers is the duty to look after the slaves when they are sick, but the young wife replies: 'This will be a most agreeable office, for those who are treated well are likely to be grateful, and more attached to me than before.'[11]

Plato: the Symposium, the Republic and the Laws

Plato (427–347 BC) was a student of Socrates and the tutor of Aristotle. Paradoxically, his philosophy has proved more important in Christian history than it ever was in Greece. Although he was not a monotheist in the full sense of Judeo-Christian doctrine, Plato could be called a believer, or perhaps a God-fearer. He said of his own writings that when he was dealing with the most serious subjects he wrote 'God', but for lesser matters he wrote 'god'. He could not believe in the riotous and immoral Olympians as described, since any real God or gods had to be wise and good. His argument for the existence of an ultimate reality beyond human knowing eventually opened the way through Stoicism and Neo-Platonism for Greeks and Christians to compare notes and seek some measure of harmonization; this was crucial to the progress of early Christianity.[12]

Plato's ethical system derives from his political theory, based on his repudiation of the ineffective form of democracy current in Athens, and his conviction that it must be replaced by a totally different oligarchic system. In the *Republic* (which expresses a philosophy he later revised), he thought the way forward was to place government responsibility with a group of carefully bred and specially educated guardians who would control the ill-directed appetites of ordinary people. His first step towards training them was to establish his Academy in 386 BC.

Plato had strong views on the relationship between political policy and private behaviour and opposed the right of individual choice, which just led to chaos. Patterns of behaviour must be imposed by those trained to discern the ultimate public good. The human experiences of sex, love and marriage should be reordered to provide opportunities to search for the highest visions of truth and beauty. He set out the theory in the *Symposium* and in the *Republic*, and proposed replacing marriage and family with communal life under strict regulation. In his old age he became less extreme, and the *Laws* has a list of precepts stressing caution and self-control that read nowadays as almost Victorian in their prudence.

The Symposium

Plato's *Symposium* uses the literary device of table talk at a dinner party to discuss the nature of love. The supposed guests are famous people, but the place of honour is reserved for Socrates, whose philosophy is presented as a corrective and development from what the others have already suggested. The conversation progresses from rather crude ideas, which are gently mocked, to the affirmation of the highest form of divine love which transcends all merely human relationships. In the middle of the dialogue the playwright Aristophanes explains the origin of human beings by the androgynous myth. There were originally three forms, male, female and hermaphrodite, and their abilities were such that they became a threat to the Gods. So Zeus decided to split them in half, with the result that they spent their time searching for their other halves. Half males searched for male lovers, female halves found each other and became lesbian couples, the hermaphrodites, who combined some of the characteristics of the other two species, found halves of the other gender and did the breeding.

The androgynous fable in various forms was widely popular in the

Ancient world. Plato may have heard of it when he visited Egypt. Genesis 2 has the obverse concept of reuniting the sundered Adam, now expressed in the colloquialism 'I have met my other half'. Aristophanes' version reflects the Greek view of the time about homosexuality, but in the *Laws* Plato rejects it. At the dinner party, the fable is not taken too seriously – the real Aristophanes was a brilliant comedian and satirist – but it paves the way for the dialogue between Socrates and Diotima, his long-time friend and 'instructress in the art of love'. She might have been a one-time courtesan or priestess, but in this dialogue she is cast in a leading role intellectually. She argues that the desire to procreate seizes people as the only way of continuing the human race, and therefore becoming themselves immortal. There is a touch of irony here because Socrates had an unsatisfactory marriage with Xanthippe, who did however care for him in his last days. Plato, himself unmarried, is here representing human procreation as a kind of animal necessity and any search for immortality by this means futile. He then goes on to argue that human desire, *eros*, is a bridge between human and eternal things because by its insatiable longing it will move on towards the search for ultimate beauty and goodness. This activity of the soul leads to spiritual procreation and those who achieve it 'will have the privilege of being beloved of God, and becoming, if ever a man can, immortal himself'.[13]

The Republic

The long dialogue we know as the *Republic* seems to have been composed *c.* 380 BC as a guide for Academy students to help them devise constitutions for newly emerging states. Strict rules are laid down for the education and lifestyle of the Guardians to be. They must live in community; private property, marriage and domesticity are to be abolished. Men and women eat together in messes, they are equal in status and training, and women are to do the same work as the men insofar as their physique allows. Since healthy bodies make healthy minds, they share in athletics, both genders unclothed, but the unruly demands of sex, as Plato thought of them, are to be strictly controlled. 'Marriage' may only take place at regular festivals designated for the purpose, and between pre-selected partners of specified ages who are reckoned to produce the best offspring. The ensuing children are to be cared for in communal nurseries to relieve their mothers of the chores of child-bearing, while they concentrate on their training and work.

Children born within these rules are to call all the men and women father or mother, and the other children are their brothers and sisters. Children conceived without permission will be treated as bastards, without civic rights. Siblings may cohabit, and senior citizens older than the official breeding age may mate, but any resulting offspring will be disposed of by abortion or infanticide.[14]

It is not always clear how far Plato intends these strict rules to apply to the ruled as well as the rulers, and certainly some of his interrogators in these dialogues doubt if they would ever be accepted by the ordinary people. Plato's reply is that they will once they are properly educated and see that it will all be for their own good, but perhaps (at least in this dialogue) he never allowed sufficiently for human free will and our dislike of being done good to. To modern minds, Plato's Utopian schema reads like a dehumanizing and totalitarian programme reminiscent of Huxley's *Brave New World* and Orwell's *Animal Farm*, but Plato is an idealist not a dictator, and he had no experience of family life or parenting. His rejection of democracy comes from his own bitter experience of its limitations; he feared the chaos it could bring. His alternative of a ruling commune specially bred and trained for the responsibility seemed to him at the time better than either tyranny or democracy. With neither money nor family of their own the Guardians too would be making sacrifices to serve the common good. The Republican model was never adopted in practice, though parallels in some respects are to be found in Christian monasticism.

The Laws

Plato's final dialogue, the *Laws*, left unrevised at his death, shows the idealism of the *Republic* being applied practically in the form of regulations to govern the proposed small city state of Magnesia. The formal institution of marriage is back in favour but must be state regulated; all other sexual relationships are to be discouraged.

> God willing, perhaps we'll succeed in imposing one or other of two standards of sexual conduct.
> (1) Ideally, no one will dare to have relations with any respectable citizen women except his own wedded wife, or sow illegitimate and bastard seed in courtesans, or sterile seed in defiance of nature.
> (2) Alternatively, while suppressing sodomy entirely, we might insist that if a man does have intercourse with any woman hired or

procured in some other way, except the wife he wed in holy marriage with the blessing of the gods, he must do so without any other
man or woman getting to know about it.[15]

The first clause would eventually find much agreement from Jews and
Christians, the second, though pragmatic, would not. Plato also gives
advice in great detail about how marriages should be arranged and
children conceived. The passage is worth reading, and at some points
one finds Plato indulging his puckish sense of humour. The following
three paragraphs provide a précis of the main points he makes.[16]

Advice is given on choosing a partner. When people are going to live
together as partners, it is vital that the fullest possible information
should be available about the bride and her background and the
family she will marry into. Preventing mistakes is all-important.
Young people's recreation must be arranged with this in mind. Boys
and girls must dance together in order that they may have a reasonable
look at each other, provided sufficient modesty and restraint are
displayed by all concerned. The partners should balance and complement each other (771–2). The headstrong must be forced into marriage with the phlegmatic and vice versa, since marriage is a mixing
bowl. Anyone set on enriching himself by his marriage should be
headed off by reproaches rather than compelled by a written law.

The purpose of marriage is that we should become partners in
eternity by leaving a line of descendants to serve God forever in our
stead, so any man still unmarried at thirty-five years old shall pay a
fine to the treasurer of the shrine of the goddess Hera.[17] Dowries are
not to be asked from poor families because the state will ensure that no
one goes without the necessities of life. But when the rich do provide
dowries they must also give an equal amount to Hera's treasurer, who
must keep a record of these payments. For the wedding feast neither
family should invite more than five friends of both sexes, and the same
number of relatives. Plato even lays down how much may be spent on
the feast, one mina for rich families, less for others, but never exceed-
ing their means.

Drunkenness should always be avoided, especially by the bride and
groom on the day of their wedding, a turning point in their lives. This
ensures that any child they may have had parents who were sober
when they conceived him, it being practically impossible to tell the day
or night when, by the favour of God, conception will take place.
Besides asking that every child should be a wanted child, a drunken

father will be clumsy and inefficient and may sow a misformed child. Further, if the foetus gets off to a careful start, there is a sort of divine guarantee that it will prosper. Plato sets up a group of women associated with the temple of Eileithua, the goddess of childbirth, to act as pregnancy advisers, distinct from midwives. Their task is to supervise newly-weds and make sure that they are concentrating on starting a family; if not they are to be admonished to abandon their sinful ways. The sin might be abortion, or contraception for which medically crude methods were available. If no child is produced after ten years of marriage, the relatives are called together and a divorce is arranged. If the wife dies without issue, the man should marry again. If the man dies but leaves children, the widow will be commended if she looks after them and does not remarry. Plato concludes his advice about marriage by setting age limits, sixteen to twenty years for a girl, thirty to thirty-five for a man.

Aristotle

Aristotle (384–322 BC), was born in Stageira, Macedonia, and studied for twenty years in the Athens Academy, leaving it when Plato died in 347 BC. Philip of Macedon invited him to become tutor to his son Alexander. That ended when Alexander began his reign, and Aristotle eventually returned to Athens to found his own school, the Lyceum. He was wealthy, married to Pythias, and after her death lived with his concubine Herpyllis, who bore him a son, Nicomachus. In his will he provided generously for Herpyllis and Nicomachus, and requested that his wife's bones should be buried with his, the normal custom.

Aristotle's natural bent was as an investigative scientist and his *Physics* was usually regarded in the Middle Ages as definitive. His *Metaphysics* was famous for his description of the final cause of the Universe as 'the unmoved mover'. His *Politics* and *Nicomachean Ethics* greatly influenced the medieval scholar Thomas Aquinas who regarded him as 'an authority it is impertinent to question'. Among the virtues, Aristotle puts great emphasis on temperance (we would say self-control), as opposed to incontinence, that is, giving way to immoderate desire for power, possessions, sex, etc. In Book One of the *Nicomachean Ethics* man is said to be a social being, i.e. belonging to a family, but otherwise self-sufficient. In Book Nine he is a social creature, naturally constituted to live in company with friends. In the *Politics* he is naturally a political animal, able to speak with others and not a recluse. Aristotle is not being inconsistent, the contexts are distinct. In Book Eight of the *Nicomachean Ethics* he analyses friendship, drawing analogies between the different kinds of human friendship and political systems. Marriage is one of these analogies, Aristotle's views in part reflecting conventional Athenian attitudes, but he also identifies friendship within families as a special category, and stresses the value of children.

> The association of husband and wife is clearly an aristocracy. The man rules by virtue of merit and in the sphere that is his by right; but he hands over to his wife such matters as are suitable for her. If the husband asserts control over everything he is turning his rule into an oligarchy, because he is acting without regard for merit and not in conformity with his own superiority. In some cases however, it is the wife that rules, because she is an heiress; such rule, then is based not on merit but on wealth and power, as it is in oligarchies.[18]

> The love of children for their parents (and of men towards the gods) implies a relation between an object that is good and superior in itself; for their parents have bestowed on them the greatest blessings; they are responsible for giving them life and sustenance, and subsequently education.[19]

> The love between husband and wife is considered to be naturally inherent in them. For man is by his nature a pairing rather than a social creature. Inasmuch as the family is an older and more necessary thing than the state, and procreation is a characteristic more commonly shared with the animals. In the other animals partnership goes no further than this; but human beings cohabit not merely to produce children but to secure the necessities of life. From the outset the functions are divided, the husband's being different from the wife's; so they supply each other's deficiencies by pooling their personal resources. For this reason it is thought that both utility and pleasure have a place in conjugal love . . . Children too, it is agreed, are a bond between parents, which is why childless marriages break up more quickly. For the children are an asset common to them both, and common possession is cohesive.[20]

In his later years Plato worked with Aristotle, so the similarity in some of their attitudes to marriage is not surprising. Aristotle was married, which probably accounts for his more positive attitude to the complementarity of partners and the family cohesiveness engendered by children. If his analysis of marriage in his day was based on his observations of family life in Greece, not just his own experience of it, then it was a more humane institution than is often assumed. Perhaps he lived before his time, but his legacy was appreciated by some Roman thinkers. As Horace subtly put it, 'Captured Greece took captive her savage conqueror and brought civilization to rustic Latium.'

Roman marriage

Historical introduction. From Etruria to Byzantium

There were two popular legends about the founding of Rome. In the *Aeneid*, a romantic version of Homer's *Iliad*, Virgil records that Aeneas, one of the Trojan heroes, fled to the place that was to become Rome after Troy was destroyed. An alternative legend, in Livy's *History of Rome*, tells of the twins Romulus and Remus, whose father was Mars, god of war, and mother a daughter of an Alban king. The twins were abandoned by the side of the river Tiber, suckled by a wolf, and brought up by shepherds. Romulus killed Remus in a quarrel and went on to found the city *c.* 753 BC. In fact, from the tenth-century BC, Rome was a small riverside settlement and bridging point in Latium, sandwiched between Etruria to the North and the Greek trading ports of Campania to the South. Under the rule of the subsidiary Etruscan king Tarquin I (*c.* 616 BC), Rome expanded as a monarchy to include its adjoining hillside communities, but won its independence as a Republic in 509 BC.

The Republic lasted nearly five hundred years, enabling Rome to emerge as the dominant power of the Mediterranean, but its system of senatorial and plebian government proved inadequate to control its vast empire, its powerful generals and their armies. After the assassination of Julius Caesar in 44 BC, his designated heir Octavian became Consul of the West. Octavian defeated Antony at the battle of Actium, and Antony and his mistress Cleopatra of Egypt committed suicide. This left Octavian without a rival for ultimate power, and he was given the title Augustus, while proclaiming in 27 BC that he would restore the Republic's former glories. In fact he became the Emperor, Pontifex Maximus (chief priest) and Pater Patriae (father of the Fatherland). He died in AD 14 and was succeeded by his son-in-law

Tiberius. The earthly life of Jesus therefore encompassed the relatively stable reigns of these first two Roman emperors; the first Christians were less fortunate. Tiberius died in AD 37, Caligula reigned for four years, and after his assassination, the moderate Claudius reigned until AD 54. Nero followed him until AD 68 and in his reign Paul and Peter were almost certainly martyred.

Roman marriage law

From Tarquin to Justinian, Rome developed three systems of government, first the monarchy, then the republic and finally the empire. Attitudes to marriage changed gradually from the traditional use of the institution to protect the property and lineage of a privileged aristocracy towards the recognition of free marriage between consenting adults and then to the partial incorporation of Christian ideals into the official legal system. The most dramatic changes were by Augustus, attempting to revive the old decencies, and by Justinian whose codification provided a system of law that became the pattern for most European countries until the nineteenth-century. England and its one-time colonies including America maintained a *sui generis* common law derived from Anglo-Saxon and Norman sources, but the canon law of the Western Church owed much to Justinian, and still does.

Freedom from Etruscan rule did not make life easy for the Romans. Apart from the cost of wars and inefficient agriculture, they were faced with a class struggle. Effective control was in the hands of the patricians while the plebeians, nine tenths of the population, were mostly poor and easily sunk in debt, for which the punishment was to be sold into slavery. The plebeian council demanded that the laws by which the patricians maintained their privileges should be published, and this was done by inscribing them on twelve bronze tablets erected in the Forum for public inspection in 450 BC. References to marriage in the tablets are sparse, mostly linked to inheritance and guardianship rules. Tablet IV says a husband may divorce his wife by ordering her to take her property with her; he claims her keys. Tablet XI forbids marriages between plebeians and patricians.

The Romans thought of marriage and domestic life as a private matter, and they did not expect the law of the state to concern itself overmuch with what happened within the family, which followed its own mores. The meaning of mores is stronger than family custom, individual conscience or 'the way we like to do things here'. It conveyed the Roman sense that they were a people who knew and practised a morality that was better than that of any other nation, including the Greeks and the Jews. State laws were only needed, they thought, as a reminder of what was proper.

In the early Republic, a woman became married by the transfer of authority (*manus*) over her from her father to her husband. The Roman pattern of *pater familias* was broader than Greek tutorship. Within the *manus* of the senior male, the Roman *familia* included his sons as well as his daughters, and his son's children, a large group that might contain several nuclear families. A wife therefore stood in a legal relationship to her husband comparable with his daughters. She could not own property of her own though she could inherit on intestacy alongside his children. Her husband could not put her to death, nor sell her. Contractual and dowry provisions were of the common pattern. Divorce for childlessness could be arranged by agreement with the woman's *familia*.

For citizens, there were three traditional ways by which the *manus* might be transferred by marriage. The religious ceremony, *confarreatio*, named after the cake offered to Jupiter, was limited to patrician families and linked with their obligation to maintain the priesthood. *Co-emptio* was a fictitious legal sale of the woman from her *pater* to her husband's *pater*. *Usus* marriage was established by a man and woman living together for more than a year without any contract or initial ceremony, provided there was evidence that the couple understood themselves to be married, and not in a concubinage relationship. This was an important distinction, because a concubine lacked the legal status of a wife and any children would not acquire citizenship nor have inheritance rights. A woman was allowed to escape from a *usus* marriage if she spent three nights a year away from home. Roman citizens could not marry foreigners without a special dispensation, and slaves could not legally marry each other unless they were freed, though kindly owners might well respect such unions.

All these three *manus* ways of getting married were virtually obsolete by the time of Augustus, having been replaced by free marriage (*sine manu*), which only required formal consent between the partners, provided they had *connubium*, that is, they were of age, not closely related and not soldiers. The great advantage of this system was that it involved no transfer of *potestas* from the bride's family, under whose tutelage she remained, though this would usually be exercised in a nominal way. Since no transfer of property was involved, divorce by consent was facilitated. Married women aged at least twenty-five with three children could acquire freedom from any *potestas*, and the right to change their curators.[21]

The wedding day

Greek women had complained that marriage for them was little more than the exchange of one kind of imprisonment for another. For a Roman woman, marriage meant escape into a dignified freedom, as her new style of dress demonstrated. She was now free to accompany her husband in public on normal social occasions, and to go out by herself, with of course an attendant to protect her from any unseemliness. Her wedding day was one to be remembered.

The date had to be chosen carefully. May was unpropitious; the last two weeks of June were best, probably because the harvest was finished by then. Having given away her toys the day before, she dressed for the ceremony in a white full-length tunic, and her hair was braided and decorated with ribbons. She wore an orange veil. The marriage took place in her family home and the key official was the *pronuba*, a respected once-married matron. After the required sacrifice to the family god, which opened the proceedings, the marriage contract was signed in the presence of ten witnesses. Then the *pronuba* joined the couple's right hands, and they exchanged vows privately. This ceremony ended with a large banquet. Then the groom 'abducted' his bride from her protesting mother, and conducted her in procession to his home. The guests threw rice as a symbol of fertility. At the threshold, he asked her name to which she replied formally (e.g. *'ubi tu Gaius, ergo ego Gaia'*) and then she was lifted over the threshold, and the guests departed. The next day, the bride received her presents from her husband and they went off to a private dinner party with members of both families.[22]

Reviving the old morality

The new system of free marriage was appropriate for the lifestyle of later Republican times, and inter alia opened the way for women to own, inherit and dispose of property, and engage in business and professional life.[23] Suitable professions for a woman were as doctor or midwife, ministering to their own gender, but they could not be

senators, magistrates, lawyers or actresses. The impression of a generally prevailing sexual decadence in the Republic comes largely from the
brilliant literature of comedy and satire of the period and directed at
the ruling clique; ordinary life was not like that. Vituperation directed at
one's political rivals, based on their public performance and intrusion
into their private lives, was standard practice among Roman authors.
Then, as now, some of this material was little more than mischief-
making caricature and not a reliable guide to shifts in general social
behaviour. That said, the economic and social changes of the last years
of the Republic meant that the wealthy élite lost their moorings in
traditional family values.

Emperor Augustus attempted to revive the old morality by a package of new laws commending marriage and discouraging adultery.[24]
He said of his proposals that they were 'to bring back into use many
exemplary practices of our ancestors which were disappearing in our
time, and in many ways I myself transmitted them to posterity for their
imitation'. The laws against adultery were strengthened. A husband
aware of his wife's adultery had to divorce her, and was liable to be
fined if he did not, but it is unlikely that such cases were pursued in
court except to justify divorce without the return of dowries. Fathers,
husbands and members of the public could bring such charges, but
they were time limited. Panderers and pimps and anyone complicit or
acquiescent in adulterous liaisons were at risk. In principle, brothel
keepers were also at risk for offending against public morality, though
prostitutes as such were tolerated. Sex between the betrothed before
marriage was forbidden, but since the period of gestation was reckoned
as between six and ten months, shotgun marriages could circumvent
this rule. A father's consent had always been required for marriage,
but his refusal, if judged unreasonable, could now be overridden by a
magistrate.

Augustus may have had a personal incentive for these rigours
because both his daughter and granddaughter were much given to
sexual licence and he finally exiled both of them. However there was a
much more pressing problem, a shortage of manpower. The incessant
wars had killed off many young men; the low birth rate, infant
mortality, the death of women in childbirth and the generally short
lifespan combined to reduce the citizen population of Rome dramatic-
ally. They were greatly outnumbered by the freed and the still bonded
slaves. So it was necessary to promote the duty of childbearing to
everyone capable of it. Marriage restrictions between free and freed

persons were relaxed and the grant of right of citizenship widely extended. Bachelors who declined marriage were to be taxed for every year they persisted in such unsociable behaviour. Widows who did not remarry had long been praised for honouring their departed spouses, but this policy was now reversed. A widow was encouraged to remarry after six months' mourning. This showed respect for the dead, but pragmatically also allowed any child she might have in that period to be counted as a legitimate heir of her dead husband.[25]

A sentimental people

Despite the tough impression they liked to give, most Roman men felt the usual slings and arrows of outrageous fortune. They were sentimental people in some ways, with romantic notions about love. Outside the patrician circle, preoccupied with property and political alliances, most fathers tried to do their best for their daughters, taking their wishes into account. They loved their wives and mourned them in touching epitaphs. When Lucretius Vespillo, an officer in Pompey's army, lost Turia, his wife of forty-one years, the inscription he wrote for the marble wall of her tomb spelled out her virtues.

> You were a faithful wife to me, and an obedient one; you were kind and gracious, sociable and friendly, assiduous at your spinning. You followed the religious rites of your family and your state. You did not dress conspicuously, nor seek to make a display in your household arrangements. You tended my mother as carefully as if she had been your own.

Turia had not led the tranquil life this epitaph suggests while Lucretius had been away from home, caught up in the civil war between Pompey and Julius Caesar. Her parents had been murdered by soldiers, her home was occupied, and she was in personal danger. Worse was that she was childless, and offered to divorce Lucretius, but he replied: 'What is the need of children compared with my loyalty to you?'[26]

In similar vein, the younger Pliny wrote to his young wife Calpurnia when she was ill after a miscarriage:

> It is incredible how much I miss you, because I love you and then because we are not used to being separated. And so I lie awake most of the night haunted by your image and during the day, during the

hours I used to spend with you, my feet lead me, they really do, to your room; and then I turn and leave, sick at heart and sad, like a lover locked out on a deserted doorstep.[27]

There was a vast amount of Roman lyric poetry, of which two examples must suffice. The first is from Catullus, on the pain of unrequited love. Catullus (84–54 BC) was born in Verona, and settled in Sirmio by Lake Garda.[28] He had fallen in love with a married woman whom he called Lesbia. She was probably Clodia, a Roman lady who dispensed her favours widely. He wrote twenty-five poems to her, moving from the first excitement of love to learning how to survive her indifference:

> Although she cannot be content with me alone, I'll bear my lady's rare discreet adventures, rather than seem to be a nagging busybody. Often the queen of heaven, mighty Juno, mastered her blazing wrath when her husband was at fault, and yet she knew the escapades of Jove. (Poem 68)

Later, he accuses himself for his foolish obsession:

> You poor Catullus, don't be such a crass-brained fool. All that is obviously lost, you must write it off. The sun shone brightly on you once in days gone by when you would follow everywhere the girl led on. The girl I loved as no girl ever loved . . . whose lips will you be kissing now with love-sharp bites? No, no, Catullus, be determined; be still bard. (Poem 8)

Ovid (43 BC–AD 17), the most famous Roman composer of love poetry, was born at Sulmo in the Appennines, and was sent into exile soon after he wrote *The Art of Love*. This was about the same time as Augustus banished his granddaughter Julia for adultery and conjecture has it that Ovid was somehow involved, though he protested innocence. However that may have been, Ovid's works might be fairly described as the best sex manuals available at his time, though of course very delicately worded. His style was never pornographic, but light-hearted and self-mocking. He wrote a humorous and slightly naughty poem to his mistress, Cypassis, maidservant to his wife Corinna.

Expert in ornamenting hair in a thousand fashions, but pretty enough to set a goddess' curls, Cypassis, my sophisticated fellow-sinner, deft at serving her, defter for me – Who could have betrayed the mingling of our bodies? How did Corinna sense our love affair? Surely I did not blush? Or stumble over a word that gave some evidence of our stolen love? Of course I said the man who loved a servant girl must be a hopeless idiot – of course! But the Thessalian hero loved the slave Briseis, captive Cassandra fired Mycenae's king. Achilles and Agamemnon fell, I am no stronger; so *honi soit qui mal y pense* say I . . . And now, tan skinned Cypassis, will you not repay me with sweet embraces for my loyalty? Do not object – I've earned it. Don't invent new dangers: to please one of your masters is enough. If you are foolish and refuse, I shall betray us, and turn state's evidence for both our guilt . . . And tell your lady where I was with you, Cypassis, how often and in what positions too. (*Amores* 2.8)[29]

A new philosophy of sex

Silencing the eroticism of Catullus and Ovid by exile seemed to Augustus a necessary part of his campaign to revive the old moralities of Rome, but it was no real solution to a culture that had grown away from its roots. A new philosophy was needed, and this was found through Stoicism, although paradoxically this was itself nothing new, since it dated back to Zeno in Athens, *c.* 300 BC. Cicero and then the Emperor Marcus Aurelius (AD 121–80) revived and reshaped Stoicism for the Romans.[30]

Stoicism and its teaching about following nature and restraining sexual appetites corresponded with the increasingly influential Christian presence in Rome and the major cities of its empire. It is not easy to assess how important these ascetic views were in the second and third centuries AD, nor how far the Christian ethos of marriage had spread by then.[31] No doubt the official attitudes reflected those of each emperor, for better or worse, and respect was countered by ribaldry, but the tide was on the turn. The change in sexual morality, at least in principle, is shown more clearly in the legal opinions of a series of distinguished third-century jurists, notably Papinian, Ulpian, Modestinus and Paulus. For example, the old custom that men could have a concubine as well as a wife was questioned. Papinian (died 212) advised that if a marriage contract included a clause prohibiting concubinage, but the husband subsequently brought one into the house, the wife could repudiate the marriage. What he did outside his home was his own business, but in due course, Constantine made a law forbidding married men to have concubines. An important element in Stoic teaching was the doctrine of Divine or Natural Law. Ulpian stated that 'all men are born free and slavery is contrary to Natural Law', and Modestinus cites this doctrine in his opinion that 'marriage is a partnership for life involving divine as well as human law'. Quotations from these jurists are extensively used in Justinian's *Digest* and became important for the Christian tradition.

4

Judaism between the Testaments

The influence of Hellenism on the Near East

There was an interval of some four hundred years between the completion of the Jewish Scriptures eventually to be included in the Hebrew Bible and the composition of the first books of the New Testament. It was a period of great change for the Eastern Mediterranean lands. Alexander had conquered Syria, Palestine and Egypt in 332 BC and on his death ten years later this part of his empire was divided between the Ptolemies in Egypt and the Seleucids in Syria, with Palestine as piggy-in-the-middle. The whole region had been caught up in Alexander's policy of Hellenization, vigorously pursued by his successors. Greek trading colonies and a Greek style of civil administration were imposed, and *koine* Greek became the universal language, hence the Septuagint. A cluster of Greek towns was built in North Eastern Galilee (the Decapolis), temples to the Greek gods were built in major towns, and a gymnasium was built in Jerusalem.

The Seleucid Antiochus III and his successors expanded their empire southwards to Alexandria, and were seen as a challenge by Rome. Pompey was sent to Syria to restore the situation there and to guard the eastern frontier of the empire against the Parthians. He occupied Judea and entered Jerusalem in 64 BC. The Romans had come to admire much in the Greek way of life, and often copied it, so they saw little point in disturbing the tenacious Hellenistic culture of the Eastern colonies now under their rule. They were on the whole content to demonstrate their authority by their military presence, statues of the emperor and taxation. They established political control by appointing governors or procurators such as Pilate and vassal local princes, of which the most famous was Herod the Great, but otherwise left the local administration in place, only interfering when their security or dignity was challenged. From their encounters with the Jewish settlements in other parts of their empire and in Rome itself by that time, the

Romans were aware that Judaism was a faith its adherents would die for. Within reason they permitted the Jews to continue their own religious practices and domestic lifestyle, and that included their marriage laws.

The effects of the Greek and Roman occupation on Jewish life in Palestine were mixed. Cosmopolitan Jews welcomed it; conservatives resisted it. But the reality was that the loss of political independence, and the inescapably pluralist nature of society thrust upon them, changed Jewish self-understanding. They were no longer a nation state; their special identity had to come from their ethnic origin and their wholehearted commitment to the Torah, so they became the people of the Book and the Sanctuary. In Jerusalem, the Temple area was a hive of activity, its sacrificial system carefully sustained by the priests, while Herod's massive building programme went on around them. In the countryside each sizeable village had a synagogue where the Law and Prophets were read through either in Hebrew or in Greek on a three-year cycle, with a rabbi or layman to translate the sacred texts into Aramaic and expound the meaning. Simple country folk hoped for better times and kept their heads down, while their children learned the Psalms at their mother's knee, usually also in Aramaic.

Some urban Jews fiercely resisted the signs of pluralism. They were outraged at the imperial statues, the pagan temples, the brothels and the naked athletes at the games, a particular embarrassment for any circumcised Jews who wished to take part. They looked for God to send them a deliverer, and a few zealots were eager to plot revolution. There had been a momentary glimpse of such a future when Judas Maccabeus led the revolt against Antiochus Epiphanes and they had achieved a measure of independence in 142 BC. The Hasmonaeans had struggled to keep an uneasy balance of the authority between the High Priest and the vassal princes, until in 27 BC Herod took total control, relying on the patronage of the Roman emperor, Octavian.

The Diaspora Jews, in Babylon, Egypt, Syria, Rome and points West, who now outnumbered the Palestinian Jews, were equally caught up in the political changes. The Romans allowed them certain privileges, which the other ethnic minorities resented. They were allowed to keep the Sabbath, assemble in their synagogues, observe their own dietary laws, and even substitute prayers for the Emperor in the Synagogue instead of offering a sacrifice in front of his statue. The Diaspora Jews were careful to maintain contact with Jerusalem, by correspondence and pilgrimage visits, and Jerusalem was in a real sense their spiritual home. It was a cosmopolitan city. Despite their respect for the Temple many Palestinian Jews were aware of Greek and Roman philosophy and culture, and could see the benefits of belonging to a freethinking pluralist society in which it was possible to value the wisdom of both worlds.[1]

The Apocryphal literature

The Septuagint, the Greek Bible from Alexandria, included the so-called Apocryphal books. These did not find a place in the Hebrew Bible, but were regarded as part of scripture by Diaspora Jews and the early Christians. Jerome included them in the Vulgate, but with a note, later ignored, that their authority was open to question. Catholic and Orthodox Churches treated them as Deuterocanonical scripture; the churches of the Reformation excluded them or printed them separately.[2] They are of diverse character, history, fable, or proverbial wisdom, and their generic name is misleading. They are not revealing hidden mysteries, as the name suggests, nor are they concealed documents in the sense of censorship. The exciting tales of Judith, Tobit and Susanna were easy-to-read reminders that devout law-abiding men and women could still depend on God's help in difficult situations. Scenes from the lives of Judith, Tobit and Susanna were often painted by Tintoretto, Rembrandt and others. Over fifty examples can be seen in the major galleries of Europe and America.[3] These Apocryphal books provide useful insights into Jewish attitudes to men, women and marriage from some two hundred years before Christ until *c.* AD 100, an essential background for understanding the New Testament teaching. Judaism at this time did not hold a dour view of marriage; it was a harbinger of joy, as well as a duty, and children were a blessing.

Tobit

The story of Tobias and Sarah is a powerful illustration of the way the themes of faithful love, romanticism, respect for parents, and above all the sense that God's blessing hovered over the marital bed. Before their marriage is consummated they pray:

Blessed are you, O God of our ancestors,
  and blessed is your name in all generations for ever.
Let the heavens and the whole creation bless you for ever.

You made Adam, and for him you made his wife Eve
  as a helper and support.
From the two of them the human race has sprung.
You said, 'It is not good that the man should be alone;
  let us make a helper for him like himself.'
I am now taking this kinswoman of mine,
  not because of lust,
  but with sincerity.
Grant that she and I may find mercy
  and that we may grow old together.

(Tob. 8.5–7)

Susanna

Susanna, an addition to the Book of Daniel, is a moral tale in the form of a detective story. She is the beautiful and pious wife of Joakim, a rich Babylonian Jew. His house is used as a courtroom by the local judges, and when proceedings for the day end, two old judges conspire to rape Susanna. They arrange to intrude on her when she is bathing unattended in the garden pool, and threaten her that if she does not submit they will accuse her of having secret sex with a young man. However she shouts out and servants arrive. The next day the judges accuse her of adultery, for which the penalty would be death under the Deuteronomic law. 'Through her tears she looked up towards Heaven, for her heart trusted in the Lord' (Sus. 35). She is condemned to death, but God stirs up the holy spirit of a young lad named Daniel, who insists that she must have a proper trial. He then cross-examines the two judges, their evidence proves contradictory, and they are put to death for making a false accusation against her.

Ecclesiasticus

A less romantic view of marriage is given in Ecclesiasticus ('The Wisdom of Ben Sirach'), a longer and probably later collection of wisdom than the canonical book, Proverbs, but similar in its teaching. There are many references to the marriage relationship, and these would have been in mind during the debates between Jesus and the Pharisees. In Ben Sirach, the truism that a good marriage is a blessing and a bad one a disaster is repeated several times and men are advised not to divorce a good woman. But they are warned to keep clear of a frustrated or cantankerous one. There is clearly an anxiety about women's character, the two faces of Eve; she is the good companion and yet the cause of sin and death. One can respect the bravery of Judith and yet remember that she was a mistress of deception and cut off the head of a king, so it is wise to be wary. Women are no longer seen as chattels, but if given too much freedom they can be a danger to themselves and to their menfolk. Thus: 'Do not dismiss a wise and good wife, for her charm is worth more than gold' (Ecclus. 7.19). The responsibilities of fathers are spelled out:

> Do you have children? Discipline them,
>   and make them obedient from their youth.
> Do you have daughters? Be concerned for their chastity,
>   and do not show yourself too indulgent with them.
> Give a daughter in marriage, and you complete a great task;
>   but give her to a sensible man.
> Do you have a wife who pleases you? Do not divorce her;
>   but do not trust yourself to one whom you detest.
> With all your heart honour your father,
>   and do not forget the birth pangs of your mother.
> Remember that it was of your parents that you were born;
>   how can you repay what they have given to you?
>   (Ecclus. 7.23–8)

And again: 'Do not go near a loose woman, or you will fall into her snares' (9.3).[4]

Fornication and adultery by men are castigated in chapter 23, followed by a warning to unfaithful wives whose children will be rejected.

> To a fornicator all bread is sweet;
>   he will never weary until he dies.
> The one who sins against his marriage bed
>   says to himself, 'Who can see me? . . .
>   The Most High will not remember sins.'
> His fear is confined to human eyes
>   and he does not realize that the eyes of the Lord
>   are ten thousand times brighter than the sun;
> they look upon every aspect of human behaviour
>   and see into hidden corners.
>   (23.17–19)

So it is with a woman who leaves her husband
  and presents him with an heir by another man.
  For first of all she has disobeyed the law of the Most High;
  second, she has committed an offence against her husband;
  and third, through her fornication she has committed adultery . . .
She herself will be brought before the assembly,
  and her punishment will be extended to her children,
  . . . her disgrace will never be blotted out.

(23.22–6)

Later, a long passage asserts that it is better to live with a lion than an evil woman, and restates the old accusation:

From a woman sin had its beginning,
  and because of her we all die.
. . . If she does not go as you direct,
  separate her from yourself.

(25.16, 24–6)

This alternation of praise and denigration of women is repeated in the remaining chapters, and one wonders why the subject of good and bad wives deserves such reiteration, while nothing is said to warn women about good and bad husbands. The answer has to be that misogyny is still embedded in these writings, though change is on the way.[5]

Other Jewish writings about Adam and Eve

Apart from the Apocryphal books, many other religious texts have survived, some virtually from the time they were written, others once well known, but then lost, and rediscovered more recently. The early Christian theologians often referred to them in their exegesis of the Adam and Eve narrative in Genesis, and they have helped modern biblical scholars to understand the original context of the New Testament documents. Being extra-canonical, they are largely unfamiliar to most Christians. Those texts, which predate the Christian era, show how Jewish thought was beginning to accommodate Hellenistic culture within the received tradition. They were seeing old truths from a different perspective from that of the post-exilic editors. They did not of course rewrite the old narratives, but they added to them in ways that were intended to make their import clearer for a later generation.

The texts are usually classified as Pseudepigrapha, Jewish history and Midrash. The Pseudepigrapha comprise a large collection of writings purporting either to be lost parts of canonical books or additional works by biblical characters. The writings date from the second century BC onwards, and often contain Christian interpolations. The Midrash is a collection of rabbinic commentaries on the Torah. Beginning soon after Ezra, it became a standard form of exegesis and appropriate sections were quoted in the synagogue after the reading from the Pentateuch. It is quite unlike modern Bible commentaries, consisting only of selected opinions from the most respected rabbis, and continually added to. All these texts include some reference to marriage and sexual morality as portrayed in the Pentateuch, and these are usually modified or commented on in ways that suggest the behaviour of the Patriarchs is no longer quite acceptable. The dilemma for the intertestamental writers was that they had to honour the sacred texts while being aware that pagans who followed Platonic and Stoic teaching would not be impressed by the apparent crudity of some Patriarchal lifestyles.

Two quotes from Pseudepigrapha

The Testaments of the Twelve Patriarchs

This collection follows the pattern in Genesis 49 of Jacob's deathbed blessing on his sons, the ancestors of the twelve tribes of Israel. Each dying son, from Reuben to Benjamin, confesses his sins and faith and exhorts his children to better ways. Reuben confesses to having taken sexual advantage of Bilhah, Jacob's concubine, while she was lying drunk and naked in bed (Gen. 35.22). Jacob learned of this and never forgave him, calling him 'unstable as water'. So Reuben warns his sons:

> See here, I call the God of Heaven to bear witness to you this day. So that you will not behave yourself in the ways of youth and sexual promiscuity in which I indulged myself, and defiled the marriage bed of my father Jacob.[6]

The Sibylline Oracles

Sibyls were women inspired with mystic visions, and were sometimes taken seriously by the Romans, whose magistrates might appeal to them for guidance in difficult cases. This collection of oracles, describing aspects of Jewish history with Christian interpolations, is falsely attributed to a daughter of Noah, and its provenance was probably Phrygia in Asia Minor. These oracles were often quoted by the Church fathers, and echoed in Dante's *Inferno*. Michelangelo painted five Sibyls alongside Old Testament prophets in the Sistine Chapel. The dating of the original components is uncertain, any time before the fourth century AD, but the first part of Book One, an account of the Creation and Fall, may well be from an early Jewish source. It is a typical attempt to explain Jewish origins for Roman readers.

> [God] fashioned an animate object, making a copy from his own image, a youthful man, beautiful and wonderful. He bade him live in an ambrosial garden, so that he might be concerned with beautiful works. But he being alone in the luxuriant plantation of the garden, desired conversation and prayed to behold another form like his own. God himself indeed took a bone from his flank and made Eve, a wonderful maidenly spouse who he gave to this man to live with him in the garden. And he when he saw her was suddenly greatly amazed in spirit, rejoicing, such a corresponding copy did he see. They conversed with wise words, which flowed spontaneously, for God had taken care of everything. For they neither covered their minds with licentiousness nor felt shame, but were far removed from evil heart; and they walked like wild beasts with uncovered limbs.[7]

> A very horrible snake craftily deceived them to go to the fate of death and receive knowledge of good and evil. But the woman first became a betrayer to him. She gave, and persuaded him to sin in his ignorance . . . He was persuaded by the woman's words, forgot about his immortal creator, and neglected clear commands. Therefore, instead of good they received evil, as they had done. And then they sowed the leaves of the sweet fig tree and made clothes and put them on each other. They concealed their plans because shame had come upon them.[8]

The historian Josephus

Josephus (37–*c.* 100) was a Palestinian Jew from a priestly family, and became a Pharisee. He was captured by the Romans in 67 AD, during the Jewish war, and eventually became a Roman citizen, trusted by the emperor who gave him a pension. His two books, *The Jewish War* and *The Antiquities of the Jews*, are the best contemporary historical sources, inevitably somewhat slanted to avoid criticism of Rome, and therefore unacceptable to the Jews who regarded him as a traitor. His work begins with the creation and ends with the start of the war. Although he embroiders the biblical narratives with much imagination, there is also some accurate background detail.[9] The opening chapter of the *Antiquities* describes the creation of Eve briefly:

> But when he [God] saw that Adam had no female companion, no society, for there was no such created, and that he wondered at the other animals which were male and female, he laid him asleep and took away one of his ribs, and out of it formed the woman; where-upon Adam knew her when she was brought to him, and acknowl-edged that she was made out of himself.

A little later the Fall is dealt with much more fully:

> The serpent, which then lived together with Adam and his wife, showed an envious disposition, at his supposal of their living happily, and in obedience to the commands of God; and imagining that, when they disobeyed them, they would fall into calamities, he persuaded the woman, out of malicious intention, to taste of the tree of knowledge, telling them that in that tree was the knowledge of good and evil; which knowledge when they should obtain, they would lead a happy life, nay, a life not inferior to that of a god: by which means he overcame the woman, and persuaded her to despise the command of God. Now when she had tasted of that tree, and was pleased with its fruit, she persuaded Adam to make use of it also. Upon this they perceived that they were become naked to one another; and being ashamed thus to appear abroad, they invented somewhat to cover them . . . But when God came into the garden, Adam, who was wont before to come and converse with him, being conscious of his wicked behaviour went out of the way. This behaviour surprised God, and he asked what was the cause of this his procedure . . .

Adam goes on to lay the blame on his wife, who in turn lays the blame on the serpent: 'But God allotted him punishment, because he weakly submitted to the counsel of his wife.'[10]

Since Josephus' purpose in writing is to explain Judaism to the Romans, he explains the Jewish laws in ways that would seem sensible to them. Thus, for the seventh commandment he offers this prudential justification:

> As for adultery, Moses forbade it entirely, as esteeming it a happy thing that men should be wise in the affairs of wedlock; and that it was profitable both to cities and families that children should be known to be genuine.[11]

The duty to be married was strongly urged in post-exilic Judaism, not only for the procreation of children, but as the antidote to loneliness, referring back to Genesis 2.18, as we have seen in the prayer of Tobias. Psalms of the period took a very positive view of marriage and children.

> Sons are indeed a heritage from the LORD,
>   the fruit of the womb a reward.
> Like arrows in the hand of a warrior
>   are the sons of one's youth.
> Happy is the man who has
>   his quiver full of them.
>
> (Ps. 127.3–5)

> Your wife will be like a fruitful vine
>   within your house;
> your children will be like olive shoots
>   around your table.
> Thus shall the man be blessed
>   who fears the LORD.
>
> (Ps. 128.3–4)

The Midrash

The Midrash Rabbah is an extended commentary on Genesis, dating from the third century AD, but with later additions. As a commentary, it consists of quotations from respected rabbis whose views are often clearly different, without any indication of which is to be preferred, reflecting the genuine dialectic between the recognized schools. This is clearly shown in the contrasting quotations below about the creation of Adam and Eve, marriage and divorce. 'He who has no wife dwells without good, without help, without joy and without atonement.'[12]

The rabbis also noted that in the Priestly creation narrative, man and woman were created together, and deduced that only together did they bear the image of God. An unmarried man was therefore incomplete and the divine image in him impaired.[13] The command to multiply, which followed directly, meant that the image of God was passed on to the whole human race by them jointly. The rabbis were of course aware of the androgynous myth, and their view of the one-flesh relationship was not totally inconsistent with it. There is here the root of the later Christian sense of marriage as a spiritual communion (*koinonia*) between God, man and woman in relationship.

The next two comments refer to God's act in taking a part of Adam to form Eve. The first seems to ignore the traditional 'rib' (Gen. 2.21–2) and suggests instead that God carefully considered which part of Adam's body to take her from. His survey rejected head, eye, ear mouth, heart, hand and foot, and settled for his 'modest part' that is the nether organs! The reasons for rejecting the other parts are given in terms of the unsatisfactory aspects of women's character that might ensue and the whole text seems to be an excuse for denigrating women.

> God said: I will not create her from Adam's head, lest she be swell-headed; nor from the eye lest she be a coquette; nor ear (eavesdropper); nor mouth (a gossip); nor heart (jealousy); nor hand (light-fingered); nor foot (a gadabout); but from the modest part of man, for even when he stands naked, that part is covered.[14]

Perhaps this kind of diatribe was not meant to be taken too seriously, but it could hardly have been read out in a synagogue. It is characteristic of Midrash to set down conflicts of opinions, and let the reader decide. A more positive view of the nature of women is given in this exchange between the Roman emperor, his daughter and the greatly respected Gamaliel, Patriarch of the Jews in Rome while their position there was temporarily secure.

> The Emperor to Rabbi Gamaliel: 'Your God is a thief, for it is written in Genesis 2.21 that the Lord caused a deep sleep to fall upon man, and while he slept took out one of his ribs.' The Emperor's daughter said 'Leave me to answer him. Give me a guard.' Her father

asked why. 'Thieves came at night and took from us a pitcher of silver, but left us a pitcher of gold.' 'If only they would come to us every day' replied the Emperor. She said 'Then is it not better for the first man that a rib was taken from him, and instead a handmaid was presented him for his use?'[15]

A very popular rabbinic story from *c.* 150 AD perpetuates the belief that marriages, if not exactly made in heaven, are arranged by God's providence. The story begins with Rabbi Jose expounding Psalm 75.7, 'but it is who executes judgement, putting down one and lifting up another'.

> A Roman lady asked Rabbi Jose ben Halafta . . . 'what was [God] doing after that time [the six days of creation]?' He answered 'He is joining couples . . . A's wife [to be] allotted to A; A's daughter is allotted to B . . .' Said she: 'This is a thing which I, too, am able to do. See how many male slaves and how many female slaves I have; I can make them consort together all at the same time.'

She goes away and arranges the slaves' marriages, but in the morning they come to her with wounded heads and eyes and elbows and legs – the result of strife. She sends for the rabbi and declares 'Your Torah is true.' The rabbi declares that even for God it is 'a task as hard as the dividing of the Red Sea'.[16]

The tradition of rabbinic commentary on scripture was continued through the Middle Ages. The most famous Jewish theologian and biblical exegete was Rashi, Rabbi of Troyes in the eleventh century. He comments on Genesis 2.18–20 that the reason for Eve's creation was to make clear that man's status was not to be divinized; only God could stand alone:

> In order that people may not say that there are two deities, the Holy One, blessed be He, the only one among the celestial beings without a mate, and this one, Adam, the only one among the terrestrial beings without a mate, He made a help meet for him. If he is worthy, she shall be a help to him; if he is unworthy, she shall be opposed to him, to fight him. When God brought all the animals to Adam he brought them male and female of each and every kind. Thereupon Adam said all these have a mate, but I have no mate.[17]

Nicholas of Lyre, the thirteenth-century Franciscan biblical exegete, who had a good understanding of Hebrew, translated Rashi into Latin. Lyre's own commentary was printed in Nuremberg *c.* 1488, and widely distributed. As valuable incunabulae, copies can still be found in some cathedral libraries. Luther quotes from Lyre extensively, so it is fair to say that Rashi was one source of Reformation theology.

The sects within Judaism

In the century before the birth of Christ, the Jewish people were united in their respect for the Torah, but divided about how it should be interpreted. As Josephus noted, the three main divisions were the Sadducees, the Pharisees and the Essenes. The Sadducees were a small group of influential people who held many seats in the Sanhedrin and were prepared to co-operate with the Romans. They supposedly took their name from Zadok the High Priest and included members of the hereditary priesthood who controlled the Temple worship. For the Sadducees, the only law that mattered was the Old Testament Pentateuch and the Prophets. They bestowed no authority on rabbinic interpretation, and did not believe in the possibility of resurrection.

By comparison, the Pharisees, whose name meant 'separated', rejected the Sadducean involvement in political affairs, but in their search for personal holiness amidst the distractions of secularism they held that the Law of Moses included the whole corpus of rabbinic interpretations. They were careful to ensure that the precepts of the Decalogue were thoroughly applied to everyday life, and to that end, for the fourth Commandment, on Sabbath-keeping, they added thirty-nine precepts to guide people as to what could and could not be done. As a predominantly lay movement, concentrated in the country districts though directed from Jerusalem, they came into contact with Jesus in Galilee. They agreed with him about resurrection but not with his emphasis on the basic principles of the Torah rather than on the minutiae of its interpretation. Their confrontation with him about marriage and divorce highlights the difference of approach.[18]

The third sect was the Essenes, taking their name from the Aramaic word *hasa*, which meant 'pious'. They rejected the urban lifestyle of the Sadducees, and everything Hellenistic, and withdrew into semi-monastic communities in the desert regions of Southern Judea. They were ascetic and commended celibacy, but not for everyone. There is evidence of marriage and family life in some Essene communities, though domestic life was thought to be a danger to the higher forms of spiritual discipline, diverting attention from minute-by-minute reflection on the Torah. Abstinence from sex, even for years, was recommended, and required for those participating in the Temple services. This went beyond the purity rules of Leviticus, but it was consonant with the normal Jewish idea that those who were called to special religious tasks should separate from their wives and embrace celibacy. The Talmud claims that the tradition that men called to prophesy should cease to have sex with their wives can be traced back to Moses.[19]

The Community of the Renewed Covenant at Qumran has become famous for its Dead Sea scrolls which have provided texts of the Old Testament texts a thousand years older than any others we have. The Qumran community led a sometimes precarious existence from *c.* 175 BC to *c.* AD 70. Part of the time, after an earthquake, the site was derelict. How far Qumran was unique is uncertain. It may have been the mother house of the Essenes, or loosely affiliated to them, and in any case would have had some contact with Essene groups in the desert on the east side of the Dead Sea, and with Masada. Like these communities, they practised abstinence for long periods, and were mocked for it by Josephus and Philo, but there is evidence from Qumran of families, wives and children in residence. Apart from the scrolls, the library at Qumran contained sets of rules for the community's life, including the Damascus Document. This was supposedly composed by the original founders of the community; their leader and a small breakaway group of priests of the post-exilic period fled to the region of Damascus when persecuted by the more orthodox Jews. The Essenes followed some of its precepts.

Incomplete copies of the Damascus Document from the twelfth century were found in a pile of documents in Cairo in 1896, but the Qumran text, although also fragmentary, is probably original. This contains a reference to Genesis 1.27, 'Male and female he created them', with the comment that a man who takes a second wife while the first is alive commits fornication.[20] The reference to the second wife while the first is still alive may be a prohibition of polygamy since the normal process in Judaism was to divorce the first wife and then remarry, but it could mean 'no divorce' and antedate the teaching of Jesus to this effect. At least one can say that the Damascus Document indicates that, either among the Essenes or from Qumran, there was a view circulating that remarriage after divorce should be prohibited. This would fit with their characteristic policy of going beyond the strictness of the law. Although Qumran was only ten miles south-east of Jericho, and Jesus was often in this area, there is no evidence of his visiting the community itself, nor do the Gospels ever mention the Essenes. One can speculate that Jesus was aware of their teaching, but his own mission strategy was very different from their exclusiveness. John the Baptist was probably familiar with the strict Essene rules. His criticism of Herod's marriage to Herodias, his brother's wife, brought him imprisonment and then execution (Matt. 14.1–12).

Jewish marriage

Jewish marriage was in principle monogamous, and polygamy, though permitted among the aristocratic class, had become rare and frowned upon in the first century. Young Jewish women were not housebound: they went to the well for water, went shopping for food, clothes, hats, etc., and could find employment making and selling them. Young men and women could meet without a chaperone, especially at folk festivals and at dances in the vineyards. Jewish girls were married young, soon after puberty, and the men were reckoned ready for marriage at eighteen. Marriage however was still a matter of negotiation between families, and since the first home would be with the groom's parents, the contract would be worked out in their favour, as they would bear most of the expense. Lineage was still important among orthodox Jews and had to be checked out before the betrothal was agreed. Once the contract was signed, a ring was given and the couple were regarded as married. There was then an interval of some months during which the couple completed their domestic arrangements. The groom set aside the usual gift to his wife, which would be given to her if he divorced her. In Judea, the woman remained in her father's house until she married but in Galilee the couple sometimes cohabited 'in order to get acquainted'. If the girl then became pregnant, they had to marry, and the boy could not claim she was not a virgin at marriage.

The actual procedures for marriage were largely the same in Palestine as in other parts of the Near East, unchanged for centuries. The ceremonies were simple, the handing over of the bride into her new family and her move into the groom's home, usually in the evening with a procession.[21] It did not involve a visit to the synagogue nor the presence of a rabbi, but this did not mean it was a civil rather than a religious occasion. Prayers and blessings would be said by senior members of the families as part of Judaism's normal perception that God was to be honoured in every home. It was not unusual for guests to join in the feasting for days after the ceremony.[22]

Jewish divorce regulations in the first century AD

We have already noted that Ben Sirach distinguishes between the good wife who should be retained and the bad one who should be divorced, and since a written bill of divorce had to be used, it became necessary to define recognized grounds. But this proved no easy matter and was much debated. The Midrash Rabbah comment on Eve as helper (Gen. 2.8) reflects the view that a man could rid himself of his partner for any trivial reason. If a man is fortunate, his wife is like that of Rabbi Hananiah, if not, she is like the wife of Rabbi Jose, who used to put him to shame. He is advised to divorce her, but he cannot afford to repay her dowry. His disciples test the matter. They go to his house where his wife angrily tells Rabbi Jose there is hash in the pot. It turns out to be chicken. So the disciples say she has not treated him with respect and he should divorce her, and they club together to collect enough money for the dowry.[23]

A more precise assessment of the conflicting views is in the Mishnah, a codification of rabbinic thought by Rabbi Judah the Patriarch, *c.* 200 AD.[24] The Mishnah has many references to the procedures for betrothal, marriage and divorce, reflecting the Pentateuchal Covenant codes, but does not resolve the dispute about the proper grounds for divorce.

> The school of Shammai says: A man may not divorce his wife unless he has found unchastity in her, for it is written: 'because he has found in her indecency in anything'. And the School of Hillel says he may divorce her even if she spoiled a dish for him, for it is written 'because he found in her indecency in anything'.[25]

The text is a commentary on Deuteronomy 24.1–4, which modern translations regard as best understood in the wider sense, the wife being found objectionable rather than specifically unchaste. The reasoning is that in the Deuteronomic legislation, wives have become legally responsible to keep the law, so if she has committed adultery, both she and her partner are guilty under the criminal law, and will be put to death. This text deals with the lesser problem of a man who finds his wife unsatisfactory even though she is not unchaste.[26] This is the interpretation followed by the Hillel school, who generally supported the liberal Pharisaic view, while the Shammai school were strict, perhaps surprisingly since they normally preferred traditional views, which in this case were liberal. Josephus followed the Hillel teaching:

> He that desires to be divorced from his wife for any cause whatsoever (and many such causes happen among men) let him in writing give assurance that he will never use his wife anymore; for by this means she may be at liberty to marry another husband.[27]

Although the Shammai and Hillel schools were influential at the time of Jesus, documents of their teaching have not survived. When the Pharisees challenge Jesus on the divorce question, they quote the Hillel view.[28]

The Mishnah also cites circumstances when a wife may require her husband to divorce her, and if he refuses she may apply to the court to force him to do so. If he remains sexually inactive for longer periods than the law prescribed, he has failed her in the 'duty of marriage'. If no children are born within the first ten years of marriage, they can agree to part, and she can insist on it and apply to the court if he refuses to agree. She may also ask for a divorce if she finds him loathsome because of some physical defect or disease not apparent at the time of betrothal. Some marriage contracts contained a clause that if the couple come to hate each other they were to be divorced. For the man that was always the case, but in Palestine, from the second century AD, a wife who had come to hate her husband could ask her husband for a divorce, and if he refused she could ask the court to compel him to do so.[29]

The general tenor of the references to divorce in the Mishnah was to maintain the old Patriarchal attitude to marriage, that it was primarily for the provision of descendants, and that a woman's role was to bear male children, run the home, and be an agreeable companion to her husband. Failure in any of these three tasks led to dismissal into an uncertain future. That undoubtedly was the tradition of the elders the rabbis found as they pondered over the scrolls of the Mosaic law.

When cases of matrimonial disharmony were referred to them for arbitration, they stuck to the rules. Their task was to sort out the consequence of failure, but that did not mean they approved, and they sometimes advised reconciliation. They suggested that when a man considered the consequences of issuing his bill of divorce, his weeping wife and daughters, and the likelihood that people would say 'such is the character of a man who divorces his wives', he would repent. If so, he was allowed to withdraw the bill. Rabbi Eleazer taught that 'the very altar weeps when a man divorces the wife of his youth'.[30]

It seems then that by the time of Jesus, there were the beginnings of a movement of thought concerning divorce that recognized the old system was, in its harshness to women, not what God had intended in creation. That recognition did not, however, much affect her position in society. Whereas in pre-exilic times, women had sometimes played a major part in Israel's history, the emergence of the Torah-driven community meant domination by the male priests and the exclusion of women from active participation in public worship. At the Temple, they were confined to an outer courtyard. As Neusner comments:

Where the priestly tradition dominated, there women were excluded. Perhaps, to begin with, the ancient pagan traditions of women as cult prostitutes led the framers of the Israelite priestly code to keep women out of the cult and Temple altogether. Whatever the original motive, the result for centuries to come proved disastrous.[31]

5

Marriage in the New Testament

Introduction

This chapter is divided into two sections, reflecting the difference in character and purpose of the four Gospels from the rest of the New Testament. Teaching about marriage is not set out systematically in either, and occurs most frequently in response to questions. For Jesus the questions were usually posed by the Pharisees, with the underlying purpose of drawing out his understanding of the Mosaic law, on which they regarded themselves as expert. In St Paul's major epistles, written some years before the Gospels were compiled, his comments on marriage similarly arise from questions put to him from young Church communities of which he was regarded as the chief guide and pastor. The problems he has to deal with concern the continued application of the marriage rules of Judaism, or conversely the freedom from any rules for the spiritual community to which Christians now belong. It is clear from his answers that he is aware of Jesus' own teaching on marriage in principle, but he has to work out the pragmatic consequences in particular local situations, usually for predominantly Gentile communities. The remaining books of the New Testament, much influenced by Paul, show how the Christian ethos of marriage and sexual relationships developed in the later years of the first century AD. The initial expectation of the imminent return of Jesus was replaced by the realization that the churches had to continue to live in this world but under the spiritual Lordship of Christ. The lifestyle of the Christians should reflect God's steadfast love.

The Gospels

References to marriage in the Gospels

The Gospels show that Jesus believed that the institution of marriage was God-given, and he had no quarrel with the standard Jewish teaching that becoming married was the normal pattern for men and women. His support is often shown indirectly, when a story or an event is set in the context of a wedding or home life, while making a teaching point. Although himself unmarried, Jesus was a family man until the start of his public ministry. He related easily with both genders, and on his journeys the Gospel authors report several personal conversations he has with individual women in public, a breach of the usual convention that surprised his disciples. These conversations show Jesus being sympathetic to women in difficulty, but also illustrate more general themes, equally applicable to men and women. His direct teaching about marriage emerges from his disputes with the Pharisees about divorce and with the Sadducees about resurrection. In these encounters the underlying issue is his approach to Mosaic law, but Jesus takes the opportunity to define his understanding of marriage. His criticism of the Pharisaic attitude to divorce shows Jesus at his most forthright.

Among the indirect references, the parable of the wise and foolish bridesmaids preparing for a wedding procession describes a familiar scene, but Jesus uses it to emphasize the need for watchfulness.[1] Similarly, John uses the visit of Jesus and his disciples to the wedding feast at Cana as the first of his signs. Jesus and his disciples have no problem about attending a wedding, but Jesus is at first hesitant about overcoming the shortage of wine, as he discloses to his mother. John asks us to perceive that the surprising miracle of turning water into wine not only shows the power of Jesus, but more significantly also teaches how the good wine of the Gospel replaces the Jewish water of purification. 'You have kept the best wine until now.'[2]

Although the Pharisees are reported in the Gospels as the fiercest and most persistent opponents of Jesus, paradoxically their views on several major doctrinal issues were similar. The aristocratic and priestly Sadducees disagreed with both Jesus and the Pharisees about the possibility of an afterlife and thought this was the best subject with which to expose Jesus to ridicule. So they put to him the hypothetical question of the woman who married seven brothers in succession: to which of them would she belong in heaven? The ancient Levirate rule (Deut. 25.5), was intended to preserve the family line, and the choice of seven is intended to expose the nonsense of survival after death. Jesus refutes the Sadducean argument in two ways. First, they underrate the power of God to give new life, and second, they misunderstand Moses who spoke of God as relating to Abraham, Isaac and Jacob in the present tense. On this issue the Pharisees agreed with Jesus. They speculated how real the life in heaven might be. Was it a restoration of Eden with gardens or fields to look after, or was the contemplation of God all-absorbing? Jesus replies that to be like angels means that the relationship to God and each other continues, but without the limitations of earthly life.[3]

Jesus and his family

Part of the mystery of the Incarnation is that Jesus grew up in an extended family in Nazareth. Joseph and family were carpenters, the Greek word *teknon* denoting a rather wider scope than carving wooden domestic and agricultural equipment. Houses of the period were timber-framed, and so, quite possibly, the family was in our terms a design and build enterprise for Nazareth and surrounding villages. The background of Jesus was therefore artisan; unlike the peasant labourers, the artisan class were what we would call self-employed.

We cannot be certain that the Gospel authors ever met Jesus in the flesh. New Testament scholars reckon that the written Gospels date from after the death of St Peter and St Paul, *c.* AD 65. They were designed to provide minimum authentic records for the new Christian communities once the original apostles and eyewitnesses were no longer available. They had available oral traditions of Jesus' life and teaching, already to some extent shaped into fixed patterns. Each Gospel author used these traditions to fit his own purpose, in part determined by the readership he had in mind but also reflecting his own theological understanding of the significance of Christ, often woven into the narratives with some subtlety.

Matthew begins with a genealogy of Jesus, stressing his human descent from Abraham, perhaps of importance for a Diaspora Jewish readership. Luke addresses his Gospel to Theophilus, probably a Roman of high rank and typical of converted Roman citizens known to St Paul. (It is also possible that the Gospel was more generally addressed to any 'friend of God' – reflecting the basic meaning of the name 'Theophilus'.) His genealogy of Jesus begins with Adam, and his birth narratives contain more human detail than Matthew's account. Only Luke records the parents of Jesus taking him to be presented in the Temple, and the later visit to Jerusalem for the Passover, when Jesus goes missing; they eventually find him talking with the scribes and rabbis in the Temple precincts. He was twelve years old, still a schoolboy by our reckoning but already in those days a working apprentice. The rest is silence until Jesus meets John the Baptist. Mark begins his Gospel with this encounter, and so, after a Prologue, does John.

That meeting marked a decisive step for Jesus. From his baptism onwards, his family life faded into the background. However, he remained in close if intermittent contact with his mother throughout his life, and his brothers and sisters are mentioned occasionally, but these terms were used loosely, and it was probably not the intention of the Gospel writers to specify the precise degree of affinity.[4] Similarly, there is no suggestion that Jesus was ever married, and that fits well within the usual Jewish understanding that anyone with a special religious vocation was expected to avoid the normal commitment to marriage and parenthood. Jesus gathered a group of male companions to form an inner committed circle, a standard custom for spiritual leaders, and conscious of the eschatological urgency of his task, he asked them to leave their families and property for the Gospel's sake.[5] Jesus was constantly on the move, but he did not withdraw from ordinary social and domestic contacts; he was even accused of not being discerning enough in attending dinner parties. There were at least two homes where he was a frequent and welcome visitor. In Galilee there was the house of Peter's mother-in-law in Capernaum; in the eastern outskirts of Jerusalem, beyond the Mount of Olives, there was the Bethany home of Mary, Martha and Lazarus, which was used as a safe haven.

Personal conversations with women

The woman of Samaria

Having used the story of the Cana wedding as the first sign, John draws out further the significance of Jesus in the somewhat puzzling account of the conversation with the Samaritan woman at the well of

Sychar (John 4.4–42). As at Cana, the conversation is somewhat blunt. Jesus surprises the woman by showing he is already aware of the chaos of her matrimonial arrangements. Obviously though, John does not record what seems to have been a genuine encounter at such length only to show that Jesus is perceptive. The real issue addressed here is the religion of the Samaritans. They were survivors of the Northern Kingdom of Israel, and thought themselves just as authentic as other Jews, who for their part regarded them as a kind of third race, neither Jew nor Gentile. In particular, Samaritan women were regarded as ritually unclean, so the disciples were astonished that Jesus should even think of talking seriously with her. However, he does, and the woman is allowed to discuss the stigma she and all her race have to bear. Metaphorically, they have no spiritual husband, nowhere to belong. In short, Jesus encourages her to accept him and worship God in spirit and in truth, and the story ends with other Samaritans deciding to follow him.

The woman taken in adultery

The dramatic story of the woman 'caught in the act' (John 7.53–8.11) has not always been accepted as authentic. It is missing from some early manuscripts and has marked linguistic differences from the rest of John's Gospel. Moreover, it does not fit well with the general trend of Jesus' teaching against adultery. In the NEB it was relegated to an appendix at the end of the Gospel, but restored in the RSV and NRSV with an explanatory footnote that 'it appears to be an authentic incident in Jesus' ministry, though not belonging originally to John's Gospel'. It actually fits better with St Luke's style,[6] but it may have been discarded from there because much the same teaching is given in other ways. But the Temple incident, probably preserved in the oral tradition, has the ring of truth about it.

The Pharisees make an attempt to trap Jesus about his respect for the Torah. While Jesus is teaching in the Jerusalem Temple area, this terrified woman is brought before him, with the suggestion that, as her guilt is clear, she should be stoned. They say to him: 'Teacher, this woman was caught in the very act of committing adultery. Now in the law Moses commanded us to stone such a woman. Now what do you say?' (John 8.4–6). After a pause, Jesus replies, 'Let anyone among you who is without sin be the first to throw a stone at her' (John 8.7). The accusers slip away, and the woman replies to his question 'Has no one condemned you?' with 'No one, sir.' Jesus then says: 'Neither do I condemn you. Go your way, and from now on do not sin again' (John 8.11).

The encounter seems bizarre. In Israel's ancient law, stoning was the penalty for a woman falsely claiming to be a virgin at betrothal or taken in adultery while betrothed, but this extreme penalty was no longer used, and may never have been. Her fiancée should have made a private complaint to her family and the local elders. Nevertheless, the Pharisees seem driven to this extreme attempt to trap Jesus, without any intention of actually killing the woman. Jesus was probably on the steps leading up to the Temple, not in its outer courtyard, but such a scene seems inappropriate in its precincts. John reports this unhappy incident to introduce a wider perspective. People who sin sexually are neither to be condoned nor condemned; they are to be offered a chance of repentance and encouraged to change their ways. The Greek word translated 'condemn' (*katakrino*) means to judge down or to find guilty, and here Jesus declines to make that final decision. By his remark to the accusers he gives them a chance to understand that since no one is sin-free, they should be wary of accusing others. 'Do not condemn, and you will not be condemned' is one of his standard teachings.[7]

Dinner parties interrupted

The synoptic Gospels record other moments when women in distress approach Jesus. When Jesus dines with Simon, a Galilean Pharisee, a woman interrupts proceedings by weeping, bathing his feet with tears, drying them with her hair, and anointing them with ointment (Luke 7.36–50). Since dinner guests were on couches, feet outwards, it would not have been difficult for her to slip in among the serving maids, and begin this action undetected. She is described as a sinner, so either an adulteress or more likely a prostitute, and Simon is outraged at this embarrassing scene – Jesus ought to have known what sort of woman she was! The story is developed as a lesson on forgiveness. Similarly, both Mark and Matthew tell of a woman who anoints Jesus' head when he is dining at the house of Simon, a leper in Bethany, during his final week in Jerusalem. This time it is the disciples who are indignant at the extravagance, but Jesus corrects them (Mark 14.3–9 and Matt. 26.6–13). Whether or not these stories refer to different incidents or are versions of one is immaterial; they demonstrate the evangelists' concern to show Jesus breaking out from the Pharisaic attitude to women.

The Pharisees' question about divorce

Jesus reveals his understanding of marriage directly when he responds to the question of the Pharisees about divorce. This is a crucial encounter, referred to in all three synoptic Gospels, a sure sign that the issue was of considerable importance in the early Church. Matthew and Mark report the incident in some detail, albeit with one significant difference, and Luke has a variant form of the key ruling. The encounter took place towards the end of Jesus' final journey from Northern Galilee to Jerusalem. His teaching was by now widely known, and the Pharisees hoped to prove his teaching on the Torah was unsound. Reports suggested that he was too soft on Sabbath-keeping, and over-rigorous on divorce. If so, the sooner his errors were exposed the better. They caught up with him on the east bank of the Jordan, opposite Jericho.

Mark's version is a straightforward account in two parts, first in public with the Pharisees, and then privately with the disciples:

> Some Pharisees came, and to test him they asked, 'Is it lawful for a man to divorce his wife?' He answered them, 'What did Moses command you?' They said, 'Moses allowed a man to write a certificate of dismissal and to divorce her.' But Jesus said to them, 'Because of your hardness of heart he wrote this commandment for you. But from the beginning of creation, "God made them male and female." "For this reason a man shall leave his father and mother and be joined to his wife, and the two shall become one flesh. So they are no longer two but one flesh." Therefore what God has joined together let no one separate.'
>
> Then in the house the disciples asked him again about this matter. He said to them, 'Whoever divorces his wife and marries another commits adultery against her; and if she divorces her husband and marries another, she commits adultery.' (Mark 10.2–9)

Matthew's version is similar, but he has already included the central ruling earlier in his Gospel. In the Sermon on the Mount, he quotes Jesus as first warning about lust and then about adultery:

> 'You have heard that it was said, "You shall not commit adultery."

But I say to you that everyone who looks at a woman with lust has already committed adultery with her in his heart.' (Matt. 5.27)

'It was also said, "Whoever divorces his wife, let him give her a certificate of divorce." But I say to you that anyone who divorces his wife, except on the ground of unchastity, causes her to commit adultery; and whoever marries a divorced woman commits adultery.' (Matt. 5.31–2)

Then, like Mark, he places the encounter much later in Jesus' ministry:

Some Pharisees came to him, and to test him they asked, 'Is it lawful for a man to divorce his wife for any cause?' He answered: 'Have you not read that the one who made them at the beginning "made them male and female", and said, "For this reason a man shall leave his father and mother and be joined to his wife, and the two shall become one flesh. So they are no longer two, but one flesh. Therefore what God has joined together, let no one separate.' They said to him, 'Why then did Moses command us to give a certificate of dismissal and to divorce her?' He said to them, 'It was because you were so hard-hearted that Moses allowed you to divorce your wives, but from the beginning it was not so. And I say to you, whoever divorces his wife, except for unchastity, and marries another commits adultery.'

His disciples said to him, 'If such is the case of a man with his wife, it is better not to marry.' But he said to them, 'Not everyone can accept this teaching, but only those to whom it is given. For there are eunuchs who have been so from birth, and there are eunuchs who have been made so by others, and there are eunuchs who have made themselves eunuchs for the sake of the kingdom of heaven. Let anyone accept this who can.' (Matt. 19.3–12)[8]

Luke's version is apparently a brief interpolation in a passage about discipleship:

'Anyone who divorces his wife and marries another commits adultery, and whoever marries a woman divorced from her husband commits adultery.' (Luke 16.18)

Reconciling the views of Mark and Matthew on divorce

Moral theologians have closely studied the teaching Jesus gives here about marriage and divorce. It shows clearly the parting of the ways between the Christian ethos and the Jewish tradition, not only on divorce itself but also on remarriage, and further, by implication, on the double standard for sexual behaviour between men and women. In their reports on the public discussion with the Pharisees, Mark and Matthew agree that Jesus bases his reply on the two Genesis texts, 1.27 (from 'P') and 2.24 (from 'J'). The one-flesh relationship is part of God's creative ordinance, and no one should separate what God has united. The union was meant to be permanent and Moses only allowed the concession of divorce because of the hardness or obduracy of men's hearts. He is warning men contemplating divorce, or would-be adulterers, to respect the marriage bond. Jesus is a realist about sexual desires, and warns against the disruptive nature of male lust. In the social mores of the time married women had little opportunity to look for extra-marital sex on their own account. Their marriages were far more likely to be broken up because the husband looked elsewhere, and since nearly every woman was either married or a prostitute, the unfaithful husband would either be committing fornication (*porneia*) or more likely adultery (*moicheia*). Jesus makes plain neither of these is God's will; there is no double standard.

In their reports of the private session with the disciples about divorce, Matthew and Mark no longer agree. This is shown by Matthew in the Pharisees' initial question (Matt. 19.3) which includes 'for any cause', their standard position, following Hillel. Matthew thinks Jesus refutes this but agrees with the Shammite teaching that unchastity (*porneia*) by a woman is the only justifiable cause for which her husband may, and indeed must, divorce her (Matt. 19.9). The inconsistency between this view and Mark's is not easy to resolve. Many New Testament scholars suggest that the best explanation is that Matthew, with a Jewish Christian community in mind, adds his exceptive clause to show that Jesus is not revoking the Mosaic law properly understood. It is also possible that the oral tradition recorded the original discussion in various forms, and that Mark chose the stricter view for a Gentile readership, to make plain that the lax ways of the Hellenistic and Roman worlds were not to be followed by Christian converts. Matthew generally introduces the exegeses Jesus gives of several of the Decalogue precepts, including adultery, by insisting that Jesus said very firmly that he had not come to abolish the law or the prophets but to fulfil them (Matt. 5.17).

Mark adds the extra comment that a wife can divorce her husband, and that may have been allowed in some non-Palestine Christian communities who followed Roman customs. As already noted, in Judaism wives could ask for divorce from their husbands, and might be able to insist on it for special reasons like impotence or refusal of conjugal rights and certain diseases. The judgement that any man or woman who marries after divorce commits adultery seems harsh to modern understanding, because we are familiar with the situation of a first wife who has been faithful and guiltless in law, but finds herself 'being traded in for a younger model'. That was the situation that 'caused the altar to weep' and the stricture Jesus puts on it fits with his dismissal of the easy divorce rules of the Hillel school. The economic situation of divorced women who failed to remarry was dire, and even if her husband had dismissed her for trivial reasons, she could well have been labelled unfairly as an adulteress. Perhaps Jesus is here drawing attention to the injustice of the system. Certainly, the variation in the texts suggests that the early church was uncertain what to do about the consequences of broken marriages, and St Paul struggles with it in 1 Cor. 7, written some years before the Gospels were finalized.[9]

From a wider perspective, it may be helpful to remember that the sins of fornication and adultery were not in biblical terms confined to immoral sexual acts between individuals. The prophets continually used these terms to refer to Israel's apostasy; they were disloyal to Jahweh and to his covenant with them, and went whoring after other gods. That brought them under the influence of cult prostitution, so the argument was that false religion leads to false sexual behaviour. The analogy is obvious. The unfaithful partner to a marriage sins against the covenant between the man and the woman; sexual immorality is an act of disloyalty which destroys the integrity of the one-flesh relationship, just as worshipping at the shrine of Baal destroys the special relationship between God and his people. In human relationships, when a partner's deception is discovered, the hurt felt at the personal disloyalty involved is often greater than the dismay at the sexual infidelity.

The Epistles

First steps towards a Christian ethos

The New Testament epistles come from Paul himself, from his disciples who reiterate his teaching, or from others claiming apostolic authorship. They were addressed to Christian communities already quite widely spread around the north-eastern rim of the Mediterranean and its hinterlands. Paul's earliest letters date back to the early or mid-fifties, some years before the Gospels were composed, and ten years before his own death. The Deutero-Pauline letters follow over the next three decades, along with the third group of epistles, and there may be some overlap between these and the first writings of the sub-apostolic age, such as 1 Clement. Nearly all these letters include some theological and pastoral teaching about human relationships, and they show how a distinctive Christian ethos for marriage and sexual behaviour was being hammered out from the rough metal of the Greek, Roman and Jewish traditions. The template for this new ethos came of course from what was known of the teaching of Christ, available in the memory of the apostles and others who had heard Jesus speak, and also from collections of his sayings now being preserved on papyrus. But, as we have seen, the Gospel authors say little about marriage apart from Christ's approval of the institution and his strictures on easy divorce. Paul and his successors had a lot of work to do, teaching the new converts what their new faith involved, not least about sexual morality.

The membership of the Christian communities they addressed was mixed, ethnically and religiously. Some were converted Diaspora Jews, long trained in orthodox Judaism; others were Gentiles of many races, some of them already 'God-fearers' attracted to some aspects of Judaism but not usually circumcised into full membership, while a few were pagans with little or no knowledge of the Torah. Given such diversity, it was inevitable that tensions would arise. Since most of the converts were already married before baptism, they wondered 'Do the legal systems of the Hellenistic and Roman cultures within which we were married still apply, or do we start again?' Given the expectation that Christ would soon return to actualize his already inaugurated kingdom, some took an ascetic view: 'No marriage, no sex please, we are Christians!' Others emphasized the new life in the Spirit, which, they thought, freed them from all merely human rules: 'What we do with our earthly bodies is no longer significant.' Paul and the other church leaders had to wrestle with both these extreme attitudes to sexuality, but to resolve them required first some theological clarity about the fundamental nature of the Church. What kind of religion was Christianity?

The first Christian missionaries to the Gentile world, however much they were influenced by the Hellenistic culture, remained, like Paul himself, respectful of Palestinian Judaism. They understood the new faith not as an alternative religion to Judaism but as a mutation growing from its roots, planned by God and achieved by Jesus. It was not a sect, rivalling the Sadducees, Pharisees or Essenes. The New Israel, as Paul called it, lived by a new covenant, but it was still Israel. The fundamental difference was that the invitation was now open to everyone, Jew and Gentile alike. As Paul expresses it to the Galatians:

> As many of you as were baptized into Christ have clothed yourself with Christ. There is no longer Jew or Greek, there is no longer slave or free, there are no longer male and female; for all of you are one in Christ Jesus. And if you belong to Christ, then you are Abraham's offspring, heirs according to the promise. (Gal. 3.27–9)

One can see immediately how attractive it must have been to many kinds of people to join a movement that assured them that this invitation was wide open to all, irrespective of their previous condition. For disadvantaged Gentiles particularly, this was good news; differences of race, status or gender no longer meant exclusion; they were all heirs together of the grace of God, as Paul firmly declared. It was not of course that the differences were obliterated. Instead of leading to conflict they could now enrich each other. However, this new doctrine required a considerable transformation of vision for any Jew wishing to convert. The raison d'être of the tradition they belonged to was the guardianship of their unique position as God's chosen people. In modern terms, they faced resocialization. What of their roots, the Torah, they are bound to wonder? If Christ came not to destroy but to fulfil the law, then do not the Mosaic codes still apply to the people of the new covenant? In human relationships, was the old double standard still applicable and divorce still permitted under the lax Pharisaic rules?[10]

To all such questions, the eventual Christian answer would be No, but there first had to be a period of hard thinking and persuading. The epistles are not systematic theological treatises or, for the most part, personal letters, but *ad rem*, mixing practical pastoral advice with relevant theological dicta. To some extent, their advice on behaviour is provisional, because of the eschatological expectation. These early Christians are living between the times – between the critical events of the life of Jesus and the time of the last judgement – and they need an 'interim ethic'. It comes to this. If maintaining behaviour belonging to the old would blur the purpose of the new Covenant, then the old is redundant. If the old rules are of such universal value that they are obviously equally appropriate for Jews and Gentiles, Christians and pagans alike, then they are to be maintained.

The Council in Jerusalem

In Acts, Luke's history of the earliest days of the Christian Church, he reports the attempt of the Council in Jerusalem, *c.* AD 50, to resolve these tensions. As a Gentile convert himself he is sensitive to their position and supports Paul's view of his mission as in no sense building a separate Church from that based in Jerusalem. Brought up in the tradition of the Pharisees, Paul was familiar with their teaching that God-fearing Gentiles were always welcome to become Jews. If they did, these proselytes, as they were called, had to give up pagan vices, be circumcised and obey the Torah. But there were other Gentiles whose respect for Jewish monotheism was genuine enough but for whom circumcision and the other details of the Torah were steps too far. For them the rabbis had looked back to the time of Noah, before the Mosaic Covenants, and devised a set of commandments, known as the Noachic commands. These included the prohibition of idolatry, blasphemy, adultery and incest, murder, theft and the eating of animal flesh not ritually killed. This list of pagan vices, with small variations, was the standard polemic of Judaism against the immorality of foreigners, and is frequently reiterated in New Testament epistles.[11]

The Council in Jerusalem applied a similar compromise for Gentile Christians. Luke first describes the conversion of Cornelius, the Roman centurion from Caesarea, and the part Peter played in it. After an overnight vision convinced him that God was no longer making a distinction between Jews and Gentiles, and the evidence that Cornelius had received the Holy Spirit, Peter agreed to baptize him. At the Council, chaired by James, the brother of Jesus, Peter, Barnabas and Paul argue strongly that God has through them done signs and wonders among the Gentiles. James sums up the Council's support:

> God first looked favourably on the Gentiles, to take from among them a people for his name . . . we should not trouble those Gentiles who are turning to God, but we should write to them to abstain only from things polluted by idols and from fornication, and from whatever has been strangled. (Acts 15.14, 19–21)

The Council's solution was to turn to the Noachian code and insist that Gentile Christians should observe three of its precepts where Jewish sensitivities were particularly strong and different from pagan culture.[12] Although the Council rejected the need for circumcision, the controversy continued and Luke refers to it again in Acts 21.17–25.[13] The prohibition of fornication (*porneia*) is best understood to refer to the standard Jewish teaching as set out in the Midrash, and including adultery, pederasty and bestiality. Some commentators have thought that in context this only refers to the prohibited degrees for marriage, and *porneia* can have this restricted meaning. Since Paul frequently includes fornication in its wider meaning as one of the works of the flesh, it seems much more likely that the Council intended the same.[14]

Who was St Paul?

After Jesus, Paul is the dominant figure in the New Testament. He was present at the stoning of Stephen, the first Christian martyr (Acts 8.1), and was then converted to Christ and commissioned as the Apostle to the Gentiles (Acts 9.15). He was born in Tarsus, the capital city of the Roman province of Cilicia in Southern Turkey, and seems to have been only a few years younger than Jesus. His family business was tent-making, enabling wealthy travellers to stay clear of the usually verminous roadside inns. Paul was brought up a Diaspora Jew and became a keen Pharisee, but even more than those in Palestine he lived in the Hellenistic environment, spoke Greek as first language, and had some knowledge of Latin, Aramaic and Hebrew. His Old Testament quotations come from the Septuagint. Luke thinks he studied for a while in Jerusalem under Gamaliel, the leading Pharisaic rabbi of the time, and a grandson of Hillel, but Paul does not mention this.[15]

Nowadays, Paul is often accused of being anti-sex and anti-marriage, but considering his Jewish background and his actual writing, this is an unfair caricature. He describes himself as 'unmarried' (1 Cor. 7.8), unusual for a Jew, but as a zealous Pharisee he may have chosen celibacy as a vocation. But he did not regard celibacy as obligatory for apostleship, and notes that he, like the other apostles and Peter, had the right to be accompanied by a believing wife.[16] Paul could have been for a while a member of the Sanhedrin, for which one had to be married, and his wife might have already died, or insisted on separation when he became a Christian. The Greek word *agamois* used in 1 Corinthians 7.8 can mean either a single man or a widower, as the NRSV notes, and since Paul is writing about unmarried men and widows in this verse, it is likely that *agamois* means widower here. The Corinthian Christians would have known his marital status but we cannot be sure. If he was a widower, his suggestion that bereaved husbands and wives do better to marry again 'than to be aflame with passion' if they do not practise self-control (1 Cor. 7.9) may reflect his personal experience that celibacy for the once married is not easy.[17]

Teaching about marriage in St Paul's epistles

Modern Bibles attribute thirteen letters to Paul, Hebrews now being regarded as anonymous. Linguistic study and the assessment of differences in theological formulations have led scholars to conclude that only seven of these letters are certainly Paul's own work, the rest probably being written by colleagues or imitators. It was standard practice in classical times to use pseudonyms. The likelihood is that these post-Pauline letters were written after his death to Christian communities with which he had been associated, and for whom the main lines of his teaching were still important, although their situations may have changed somewhat.[18]

Paul's teaching about marriage for Christians in the interim period is an amalgam of standard rabbinic sexual morality, some Stoic asceticism, what he knows of Jesus' own teaching, and a pragmatic response to problems in his local churches. When in doubt he relies on the Spirit's guidance or makes clear that he is giving his own opinion. His excitement with the gospel was tempered by his profound respect for the truths of the Old Testament. His advice to his congregations is often: 'If it ain't broke, don't fix it.' While Christians looking for the new era should keep free from unnecessary commitments, in personal morality they should preserve what did not need to be changed. For Paul, deciding between his basic vision of the new life in Christ and the tug of his abiding respect for the Torah as expounded by his rabbinic teachers was not always easily managed. And he lived in a changing situation. As time passed the Christian communities became pre-dominantly Gentile rather than Jewish in membership, and he wrote accordingly. A good example is 1 Thessalonians. Probably written from Corinth *c.* AD 50 or even a little earlier, it is the first extant letter of St Paul, and the earliest document in the New Testament. He reminds the Thessalonians of his instructions on how they ought to live and please God:

> For this is the will of God, your sanctification: that you abstain from fornication; that each one of you knows how to control your own body in holiness and honour, not with lustful passion, like the Gentiles who do not know God; that no one wrongs or exploits a brother or sister in this matter. (1 Thess. 4.3–6)

The main point here is that Gentile converts must recognize the Christian way is different from the pagan, not least in sexual morality. Some manuscripts replace the reference to knowing how 'to honour one's own body' with 'how to take a wife for himself' (NRSV margin); either makes sense in the context. It is an important element of Paul's theology of sex that it involves the whole body of a person, as we shall see later. The reference to the holiness and honour of the body is probably a conjunction of Jewish and Stoic ideals, and he adds two further points against fornication: the usual one that it is a vice of the Gentiles, and in the Church it is an exploitation of a fellow Christian. All that said, rejecting this rule is rejecting God (1 Thess. 4.8)!

Trouble in Corinth

Corinth had been for some centuries a prosperous Greek city on the direct East–West trade route between the Aegean and Ionian Seas. Destroyed in 146 BC, it was revived by order of Julius Caesar as a Roman colony and capital of the province of Achaia, in 44 BC. Although infamous in Greek literature for the prevalence of its prosti-tution, by the time Paul visited it, it was no more vice-ridden than other sea-ports. It had a large temple to Athena in the agora, typical of the times, and a small Jewish settlement.[19]

Paul founded the church in Corinth during an eighteen-month stay not later than AD 50 and kept in contact with the Christians there by the exchange of letters, and reports from visitors.[20] The letters from Corinth have not survived, but two of Paul's to them have, the first written from Ephesus *c.* AD 53. This contains his most direct thoughts about marriage, given as his answers to questions raised in their letters, which he quotes. As Rowan Williams puts it, 'If this letter had been lost in the post, Christian Ethics would have been very different, since there is more here on sexual relationships than in all the rest of the New Testament.'[21] Whereas the news from Thessalonika enables Paul to write to them with approval and encouragement, the news from Corinth is bad and Paul is disappointed and angry. He refers to a number of their failures in this letter, characteristically moving from one subject to another and then resuming a previous line of thought, and quoting from their letters at various points. Disentangling his words from theirs is not always easy.[22]

The social composition of the Corinthian church was typically mixed, a few rich people, merchants, artisans, shopkeepers, some urban poor, many of them freed slaves. For the Gentile majority, learning that the Old Testament mattered was difficult; for the Jewish minority, conversion meant accepting as equals those they had been trained to despise. It was natural for small cliques to form and Paul was anxious to overcome the dissensions within a community at odds with itself. One influential group favoured asceticism, especially with regard to sexual activity. Another group was interpreting its freedom from the law too literally in various forms of sexual irregularity. Their argument was that since they are now spiritual beings what they do with their bodies no longer matters. Paul strongly disagrees with this dichotomy. Soul and body are not separate entities, the one indwells the other; they do not yet have resurrection bodies! Jewish thought did not separate existence from embodiment, so when Paul refers to flesh and spirit he does not mean simply the transient body over against the immortal soul, a Greek notion, but the orientation of a person's whole being away from or towards God.[23]

1 Corinthians 5—6

All this is worked out in 1 Corinthians 5—6, starting with the scandal of a member of the congregation living with his father's wife, forbidden by both Roman and Jewish law. It is likely that she was his step-mother, and perhaps a widow and maybe not a believer, but in any case the offence is sexual, and Paul rules that the man is to be excluded from the community.[24] He then refers to a previous letter where he warned them not to associate with sexually immoral persons in the church. He is realistic enough to admit that this will happen in the world but it is not to happen 'among the brothers and sisters' and adds a list of other offences that would justify exclusion (1 Cor. 5.9–11). In 1 Corinthians 6, he repeats the warning that those who commit the pagan vices will not inherit the kingdom of God, and then returns to the problem of fornication and introduces an analogy between the Church as the body of Christ and the human body. Theologically Paul makes a bold leap here, placing the sexual behaviour of Christians firmly within his doctrine of the Church.

> The body is meant not for fornication but for the Lord, and the Lord for the body. And God raised the Lord and will also raise us by his power. Do you not know that your bodies are members of Christ? Should I therefore take the members of Christ and make them members of a prostitute? Never! Do you not know that whoever is united to a prostitute becomes one body with her? For it is said, 'The two shall be one flesh.' But anyone united to the Lord becomes one spirit with him. Shun fornication! Every sin that a person commits is outside the body, but the fornicator sins against the body itself. Or do you not know that your body is a temple of the Holy Spirit within you, which you have from God, and that you are not your own? For you were bought with a price; therefore glorify God in your body. (1 Cor. 6.13–20)

Understanding this text is easier if the phrase about sins 'outside the body' (v. 18) is identified as a slogan of the Antinomian group, since it is difficult to see why other sins such as drunkenness or gluttony can be said to occur outside the body. It is equally obvious that sexual sin involves bodies in an intimate way, but that is not the main point Paul is making here with his claim that 'the fornicator sins against his own body'. (This is a better translation than the 'body itself', in the NRSV as above.) The word 'body' (*soma*), is often used by Paul to describe the corporate nature of the Church, of which each Christian is a member. 'Just as the body is one and has many members, and all the members of the body, though many, are one body, so it is with Christ.'[25] Since all Christians are members of the same spiritual body, one person's sin affects them all, and mingling a human body which is sanctified by the Spirit with the unholy body of a prostitute is a duplication of Israel's old sin of idolatry and sacred prostitution. It is an act of disloyalty against the Christian community, a kind of spiritual apostasy. Personal integrity is lost by this sin against one's own body. The human body has a positive connotation for Paul; it is the temple of the Holy Spirit, and therefore deserves respect. He argues that intimate sexual acts involve the whole person, not just one small part of a man and a woman's anatomy.

This doctrine is different from the Stoic argument for avoiding passion; it affirms the positive and unitive value of sex as a means of honouring God, and this is a distinctively Christian development. It does not depend on the argument for procreation, derived from Genesis, since the Christians are not taking a long-term view, nor is it a process which considers the meaning of sex *sui generis*. The nature of the body of the Church is the a priori consideration, which leads on to a fresh appraisal of what makes for good human behaviour. The guiding principle of this is the selfless love of God, *agape*, which Paul considers later in this epistle (1 Cor. 13). Paul's application of his doctrine of the body of Christ corporately married to God is paralleled in Isaiah 62.4–5.

1 Corinthians 7.1–7

The ascetic movement among the Corinthians has been described as a form of 'over-realized eschatology', which is theologian speak for an excessive preoccupation with being prepared spiritually for the return of Christ. Paul is asked whether or not in the circumstances it would be better to avoid or abandon marriage, and renounce sex altogether. They say, 'It is well for a man not to touch a woman' (1 Cor. 7.1). Having already set down his basic theology, and declared his mind about the incestuous man, Paul answers this question pragmatically. Each man should have his own wife and each woman her own husband, and they should give each other conjugal rights since they have authority over each other's bodies. As Jesus has taught, there is to be equality in the relationship, and Paul reiterates this novel teaching some twelve times in this epistle. Within marriage, the old Jewish rule about sexual abstinence should still apply. They could agree together to do without sex during periods of prayer and fasting, but not otherwise, lest lacking self-control they may be tempted to find other partners. Paul admits that this advice does not have Dominical authority, presumably because he knew Jesus had suggested celibacy for disciples called to it, as Paul himself had been; to be married or celibate are both gifts (*charisma*) from God.

1 Corinthians 7.8–40

After the brief advice to widows and widowers to remain unmarried if they can (vs 8–9), Paul turns to the twin problems of separation and divorce. In the simple case, he knows the command of Christ (Mark's version) and repeats it. Neither Christian partner may divorce the other, but if they separate they must seek reconciliation or remain unmarried (vs 10–11). The more difficult case, for which Paul cannot refer to a Gospel saying and can only offer his own discernment, is the situation of marriage between Christians and pagans. Becoming a Christian does not of itself necessitate a divorce from an unbelieving partner, though it may well cause stress. If the relationship breaks down irretrievably, the Christian partner should accept it. If the spouses agree to stay together, they should continue the marriage and the believer will make the other holy. The Greek word here, *hagiastai*, comes from *hagios*, meaning holy or saintly, and is commonly used as a generic term for the Christian people, who are not necessarily of excellent moral character, but who are 'in Christ' acceptable to God. Paul suggests that the unbelieving spouse should be drawn within the ambience of the Holy People despite his or her unbelief, and who knows what God's grace might do? Apart from this missionary hope, Paul believed that marriage is part of God's general provision for humankind, not just for Jews and Christians, so provided there is consent, rejection of the unbelieving spouse is not justified; they should feel welcome in the community. And whereas, in the old system, the children of a mixed marriage between a Jew and a foreign wife would not be accepted as Jewish, now any child of an existing marriage in which either one of the partners was Christian would be included. The collective sense of family justifies this. There remains the unsolved problem of whether or not Christian men or women rejected by their unbelieving partners can marry again, or have to remain bound by the no-divorce rule. Some commentators note that the word 'bound' is in Greek *dedoulotai*, literally 'enslaved', which they take to mean unreasonably locked into a situation from which they should be freed, or at least they think that was Paul's view of the matter (vs 12–16).

The next section begins with a general principle that since the time is short, converts should not change their human status for change's sake. 'Remain in the condition in which you were called.' There follows a further, somewhat convoluted discussion addressed to those who are betrothed and not yet married, and the Corinthians may have raised this precise question. Should they go through with it? They are in principle promised to each other but not as yet cohabiting. Paul's opinion is that they need not marry, because the times are short, but equally there is in principle no shame in becoming married. He amplifies this with his typical view that married people have to put each other first while the unmarried are more free to attend to the Lord. Since Paul worked closely in his care for the churches with several married missionary couples, he was probably not allowed to argue this too strongly![26]

1 Corinthians 11.2–16

The questions here concern worship in the community: who should lead it and how are they to be dressed? These issues were causing serious controversy in Corinth, not least about the roles permitted to women. One commentator has described these verses as a theological quagmire,[27] as Paul wrestles between his basic conviction of sexual equality in the Church and his awareness of the old tradition of subordination. Several phrases in Paul's reply have proved a happy hunting ground for those for and against women's ministry.

The Corinthian Christians lived in a predominantly Roman culture. Roman women put their hair up in braids, but if they attended Hellenistic style cults, not uncommon in Corinth, they let their hair flow loose. Outside their homes, married Jewish women bound their hair up under a simple cloth, not the full veils in the Islamic style we now know. Some rabbis taught that a wife who let her hair down in public should be divorced. One can imagine the consternation among the more conservative Jewish Christians in Corinth if Gentile women came to worship with unbound hair. Was this because they did not know better, or because they wanted to make a liberation point, or even because from past experience with the mystery cults they assumed this was the correct thing to do? Hence the question, 'is it proper for a woman to pray to God with her head unveiled?' (v. 13).

Paul's answer is a somewhat hesitant Yes because a woman's long hair has been given to her for a covering and her glory instead of a veil, so she does not need to wear anything else on her head. He then turns to the two Genesis creation narratives, the 'patriarchal' view of Genesis 2.18, and the 'interdependence' view of Genesis 1.27. The difference in the status of women in these two narratives had been a subject of endless argument among the rabbis, as Paul well knew. He favours the interdependence view, but does not press it overmuch. His primary consideration, at least as far as the Corinthian church at worship is concerned, is to cool the dispute by advising that the ordinary customs of Judaism should be observed in this respect. That is, women and men can worship together as they did in the synagogues, and not be segregated – a much later Jewish custom. Then, married women should keep their hair up, both in church and out of it in the normal Jewish fashion, the point being that gender difference, a good thing and God-given, should not be obscured.[28]

Galatians

Soon after the meeting of the Jerusalem Council, Paul visited the churches he had previously founded in Galatia, the central part of Turkey. They had come under the influence of Judaizers who had taught them that circumcision was required for Gentile Christian converts. This letter is his reply: in Christ there is neither Jew nor Greek, male nor female (Gal. 3.28). Having dealt with the circumcision issue in forthright terms, Paul changes mood, and pleads for harmony in the community, quoting Jesus: 'The whole law is summed up in a single commandment, "You shall love your neighbour as yourself"' (Gal. 5.14).

Apart from the Judaizers, the Antinomians are also active, so he argues that Christian freedom is not to be used as an excuse for self-indulgence. To illustrate what this means within the community, Paul draws out the difference between the downward pull of the lower nature, gratifying the desires of the flesh (*sarx*) and life in the Spirit. This is the best-known delineation in the New Testament of the contrast between worldly and Christian lifestyles. The various aspects of sexual morality (*porneia*) are condemned, to be replaced by faithfulness and self-control (Gal. 5.19–26).

Marriage in the Deutero-Pauline letters

The remaining six letters attributed to Paul in the New Testament include much of his main-line thought. But their language and theology, and the church situations they address, suggest either that he wrote them towards the end of his life, when his own views had altered, or, more likely, that they were written by disciples who were close to him and wished to preserve his teaching. Either way a distinction should be made between the two letters addressed to churches, Colossians and Ephesians, and the obviously later 'Pastoral letters' 1 and 2 Timothy and Titus which have little to say about marriage.

Colossians

The church in Colossae, a town some 100 miles inland from Ephesus, was founded by Paul's colleague, Epaphras. The purpose of the letter, set out in the first two chapters, is to correct false ideas about Christology and resurrection, and then to give some ethical instruction. The Christians are to move away from their old lifestyle, the fornication, greed, lying, etc., and to seek the things that are above, where Christ is seated at the right hand of God (Col. 3.1). Christian family rules are briefly mentioned:

> Wives, be subject to your husbands, as is fitting in the Lord. Husbands, love your wives and never treat them harshly.
>   Children, obey your parents in everything, for this is your acceptable duty in the Lord. Fathers, do not provoke your children or they may lose heart. (Col. 3.18–21)

Lists of this kind, brief summaries of the 'rules of the house', occur frequently in the epistles, but not only there. They date back at least to Aristotle, who suggested that the simplest form of human association, the family household, provided the starting point for analysing how a political system worked. Within the household, there were three relationships, husband and wife, father and child, master and slave, and these three relationships set the pattern for the lists commonly found on the walls of both classical and Jewish homes. They served as a reminder of the expected style of domestic family life, both defining and conforming to the accepted norms of behaviour in the community to which they belonged. The Christian family rules, as here in Colossians, conform to this pattern; they were distinctive in their Christological basis, but the rules were otherwise commonplace – no Jew would have disagreed with them. These Christian household codes (Luther called them *Haustafeln*), appear quite regularly in

Christian literature from the end of the first century onwards, notably in 1 Clement, as an embryonic form of Christian morality.

Ephesians

Ephesus was Paul's base for some years during his mission to Eastern Turkey and he could have written this letter to the Christians there from his prison in Rome. But their situation, as the letter describes it, has moved on; there is less anxiety about the imminent return of Christ and more attention to the problems of living as Christians in this world. It seems more likely that a disciple of Paul, who had remained in Ephesus, compiled this letter soon after Paul's execution (probably in AD 65). He worked from copies of Paul's own letters, as well as Colossians, and includes a major section about marriage (Eph. 5.21—6.9). Although the themes of Paul's own letters reappear, they are as it were re-wrapped here within a new overarching theological concept that the married experience is a paradigm of the relationship between Christ and his Church.

Christian marriage is an opportunity for husbands to love their wives as Christ loves the Church, and wives should respect their husbands as the Church respects Christ.[29] This paradigm is not so much an elaboration of Colossians and similar Christian household codes as a reworking of their precepts that alters them fundamentally. There are three clear rules: be subject to one another, wives be subject to your husbands, husbands love your wives, but the reasons for them are explained in new ways which give a different character to Paul's doctrine of marriage. It may be that this section of the epistle originally existed as a separate document in the form of summary notes dictated by Paul himself, as an *aide mémoire*, a précis of his own developed thinking about Christian marriage. The text seems very condensed, and includes towards its end the inclusion of parenthetic but very important references to baptism and the one-flesh relationship. As set down, these references seem like interpolations, but make better sense if they are actually speaker's notes, to be given proper exegesis later. The author of the epistle seems to be content to leave them in the abridged form he has to hand.

Be subject to one another out of reverence for Christ.

Wives, be subject to your husbands as you are to the Lord. For the husband is the head of the wife just as Christ is the head of the church, the body of which he is the Saviour. Just as the church is subject to Christ, so also wives ought to be, in everything, to their husbands.

Husbands, love your wives, just as Christ loved the church and gave himself up for her, in order to make her holy by cleansing her with the washing of water by the word, so as to present the church to himself in splendour, without a spot or wrinkle or anything of the kind – yes, so that she may be holy and without blemish. In the same way, husbands should love their wives as they do their own bodies. He who loves his wife loves himself. For no one ever hates his own body, but he nourishes and tenderly cares for it, just as Christ does for the church, because we are members of his body. 'For this reason a man will leave his father and mother and be joined to his wife, and the two will become one flesh.' This is a great mystery, and I am applying it to Christ and the church. Each of you, however, should love his wife as himself, and a wife should respect her husband. (Eph. 5.21–33)

This exposition of Christian marital obligations begins with the linking preface 'be subject to one another out of reverence to Christ' (v. 21). This underlying principle informs all that follows but connects with the precepts of behaviour listed from the beginning of chapter 4 onwards under the general heading that Christians are to live in a style 'worthy of their calling' (Eph. 4.1). This 'style' is in practice an imitation of Christ's own action in loving the Church and giving himself up for her, and the Church's response in submitting to him. Within marriage then, both husbands and wives are subject to one another, as both are to Christ. This preface differs markedly from Colossians (3.18) by bringing husbands as well as wives under the same obligation. This is a logical step in relation to the earlier precepts which refer without gender distinction to all being 'members of one another' (Eph. 4.25) but it boldly breaks out of the patriarchal mould that assumes the subject status of women, otherwise often maintained in the Household Codes. In fact it reappears immediately in the next verse, as in Colossians, but then is justified differently. The women are not subject to their husbands 'as is fitting', that is, according to custom but instead 'as you are to the Lord'. This is clearly not meant to be the same system under a new name (though Christian history amply demonstrates that supposition), but is a rethought definition of human relationships vis-à-vis each other as members of the one body – they are to be as Christ to each other. This point is clearly made in verse 25.

Rather than repeat the same injunction to the husband, his obligation to his partner is specified as loving her as Christ does, and then comes the parenthesis about the purifying water of baptism. The connection intended here, but not immediately obvious to us, is that baptism makes for a new start in human relationships on an equal basis. Any lingering attitude that womankind is tainted for ever by the sin of Eve, a commonplace among the rabbis, is to be rejected; they are now, by Christ's action, holy and without that inherited blemish. Some commentators identify this washing with the pre-nuptial ceremonial bath of a Jewish bride, but it is a standard metaphor of Paul.[30] The next step in the argument equates a man's love for his own body with that due to his wife and draws an analogy between that and Christ's tender care for the Church 'because we are members of his body' (vs 29–30). In parenthesis again, the reference to the one-flesh relationship (Genesis 2.24, 'J' narrative), gives added weight to the stress on mutual care for the partners and explains further the perhaps surprising suggestion that to love one's wife is to love oneself. But the major point is that the mutuality between man and woman in Christian marriage is no innovation; it was part of the original creation ordinance. Therefore it is appropriate to refer to it as a great mystery, one of the hidden ways in which God's plans slowly come to fruition, as indeed is the coming of Christ and his Church. The final reiteration suggests that the author while returning to the principle of verse 21 still links it with caution about wifely status. It is not to be expected that patriarchal attitudes could be eliminated completely from first-century patterns of thought, but this text gives it notice to quit.[31]

These verses have been one of the most-favoured texts used in Christian marriage ceremonies from the earliest times, predominantly in the Eastern churches, but also in the Anglican rites based on the work of Cranmer, who was influenced in this respect by Luther's marriage service. Most people married in the Church of England in the past five hundred years will have heard this paradigm, either as a Bible reading or mentioned in the prayers. It is a popular theme in sermons and marriage preparation courses, especially if the woman's response (BCP) 'love honour and obey' is being discussed.

The Pastoral Epistles

Despite appearing to be letters from Paul to his one-time companions Timothy and Titus, who are now responsible for the churches in Ephesus and Crete respectively, Paul was probably not the author. Since the eighteenth century they have been called 'the Pastoral Letters' and are best read as just that – advice from an unidentified senior church leader to a group of churches in Asia Minor under his care. They probably indicate a system of church order from about AD 90 onwards, and the advice given addresses the need to regulate the daily life of the churches in a more settled period. The Jewish problem has by now faded away, and the references to marriage and sexual morality are typical of the Household Codes of that period. Domestic harmony is stressed, and women are again relegated to a subordinate position (1 Tim. 2.8–14). The reference to their being 'saved through childbearing' (1 Tim. 2.15) is perplexing to modern readers, and much debated.[32] Christian leaders, bishops or presbyters and male and female deacons are meant to set a good example by managing their children and households well (1 Tim. 3.4 and 12). They should be married only once, which presumably means not allowed to divorce and remarry (1 Tim. 3.3 and 12). Paul's advice to the Corinthian widowers and widows forty years earlier may still be relevant. Unless they were still young they should give themselves to prayer and good works, and not remarry. The duty to support aged parents should be first met by their children, but for women over sixty the charge often fell on the Christian community, which was proving expensive.[33]

Other New Testament Epistles

Hebrews

This letter is obviously written for Jewish converts to Christianity by one of them who is particularly well versed in the Old Testament and the way it was interpreted in Judaism *c.* AD 70. He expected his readers to share that familiarity; without some knowledge of that kind, the epistle is barely accessible. The author may have been Apollos, a colleague of Paul in Ephesus, and the letter could have been specifically designed for the Jews at Corinth, which Apollos had visited with Paul's approval. It is typical of such letters to end with a series of moral injunctions introduced by the general principle 'let mutual love continue'. The only reference to marriage occurs here, a conventional

Jewish view, which Paul has already commended to the Corinthians. 'Let marriage be held in honour by all, and let the marriage bed be kept undefiled; for God will judge fornicators and adulterers' (Heb. 13.4).

Peter's epistles

The dates of the Petrine letters are uncertain, and the authorship is questioned. As with Ephesians, Peter might have written 1 Peter from prison from Rome, or it might have been the work of a disciple soon after his death, though it could have been compiled much later. In favour of a disciple soon after AD 65, the letter shows a closer affinity with Paul's own thinking than the Pastoral Epistles do. This is noticeable in the section devoted to slaves, wives and husbands (1 Peter 2.17—3.8). In précis, 'Wives are to accept the authority of their husbands', so that, even if some of them do not obey 'the' word, they may be won over without 'a' word by their wives' conduct, a hint that conduct rather than argument will convert them. So they are not to braid their hair nor wear gold ornaments, but adorn themselves with the lasting beauty of a gentle and quiet spirit, which is very precious in God's sight. Sarah, Abraham's wife, is cited as a model. Husbands, in the same way, are to show consideration for their wives in their lives together, paying honour to the woman as the weaker sex, since they too are heirs of the gracious gift of life.[34]

The meaning of love in the New Testament

Paul's famous panegyric of love (Greek *agape*) in 1 Corinthians 13 is not quoted directly elsewhere in the New Testament, but as an ethical imperative for Christians it permeates much of its teaching about marriage. Sometimes regarded as originally a separate text, composed as a meditation, Paul includes it in 1 Corinthians to distinguish the essential spiritual grace available to all from the charismatic gifts which are being claimed by the few, a claim he regards with some misgivings. Although the panegyric is unique in form, the aspects of love it commends reappear in Romans 8.9–21, recast in a way that suggests some parallels with Christ's Sermon on the Mount. Apart from Paul's own writings, the theme of God's love is dominant in John's Gospel and epistles, less so in the synoptics, though they all report the duty to love God and neighbour.[35]

To understand what *agape* means in the New Testament we have to look back to the Old Testament and the Hebrew language which, like English, had only one general word for love, *ahabah*. Thus, the types of love between the Patriarchs and their wives, powerful and sensual, passionate and patient, are all described with this word, and only the context makes clear what kind of love is meant. Solomon can be praised for loving the Lord and damned for loving many foreign wives.[36] As Israel's perception of the real nature of God developed, and his loving patience with his wayward people became more understood, it seemed a more focused word than *ahabah* should be used, and so *chesed* was chosen. The ordinary meaning of this word was human forbearance or compassion so it was also suitable to express God's steadfast and loving kindness to Israel, and his undeviating commitment to their well-being, whatever sins they committed or whatever disasters consequently fell upon them.

This special meaning of *chesed* appears very frequently in the Psalms and occasionally in Isaiah, Jeremiah and Hosea.[37] 'When Israel was a child, I loved him, and out of Egypt I called my son' and 'I led them with cords of human kindness, with bands of love' (Hos. 11.1 and 4).

Anglicans familiar with the BCP or the old form of Compline will recognize Psalm 17.7–8, but are unlikely to know that they are reading Coverdale's unique and felicitous translation of *chesed*: 'Shew thy marvellous loving-kindness, thou that art the Saviour of them which put their trust in thee . . . Keep me as the apple of an eye: hide me under the shadow of thy wings.'[38]

When the work on the Septuagint began in Alexandria, the translators had to decide how to translate *ahabah* and *chesed*. The Greeks had several words for loving, but the distinction between them was not sharply drawn. *Eros* commonly meant sexual love, but Plato and Aristotle used it for spiritual love, while *philia* described human friendship and affection. The verb *agapao*, from which *agape* was derived, meant the kind of unemotional love that was linked with duty and obligation. It was decided that *eros* and *philia* had some all too human connotations, so *agapao* became the well-nigh universal translation of *chesed*. For example the Septuagint version of the command to love God with heart, soul and might has *agapeseis*.[39]

The New Testament writers, facing the same difficulty over which Greek word to use, and being familiar with the Septuagint, adopted *agapao* and *agape* throughout, so in every New Testament reference to God's love or the Christian response to it the special meaning of *chesed* is implicit. This kind of love involves constancy and selflessness, initiated by God, revealed in Christ and reciprocated by Christians.

The defining use of *agapao* is in Christ's response to the scribe's question, 'Which commandment is the first of all?' (Mark 12.28, and parallels). Christ's answer – love God and your neighbour – is rendered in Greek by *agapeseis*.[40] This definition is reiterated by Paul: 'God's love has been poured into our hearts through the Holy Spirit that has been given to us' (Rom. 5.5) and by John: 'We love [*agapomen*] because he first loved us' (1 John 4.19).

Given the somewhat complicated journey, etymologically, from *chesed* to *agape*, it is not surprising that translators from the Greek into European languages have had their own problems. For 1 Corinthians 13, Latin Bibles used *caritas*, hence the French *charité* (Jerusalem Bible), and the English 'charity' (AV and RV), which now has a limited meaning. Luther used love (*Liebe*), and that is still standard in German Bibles, but in France *amour* might not seem quite right. Modern English Bibles replace 'charity' with 'love', but this omnibus word with its ambiguous use in our culture now seems too imprecise to convey the particularity of *agape* in scripture. Whereas 'steadfast love' is quite suitable for the Psalms, it would seem a clumsy expression in 1 Corinthians 13. Perhaps when the chapter is read as a whole its meaning is clear enough. The alternative Latin word for love is *dilige*, from which comes our 'diligence', with the modern meaning of being assiduous in duties. In the Vulgate, for 1 John 4.21, *agapao* is translated with *diligere*: '*Qui diligit Deum diligit fratrem suum*', which becomes in English, 'he who loves God must love his brother also'. The shift in meaning of 'diligence' has had a confusing effect on Christian ethics, which are as much to do with the will as with the emotions, a subject for the next chapter.

6

Constructing the Christian Ethos

The first five centuries

The Christian mission to the Roman world

By the end of the first century AD, Christianity had established itself as one of the many cults of the Roman world. Although the Christians thought of themselves as a distinct community, to the Romans they appeared to be a new sect within Judaism. Despite its segregationist tendencies, Judaism was usually tolerated as an Eastern religion posing little threat to the empire and respected for its ethical monotheism. Large communities of Diaspora Jews were spread throughout the empire, with at least eleven Jewish synagogues in Rome itself. The Roman people were eclectic towards such cults, quite ready to pick and mix among them and insufficiently certain of the ultimate authority of any of them to inhibit local freedom of choice. The chief religious obligation was to honour the emperors, who were inclined to self-divinization. Beyond that civic duty, each city of the empire had its own patron deity, as did each household.

Whereas the mission of Jesus had found its best response in rural Galilee, Paul and his associates planted most of their churches in urban settings, the converts coming mostly from among the Diaspora Jews and the God-fearers. In any case, the destruction of Jerusalem in AD 70 meant the dispersal of its population and the end of the city as the leading Christian base. Apart from Rome, the main Christian centres were Antioch in Syria and Alexandria (with an estimated population of a million Jews). The Christians kept in touch with each other easily enough by road or sea and through the efficient imperial courier system. To their copies of the Septuagint, in new translations, they added copies of Paul's letters and the Gospels as these became available, together with letters from other apostles, including some spurious ones. As the leadership pattern changed from travelling apostles and prophets towards that of more local and residential teachers and pastors, bishops and presbyters, so their more substantial writings were also preserved.[1]

The alliance with stoicism

As we have seen, St Paul's understanding of the way of life of the people of the new covenant was to be imitators of Christ.[2] In essence this required a recasting of the basic precepts of the Torah in the light of Christ to define a new community, whose social character was as far as possible an image of his. Thus for violence, peace; for arrogance, humility; for deceit, honesty; for anarchy, obedience to lawful authority; for religion, one God, not many. In marriage there had to be mutual honour and fidelity, and for the sexual drive apart from marriage, chastity was to replace lust. But these characteristics of the Christian community were not in practice as strange to Roman minds as the notorious decadence of their culture might suggest. Most Romans had a robust and light-hearted attitude to the physical aspects of sexuality, often thought obscene by Judaism. Priapus, son of Dionysus and Aphrodite, was the god of fertility and the subject of explicit poetry; naked statues of him, well equipped, adorned Roman temples and gardens. Confronting this culture, proponents of the Christian ethos were able to form a ready alliance with the new teaching of discipline and asceticism being promulgated by the Stoics and Neo-Platonists.

Alliance is perhaps not the best word to explain the convergence of thought, not least about marriage and sex, between the Graeco-Roman and Christian thinkers at this time. It was not so much a conscious decision on either side to promote the same policy as a recognition by the Christians that the teaching of Plutarch, Seneca and Musonius about marriage and sex had close affinity with that of St Paul. In very simplified terms, the philosophers, following some of Plato's insights, held that reason must conquer the emotions; the good life had be lived by rational control, choosing always the dictates of the higher nature, and resisting the lower impulses, not least the sexual drive. As an example of the range of this teaching, an anonymous tract *The Education of Children*, once attributed to Plutarch, reads much like the household codes of the New Testament.

What is honourable and what is shameful, what is just and what is

unjust, what, in brief, is to be chosen, and what to be avoided? . . .
one ought to reverence the gods, to honour one's parents, to respect
one's elders, to be obedient to the laws, to yield to those in
authority, to love one's friends, to be chaste with women, and not to
be overbearing with slaves.[3]

Many of the Stoics were cautiously in favour of love and marriage.
Sex between married partners was acceptable if restrained, not dominated by lust. But since completing the act necessarily involved some
loss of control, the possibility of sexual abstinence even within marriage was sometimes commended. It was suggested that even the sight
of a neighbour's wife naked should not disturb the tranquillity of a
rational husband! Seneca wrote that 'unchastity is the plague of our
time'. Ironically, he was already banished to Corsica for adultery
when he wrote this.[4] The teaching of Musonius Rufus (*c.* AD 35–100)
was probably the most influential in Rome at this time, and was highly
regarded by the Christian apologists.

The only sources we have are from his students' notes. In Fragment
14 he refers to the androgynous myth, saying:

> To what other purpose did the creator of mankind first divide our
> human race into two sexes, male and female, and then implant in
> each a strong desire for association and union with each other? . . .
> Is it not then plain that he wished the two to be united and live
> together, and by their joint efforts to devise a way of life in
> common?

A little earlier, in Fragment 13A, he says:

> Husband and wife should come together for the purpose of making
> a life in common and of procreating children, and furthermore of
> regarding all things in common between them, and nothing peculiar
> or private to one or the other, not even their own bodies . . . In
> marriage there must be above all perfect companionship (*symbiosis*)
> and mutual love (*kedemonia*) of husband and wife, both in health
> and sickness and under all conditions, since it was with desire for
> this as well as for having children that both entered upon marriage.[5]

Early Church thoughts on marriage

The Apostolic Fathers

The authors of the surviving non-canonical documents of the early Church, known collectively as the Apostolic Fathers (who wrote in Greek), had greater issues on their minds than sex and marriage, so they only refer to them *en passant*. There was no separate Christian marriage ceremony, only civil law and custom, and for the most part the Fathers were content to reiterate the standard moral teaching of the household codes. But it is possible even at this early stage to see the initial developments of a particular Christian attitude, largely based on phrases from 1 Corinthians and Ephesians. The epistles of Clement and Ignatius are complemented by less weighty manuals of instruction for new converts, notably the *Didache* and the *Shepherd* of Hermas.

Clement of Rome

Clement's first epistle was written from Rome in AD 96 by a leader of the church, and is addressed to the church in Corinth. Clement was possibly a bishop in Rome[6] and Eusebius says he was a pupil of the apostles. The Corinthians had asked Rome for advice about local rivalries leading to the dismissal of some of their presbyters. Clement replied, on behalf of his church, in a fraternal if somewhat long-winded style, advising the restitution of the elected leaders. Clement was probably a Hellenistic Jew, and his letter shows he knew both the Old Testament and St Paul's epistles, and parts of the Gospels, from all of which he quotes extensively. He was also familiar with the particular character of the Corinthian congregation, and commends them that they have

> instructed your women to do everything with a blameless and pure conscience, and to give their husbands the affection they should. You taught them, too, to abide by the rule of obedience and to run their homes with dignity and thorough discretion. (1 Clem. 3)

Later in the epistle, he gives his own version of personal Christian morality:

> Since then we are a holy portion, we should do everything that makes for holiness. We should flee from slandering, vile and impure

embraces, drunkenness and rioting, filthy lusts, detestable adultery and disgusting arrogance. For God, says Scripture, resists the arrogant, but gives grace to the humble. (1 Clem. 30)[7]

Ignatius of Antioch

Ignatius was the Bishop or chief presbyter of the church at Antioch in Syria. He is only known for his journey to Rome, for martyrdom in the Coliseum (*c.* AD 107) and for his seven letters to churches he passed by during the middle part of his journey. He was a friend of the much respected Polycarp, Bishop of Smyrna (later himself to be martyred in AD 155 or 156) and his advice about marriage reflects his endorsement of 1 Timothy and Ephesians:

> Tell my sisters to love the Lord and to be altogether contented with their husbands. Similarly urge my brothers in the name of Jesus Christ 'to love their wives as the Lord loves the Church' (cf. Eph. 5.24–5).

> If anyone can live in chastity for the honour of the Lord's flesh, let him do so without ever boasting. If he boasts of it, he is lost; and if he is more highly honoured than the bishop, his chastity is as good as forfeited. It is right for men and women who marry to be united with the bishop's approval. In that way their marriage will follow God's will, and not the prompting of lust. Let everything be done so as to advance God's honour. (Ep. Poly. 5)

There are a number of important insights here about marriage. First, the reciprocity between husbands and wives is quoted from Ephesians. When Ignatius commends chastity as 'for the honour of the Lord's flesh', he means the physical body of Jesus (Greek *sarx*), not the Church, a reference to his celibacy. It is an early hint of the later doctrine that in the imitation of Christ, celibacy was the more perfect way, but was not something to boast about. Ignatius was aware of the danger of Gnostic teaching that human flesh is of the devil.[8] He therefore asserts that marriage is right for men and women, and adds that the bishop should approve. But, as Schillebeeckx observes, there was no question of ecclesiastical jurisdiction implied here, that came much later. Following Jewish and Roman custom, marriages remained family affairs, but the chief presbyter would be interested in special categories such as presbyters, catechumens and orphans, and in avoiding consanguinity.[9]

The Didache and Hermas

The *Didache* has been variously dated between AD 60 and 150, and appears to be a composite work describing church practice in Syria throughout this period. Its first part is a simple catechism contrasting the way of life and the way of death, and the second part deals with church order, including simple instructions for baptism and the Eucharist and a version of the Lord's Prayer. In part one, adultery, fornication and the corruption of boys are included in the ways of death.[10]

The *Shepherd* of Hermas is a very long document, written by an author who claims to have been a Christian slave in Rome, later emancipated. It dates from *c.* AD 150 and records a series of visions, mandates and principles of Christian behaviour. It was popular in the Eastern churches. Mandate 4 begins:

> I charge thee (saith he) to keep purity, and let not a thought enter into thy heart concerning another's wife, or concerning fornication or concerning any such like evil deed; for in doing so thou committest a great sin. But remember thine own wife always, and thou shalt never go wrong.[11]

Hermas addresses husbands here, and rules that if a wife commits adultery she has to be dismissed, but the man is not to remarry (following Mark 10.11). If she repents, he must accept her, but only once, since it is necessary to welcome back a sinner who repents. If the husband is the adulterer, the wife must follow the same rules. As we have seen, the Augustan rule was that Roman citizens must divorce adulterous wives, and not condone them. Hermas agrees, but allows that repentance is now possible. The Church was working out its doctrine of repentance and restitution, chiefly for Christians who became apostate under the threat of execution and then wished to be readmitted; this was allowed only once. The same rule is now being applied to adultery.

Second and third-century developments – the Latin Fathers

The effect of persecution

As the Christians became more numerous, outnumbering the Jews, they were at risk of being made the scapegoats for any kind of disaster. After Nero, the persecutions were intermittent, but whenever things looked bad in Rome, even from natural disaster like the flooding of the Tiber, the cry went up: 'Christians to the lions.' Among the emperors, Marcus Aurelius, who ruled from 161 to 180, stands out as the humane Stoic moralist, but surprisingly he ordered the execution of those Christians who would not recant. In contrast, as a corrective to the prevailing decadence, it was his policy to reinforce the growing status of decent nuclear family life by emphasizing the harmony (*concordia*) of his own marriage. His wife Faustina was the daughter of the Emperor Antoninus, and when Aurelius succeeded him, he had her portrait on the obverse of his coins. After her death, he lived separately with his concubine, not wishing to upset his family with step-children.[12] In reaction to the harsh policy of Diocletian and Galerius which had been intended to kill the clergy and close the churches, Constantine introduced the era of tolerance by his Edict of Milan in AD 313.

The Christians never knew when persecution would fall on them again. To honour those who were butchered in the Coliseum and many other places for being faithful unto death, the martyrs' dates of death were commemorated annually as their heavenly birthdays, the day when they received the crown of life (Rev. 2.11). The resurrection promise was made to all the faithful, not just the martyrs, and this altered the Christian perspective of ordinary life. As Paul put it, his personal aim was 'to depart and be with Christ, which is far better' (Phil. 1.23). The corollary of this mindset towards eternity was to loosen the ties between one's earthly body and one's ultimate significance. Paul sets this new perspective with tremendous verve towards the end of 1 Corinthians: 'This perishable body must put on imperishability . . . Therefore, my beloved, . . . you know that in the Lord your labour is not in vain.'[13] The consequence was a change in the Christian attitude to sex, marriage and children; they seemed less important. If it was better to depart this life and be with Christ then it was also clear that the natural drives of the human body should be subordinated to or even superseded by the spiritual drives of those preparing for heavenly citizenship. As we have seen, some of the Corinthians had tried to press this freedom too far, as did the Gnostics and the Montanists, but the more balanced view continued to dominate, echoing the epistle to the Hebrews: 'Let marriage be held in honour by all, and let the marriage bed be kept undefiled; for God will judge fornicators and adulterers' (Hebrews 13.4).

Virginity preferred

A change in attitude, making marriage second best to virginity, becomes very clear in the writings from the second- and third-century Latin Fathers, so called because of their first language. The Fathers used the Old Testament to support their teaching generally, but they began to lose touch with its unreserved affirmation of procreation, questioning its continued relevance. They replaced it with an eschatological emphasis, which, while linking at points with Stoic asceticism, was mostly concerned with preparing for eternity. Equally important was their study of the incarnation. The difficult but essential task of defining the nature of Christ vis-à-vis his divinity and humanity required careful study of the birth narratives in Matthew and Luke. Paul had simply recorded that Jesus was born of a woman (Gal. 4.4); however, the medical understanding at this time was that the woman was merely the incubator of the male seed, so it was from the male that the entail of human sinfulness was passed on. Mary had conceived Jesus by the direct intervention of the Holy Spirit; that marked her out as most highly favoured, and meant that Jesus was without sin, but it led to speculation about the role of Joseph, who, it was suggested, had been absent on business elsewhere between the betrothal and Mary's realization that she was pregnant. Although this kind of speculation went beyond the canonical Gospels, it was set out in various apocryphal writings, and the effect was to exalt the status of virginity, enhanced of course by Jesus' own celibacy and suggestion to his disciples that they should renounce family ties for the sake of the kingdom (Matt. 19.29). The speculation was encouraged by popular legends about young virgin martyrs and married couples who refused to consummate their marriages sexually.

One of Paul's more vigorous metaphors for the relationship between Christ and his Church was the spiritual marriage between them. 'I feel a divine jealousy for you, for I promised you in marriage to one husband, to present you as a chaste virgin to Christ' (2 Cor. 11.2).

The metaphor has Old Testament precedents, and there is a loose parallel in the vision of Revelation 21, but it is clearly a corporate image. However, the notion that Christian virgins would be united in heaven as brides of Christ was seen as another argument for their renunciation of earthly marriage. Cohorts of saintly virgins surrounding the figure of their ascended Lord become a popular theme in Christian art,[14] but common sense suggests that the ordinary vision of most people looked towards marriage and children, as they always do. And the frequency of admonitions against fornication and adultery in Patristic writings shows that the old Adam was not so easily quenched. That admitted, the shift in attitude towards virginity for both men and women won wide acceptance among Christians. The great principle was the priority of following Christ, for which all else had to be given up. The Jewish tradition had understood human life as an opportunity for obedience to God within the constraints of his created order. The Stoic tradition understood human life as an opportunity for self-improvement through unrelenting education in certain forms of truth which might lead one into the summit experience of the good, culminating in the beatific vision. The third-century Christians understood human life as a limited and temporary state, from which by faith and the imitation of Christ one could prepare to escape the unfortunate encumbrance of the earthly body and join the resurrection life.

Apart from the eschatological and Christological considerations, there were several other factors that help to explain why the official Christian emphasis turned away from marriage to virginity as the preferred choice. The teaching of Musonius and other Stoics that sex was irrational has already been mentioned. Then, among the Christians the advice that widows should remain unmarried was extended to younger women. Some of the widows would have been powerful matriarchs in their own families, and welcomed the opportunity in later life to exercise leadership roles in the congregation. They might be rich enough in their own right to endow churches. Equally, for younger women the positive effect was gradually to gain more choice about the kind of life open to them: childbearing and domesticity ceased to be the only options. Among the Patrician Roman families influenced by Christianity, the daughters no longer had to be married off; they could stay at home, declaring themselves committed to virginity.

[The teaching that celibacy, adopted for the best reasons, is an intrinsically higher state than that of marriage was reaffirmed as official Roman Catholic teaching in the 1954 papal encyclical *Sacra Virginitatis*. Many Christians disagree, claiming that marriage and virginity, when chosen for the right ends, are of equal standing. Ed.]

Monasticism and celibacy

More broadly, the growth of Christianity coincided with and maybe even caused a period of social change. The local church and its house groups, with their sense of fellowship (*koinonia*) and being open to both genders and all ages, could offer all kinds of interests beyond being stuck at home for the women and the struggle of men to stay in the swim of economic or political security, and provided for some of them a respectable reason for avoiding family commitments. There was the opportunity to join cells of like-minded people working with and supporting particular teachers, similar to the pattern Jesus used with his disciples. These informal communities, sisterhoods and brotherhoods, had obvious risks and led to the more formal construction of monastic communities, with their strict rules, matched for a time by the hermit life of the Desert Fathers. The life of religious communities may seem to us restrictive, especially with their threefold vows of chastity, poverty and obedience, but there was a positive side to the life of monks and nuns. Not all religious houses were remote from civilization; they had to be within reach of a village to sell their handicrafts and obtain food. Or, if they were in fertile places, their developed agricultural techniques provided a good life and a steady income. The vow of poverty meant handing over one's personal property to the community common fund, but some parents noted that the dowry required for their daughter by the convent would be less than if she were to make a prestigious marriage. For poor peasants, joining a community was a way out of rural poverty and subjection to rapacious landlords. Celibacy was a vocation for the future, deliberately chosen, irrespective of the past, but it implied the end of any existing marriage, and sometimes therefore a church sanctioned exit from a disagreeable one.

Tertullian

Tertullian (AD 160–225) was a very able but in some ways maverick theologian from North Africa, who proved to be a continuing and persuasive influence on the Christian attitude to marriage throughout the Middle Ages. Growing up in Carthage as a pagan and trained as a lawyer he was converted to Christianity in Rome in AD 195. Henry Chadwick has described him as 'brilliant, exasperating, sarcastic, and intolerant, yet intensely vigorous and incisive in argument . . . a powerful writer of splendid torrential prose'.[15] Tertullian may have witnessed the execution of Perpetua and her companions in the arena at Carthage in AD 203. In later life, he became a member of the ascetic and apocalyptic Montanist sect. In a letter to his wife written *c*. 205, he asks her not to remarry after his death:

> You will confer no benefit on me by this action, other than the good you do for yourself. In any case there is no promise of a restoration of marriage after the day of resurrection for Christians who have departed this life, for at that time they will be transformed into a state of angelic holiness. Therefore, there is no cause for that anxiety which comes from carnal jealousy . . . [he cites Jesus' saying about the woman with seven husbands that there would be no marriage in heaven] . . . Do not think that I have counselled you to remain a widow in order to reserve to myself the integrity of your body because I am afraid that someday I might suffer hardship. On that day we will not resume any disgraceful pleasures. God does not promise such frivolous filthy things to those who are his own . . . Of course, we do not reject the union (*conjunctio*) of man and woman. It has been blessed by God to be the seedbed of the human race; it was devised to fill up the earth and to set the world in order. Thus it was permitted, but only once. For Adam was the one husband of Eve, and Eve his one wife; one woman one rib. It is true that our ancient forebears, the Patriarchs, were allowed not only to marry, but also to practise polygamy; they even had concubines. Now although the church existed in a figurative way in the synagogue, we can give the simple interpretation that it was necessary in the past to establish practices that would be later abrogated or modified . . . I have not set forth these remarks about the liberty of the old in order to argue that Christ came to dissolve marriage or to abolish sexual relations, as though from now on marriage is to be outlawed. Let them beware, who among their other perversities teach the separation of the two in one flesh, rejecting him who first derived the woman from the man and then reunited in the marriage compact the two bodies that were taken from the harmonious union of the same material substance.[16]

In later writings on marriage, Tertullian moves towards a firmer Montanist position. Their view was that they were the chosen few who would shortly be released from the evil drag of human bodies by the return of Christ, and there was therefore no need to breed children. Montanism was condemned by Pope Zephyrinus *c.* AD 210, but Tertullian's suggestion in the letter to his wife that marriage was little more than a regrettable necessity, was an idea that embedded itself in the Christian tradition for a long time. The sense among these ascetics that they were ashamed of their bodies, not least for the filthy frivolity of sex, would of course produce howls of derogatory laughter among the rabbis that the positive good of procreation could be so despised, and one wonders what his wife thought, if she read it. Actually, it reads more like a tract for the times than a personal letter.

Clement of Alexandria

Little is known of the life of Clement of Alexandria (AD 150–215), though Eusebius records that he had copies of some of his books. He was born in Rome and studied in Alexandria, where he was head of the school for Catechumens, but had to flee from there under persecution *c.* AD 202. His basic teaching on marriage comes from his *Instructor* (*Paedagogus*), a manual designed for the moral education of new Christians, and from his *Miscellanies*, where the doctrine of creation is emphasized. In *Paedagogus* he is for marriage but against fornication and abortion:

> (95) Wise then was the person who when asked his opinion of the pleasures of love replied 'Silence Man. I am very glad to have fled from them as from a fierce and raging tyrant'.[17] Nevertheless, marriage should be accepted and given its proper place. Our Lord wanted humanity to multiply (Genesis 1.28) but he did not say that people should engage in licentious behaviour, nor did he intend for them to give themselves over to pleasure as if they were born for rutting. Rather let the Pedagogue put us to shame with the word of Ezekiel: Put away your fornications (Ezek. 43.29). Even irrational animals have a proper time for sowing seed. But to have intercourse without intending children is to violate nature which we must take as our teacher . . . So marriage is the desire for procreation, but it is not the random, illicit, or irrational scattering of seed.
>
> (96) Our entire life will be spent observing the laws of nature, if we

control our desires from the start, and if we do not kill off with
devious instruments the human creature that has been conceived
according to divine providence. For women who, in order to
conceal their incontinence, make use of death-dealing drugs that
completely expel the mortal creature, abort not only the embryo,
but also human kindness.[18]

Clement was learned in classical literature, and uses a wide range of
references from them, particularly Plato, but they are somewhat
contrived. Thus he warns that couples should not be like Penelope at
her loom, weaving industriously during the day and unravelling her
work during the night. So couples should not practise self-restraint in
the day, and be intemperate at night under the cover of darkness.

(II. 145) . . . we rise from our sleep with the Lord and go to sleep
with thanksgiving and prayer . . . Scripture recommends marriage
and does not allow release from the union; this is evident from the
precept 'You shall not put away your wife except because of fornication' (Matt. 5.32). It is regarded as adultery if either of the
separated partners marries while the other is alive.[19]

Later in the *Miscellanies* he discusses the celibacy of Jesus:

(III. 49) Some openly declare that marriage is fornication and teach
that it was introduced by the devil. They boast that they are imitat-
ing the Lord himself who neither married nor possessed anything in
the world, and they claim to understand the gospel better than
anyone else. Moreover, they do not know the reason why the Lord
did not marry. First, he had his own bride, the church; second he
was no ordinary man who had need of a helpmate after the flesh
(Genesis 2.18). Nor did he need to beget children, since he lives
eternally and was born the only Son of God.[20]

The Apocryphal Acts of the Apostles

These were a group of five pseudo-biographies of the third century AD,
designed to supplement the sparse details of the lives of the Apostles
John, Peter, Paul, Andrew and Thomas given in the Gospels and Acts.
To us they read like a mixture of credible legends built on real events
and added fables. Thus, the account of Paul's life is an embroidered

version of his missionary journeys, including his encounter with the lion in the arena at Ephesus. They recognized each other as Paul had previously baptized him, and so they conversed amicably, to the annoyance of the crowd. Both Paul and the lion survived.[21] Although widely read, these Acts were eventually condemned as spurious, not because of their legendary character but because they included gnostic teaching, notably about the evils of sex.

The *Acts of Thomas*, not to be confused with the *Gospel of Thomas*, has a historical basis since Thomas is honoured as the founding patron of the Syrian Orthodox Church of India, and may have reached there or Parthia before being martyred. His legendary *Acts* come from Edessa in Syria, *c.* AD 220, and claim that Judas Thomas, as he is called, was actually the twin brother of Jesus. He is taken to India as a slave carpenter, but is soon recognized as a miracle worker. Invited to the wedding celebration of the king's daughter, he is asked to pray over the couple and does so with these ambiguous words: 'Lord Jesus, do thou for them the things that help and are useful and profitable.' The result is that when the groom prepares to meet his bride in the bedroom, he sees a vision, which he assumes is Thomas, but is in fact Jesus, who says to them:

> If you abandon this filthy intercourse you become holy temples, pure and free from afflictions and pains, both manifest and hidden, and you will not be girt about with cares for life and for children, the end of which is destruction.[22]

When the young couple heard this they abandoned their passion, remained chaste overnight and surprised everyone the next morning by saying so, not least the outraged king. The bride said she had a new husband, Jesus, and the groom gave thanks to God that he had put him far from corruption and sown new life in him. Thomas escaped the king's wrath and sailed to India the next day.

The better known story of Thecla was originally an independent account, with some historical basis, but later elaborated and incorporated in the *Acts of St Paul*. Paul, described as a small man with a bald head and crooked legs, was in Iconium teaching at the house of Onesiphorus (2 Tim. 1.16). Thecla, a young lady betrothed to Thamyris, watched Paul from her window opposite and decided to become one of his followers. Thamysis, bitter at losing his fiancée, accused Paul of sorcery before the governor, who ordered him to be scourged and Thecla to be burned. In the theatre, she prayed and had a vision, and then 'God in compassion' sent a great hailstorm to put out the fire, and she escaped. She had further similar adventures and died naturally. She remains as a saint in the calendar of the Orthodox Church, but not in the West. Included in this story is an extraordinary example of the teaching St Paul was said to be giving, in the form of a revised set of Beatitudes:

> When Paul entered the house of Onesiphorus, there was great joy, and bowing of knees and breaking of bread, and the word of God concerning continence and the resurrection, as Paul said: 'Blessed are the pure in heart, for they shall see God, Blessed are they who have kept the flesh pure, for they shall become a temple of God, Blessed are they who have renounced this world, for they shall be well pleasing to God. Blessed are they who have wives as if they had them not, for they shall inherit God.'[23]

Methodius

Methodius was a teacher, and Bishop of Lycia (in Southern Turkey), who died *c.* AD 311, probably martyred in the last years of Diocletian. He follows Clement in accepting that virginity is the higher calling but maintains that marriage is to be continued as a good provision of God's creation. He sets out the case in his *Symposium*, a deliberate copy of Plato. Here the guests at the banquet are ten virgins, praising virginity, but he allows one of them, Theophila, to defend marriage.

> [The] suggestion that it is no longer necessary to produce children is mistaken. It is very clear to me from scripture that with the coming of virginity the Logos did not completely abolish procreation . . . We will begin with Genesis in order to pay the highest respect to Scripture. God's declaration and command regarding procreation, all agree, is still being accomplished even now, since the Creator is still fashioning human beings. Everyone can see that God at this very moment is at work on the universe, like a craftsman, as the Lord himself has taught us: My father is at work even now (John 5.17) . . . And when the predetermined number of human beings is fulfilled, only then must there be no more procreation. But now it is necessary that human beings co-operate in producing the image of God, since the universe continues to exist and to be created. Increase

and multiply, scripture says (Gen. 1.28). We must not recoil from the commandment of the Creator, from whom we too have received our existence. Human reproduction begins with the sowing of seed into the furrows of the womb, in such a way that bone from bone and flesh from flesh is taken by an invisible power and fashioned by the Craftsman himself into another human being . . .

This perhaps is what was signified by that ecstasy which fell upon the first man in his sleep (Gen. 2.21); it prefigured the enchantment that men would find in love, when thirsting for children he falls into ecstasy and is lulled into sleep by the pleasures of procreation, so that once more another person might be created from that bit that was torn from his bone and from his flesh. First the harmony of the body is greatly agitated in the excitement of intercourse (so I have learned from those who have consummated the marriage rite); then all the marrow in the blood, which has generative power and is liquid bone, is gathered from every part of the body, worked into a foam and coagulated, and then rushes out through the reproductive organs into the living soil of the woman. For this reason, it is well said that a man will leave his father and mother (Gen. 2.24), because a man forgets everything else when he is joined to a woman in tender embrace, overwhelmed with a desire for children. He offers his rib to the divine Creator to be removed, so that he the father, might reappear again in his son. Since then, even now God is still fashioning human beings, would it not be arrogant for us to loathe procreation, which the Almighty himself is not ashamed to accomplish with undefiled hands? 'Before I formed you in your mother's womb, I knew you,' he says to Jeremiah (Jer. 1.5).[24]

[The idea that there is to be a definite number of created human beings is common to many Christian writers. According to Anselm's *Cur Deus Homo*, the number will correspond to the number of fallen angels, thus making up for their loss. Ed.]

Constantine

In the fourth century, Christianity was officially declared the most favoured religion of the Roman world. Put like that, Constantine's Edict of Milan in 313 suggests a straightforward victory for the Christians, but in reality it was one decisive step in the slow but steady process of movement towards Christianizing the empire. The Christian takeover was bound to be patchy because, politically, the empire was no longer an effective unity. The two emperors, Constantine in the West and Licinius in the East, had made a personal agreement that persecution of the Christians should cease but this only became fully effective when Constantine became sole emperor and founded his new capital at Byzantium, renamed Constantinople.

The consequences of all these changes for the Christian Church were mixed. The majority of the empire's population would have had little idea who Christ was, but the church was steadily growing in influence in the corridors of power. With hindsight one can say that the empire and the Church needed each other. Just as the expansion of the Church had reached the boundaries of the Roman world, but scarcely beyond, so Constantine knew he relied on the one and only God of the Christians to win his battles, as he explained afterwards to his friend, the Church historian Eusebius. Despite delaying baptism until death was near, not unusual in those days, Constantine was far more than a nominal Christian, and he understood himself called upon to provide a watchful oversight of the church. Some of his legislation about marriage, but not all of it, reflected modifications towards Christian morality.

Virginity or marriage debated in the fourth and fifth centuries

It might be expected that by now the Christians would have constructed an agreed ethos for marriage that could be commended to everyone. But the diverse views about virginity and marriage continued, as the quotations that follow from five of the most influential theologians illustrate. All were born within fifteen years of each other, from 339 to 354, and lived through the final years of the united empire under Theodosius. From the west, Ambrose praises virginity but accepts marriage, while Jerome takes a negative view of marriage. From the East, Chrysostom and Basil are more positive and Augustine hesitantly achieves a synthesis.

Ambrose

After Constantine, the empire reverted temporarily to anarchy and attention was concentrated on resisting the invasion of the tribes from the North. Only with the accession of Theodosius, a successful Spanish general, as sole emperor (378–95) was the Christian status in the whole empire consolidated. The incident usually reckoned to demonstrate this change was the confrontation between Theodosius and Ambrose. Ambrose (339–97) came from a patrician and Christian family and was a provincial governor before being suddenly elected, while still a layman, to be Bishop of Milan, for the lack of an agreed clerical candidate. A mob in Thessalonica murdered the captain of the imperial garrison for putting their favourite charioteer in prison. In fury, Theodosius ordered reprisals, and despite Ambrose's plea that the punishment was excessive, the soldiers killed some 7,000 of the citizens. Ambrose threatened to excommunicate him until he did public penance. The emperor duly attended the mass without his royal regalia and publicly confessed his sin to clear his own conscience for a decision he now regretted. He did not lose his authority by this confession, nor did Ambrose wish him to, but the point was made: Christian emperors were not above Christian morality.

For Ambrose, the integrity of the Christian life was a key principle, not only for emperors but equally in the use of sex. Although not forbidding marriage, in his most influential treatise *On Virginity* he stresses the perpetual chastity of the Blessed Virgin Mary, preserving her integrity from the taint of sexual sin. He then cites the popular stories of Agnes and Thecla as contemporary examples.

> I am not discouraging marriage, then, if I enumerate the benefits of virginity. This latter, to be sure, is the work of a few, while the former is for all. Virginity cannot exist unless there is the possibility of being born. I am comparing good things with good things, so that what is superior may be much more apparent. It is no judgement of mine that I am adducing; rather I am repeating the one that the Holy Spirit proclaimed through the prophet; 'Better', he says, 'is barrenness with virtue' (Wisdom 4.1).[25]

Jerome

Jerome (345–420) is justly famous for his achievement in producing the Vulgate, and has been the target of occasional and probably undeserved ribaldry for the clique of aristocratic Roman virgins who formed a devout circle round him in his Roman period. Born in Dalmatia, Northern Italy, and teaching for a while in Rome, his sardonic tongue led to his exile to Palestine. He had suggested that only men who were afraid to go to bed alone should marry! He founded a small monastery in Bethlehem, close to the cave where Jesus was supposedly born, and encouraged his close collaborator, Paula, to build a convent nearby. Jerome supported the doctrine of the perpetual virginity of Mary, and used it to argue for virginity for both sexes. Further, he believed that since the apostles had been either celibate or sexually abstinent in their marriages, bishops, priests and deacons should be chosen from people who had been either celibate or were widowers.

Jerome enjoyed dialectic, and although he could not actually forbid marriage, he could be very scathing about it, as this comment on Matthew 19.10 shows:

> Having a wife is a heavy burden if one cannot dismiss her except on the ground of fornication. For what if she were a drunkard, hot-tempered, badly behaved, lustful, a glutton, inconstant, quarrelsome or abusive? Must one retain a wife of this sort? Like it or not, one must put up with her, for one has subjected one's self to servitude while one was still free. Seeing what a heavy yoke having a wife must be, the disciples spoke out from their hearts, saying: 'If such is the case of a man with his wife, it is not expedient to marry'.[26]

Some scholars have criticized Jerome for his translation of 'mystery' as 'sacrament' (Greek *musterion*) in the Ephesians analogy between the marriage relationship and that of Christ and the Church (Eph. 5.32), supposing that Jerome was intending to equate marriage with baptism and the eucharist. This seems unlikely, partly because Jerome had no great opinion of marriage, but also because in classical use *sacramenta* were the oaths taken by soldiers on recruitment, and similarly described initiatory vows to the cults.

Basil of Caesarea

Classically educated at Constantinople and Athens, Basil (329–79) renounced the world and became a hermit monk, and as a brilliant organizer he created by his rule the enduring administrative system of eastern monasticism. Brought back to Caesarea in 370 as bishop, his advice about marriage comes in three letters to his neighbouring bishop, Amphilochius of Iconium. He is not afraid to question, at least in principle, the double standard for men and women:

The decree of the Lord, that it is forbidden to withdraw from marriage except in the case of fornication (Matt. 5.32; 19.9) applies equally to men and women, at least according to the logic of the idea. But the custom is different, and we find much stricter prescriptions for women. [He cites 1 Cor. 6.16, Jer. 3.1 and Prov. 18.22.] But custom requires wives to keep their husbands, even if the husbands commit adultery and fornication.

Basil concludes that the wife should bear being beaten or lack of money, and stick with him if a pagan. But if the woman commits adultery, abandoning her husband, he is not to be condemned, nor is his subsequent partner an adulteress. Basil seems here to be recognizing the status of an 'innocent party'. Similarly, he questions the inequality of treatment:

If a man who is living with his wife becomes dissatisfied with the marriage and falls into fornication, I judge him to be a fornicator and extend his period of punishment. We have however no canon to accuse him of adultery if the sin is committed against an unmarried woman . . . But the man who commits fornication is not to be excluded from cohabitation with his wife. Thus the wife will take back the husband who returns from fornication, but the husband will expel the defiled wife from the house. The logic of this is not easy to grasp, but this is the custom that has obtained.[27]

John Chrysostom

John Chrysostom (347–407), from Pontus in Northern Turkey, is best remembered as a great preacher (his name means 'golden-mouthed'), and as the author of the closing prayer in the BCP Office.[28] He studied in Antioch, became a hermit briefly, and then returned to Antioch and ordination. He was appointed Patriarch of Constantinople in 398. In his Homily 20, addressed to men, expounding Ephesians 5, he describes the love between man and woman, an early indication that the Eastern Orthodox tradition would tend to affirm marriage more strongly than did the Catholic West.

This love is more tyrannical than any other tyrant. Other passions may be strong; this passion is not only strong, but also imperishable. For deeply implanted in our nature there is a certain desire (*eros*) that, without our noticing, knits together these bodies of ours. That is why from the beginning woman came from man, and later, man and woman came from man and woman. Do you see the bond and connection, and how God did not allow any other substance from the outside to come between them? . . . The man was not allowed to marry his own sister . . . but his very own flesh . . . From the beginning [God] constructed the whole edifice, like a building made of stones, gathering them together into one.

In the second section he comments on Ephesians 5.23–4, noting the husband's duty to lead and provide and the woman's to obey, and then elaborates on the husband's obligation. No decent man would wish his wife to be afraid of him, as if she were a slave:

Hear what he [Paul] demands of you . . . Would you like your wife to obey you as the church obeys Christ? Then you must care for her as Christ does for the church. Even if it is necessary to give your life for her, even if you must be cut into a thousand pieces, even if you must endure any suffering whatever, do not refuse it. Even if you do suffer like this, you will never suffer as much as Christ did. For you are doing it for one with whom you are already joined, but he did it for one who rejected him and hated him . . . Even if you see her looking down at you and despising you . . . you will be able to lay her at your feet by showing great care and affection for her. For nothing has greater power than these bonds, especially between husband and wife.

Later in this homily, Chrysostom reflects on the deceitfulness of a woman's physical beauty or lack of it, over which she has no control, for Christ did not detest the church for her ugliness:

Do not praise her for her beauty, that sort of praise and hatred is typical of intemperate souls. You should seek after the beauty of the soul. Imitate the bridegroom of the Church. External beauty is full of arrogance and foolishness; it leads to jealousy and often makes you suspect something foul is afoot. Perhaps external beauty gives pleasure? For the first month or two, or at least for one year, but no longer. After a while, familiarity will cause your interest to wane. Yet the evils bred by her beauty will remain; the vanity, foolishness, and contempt. But if your love is not based on that sort of beauty, this will not happen. If love has begun properly, that is if it is love of the soul's beauty and not of the body's, it will remain strong.[29]

Augustine

The troubled life story

Aurelius Augustinus, to give him his proper name, was a North African, born in 354 at Thagaste, a small inland Roman provincial town, some 200 miles south-west of Carthage. His father, Patricius, was a pagan, though later converted, and his mother Monica was a Christian. They had four children, two boys and two girls. Augustine was first educated locally, chiefly in classics and philosophy, and he was enrolled as a catechumen. It was common practice for children to register thus as 'under instruction' (which could be either serious or nominal) but to delay baptism until ready to undertake full Christian commitment as an adult. They were admitted to the ministry of the word, but had to leave the service before the eucharist proper. In 371 Augustine, then 17, went to Carthage to be trained as a rhetorician, and the next year set up house with an unnamed concubine, with whom he cohabited for fifteen years. They had a son, Adeodatus, a clever boy who died aged 17.

While in Carthage, Augustine had joined the Manichaean movement, a variant form of Gnosticism, centred on the opposition of the powers of good and evil. The Manichees believed the human soul was a fragment of light imprisoned in an evil body, longing to escape. Although Augustine abandoned this heresy when he moved to Milan and came under the influence of Ambrose, who baptized him in 387, traces of negative Manichaean attitudes to the human body may have influenced him in his stern teaching about the stain of original sin. Being, as we would say, highly charged sexually, Augustine freely admitted he found continence difficult and delayed baptism on that account until he was assured that as a committed Christian he would be able to rely on God's help. So Monica set about getting him married:

Active efforts were made to get me a wife. I wooed, I was engaged, and my mother took the greatest pains in the matter. For her hope was, that once I was married I might be washed clean in baptism, for which I was being daily prepared, as she joyfully saw, taking note that her desires and promises were being fulfilled in my faith.[30]

However, the girl was only twelve, and her parents sensibly decided she was too young. Augustine offered to wait for her and turned briefly to another concubine, but Monica's hopes to get him settled were thwarted. He never married, and perhaps he was relieved that this particular plan came to nothing.

After his mother's death, Augustine returned to Thagaste in 388, and was ordained priest three years later. In 395 he was made coadjutor Bishop of Hippo, and took sole charge of the diocese soon after. At the time of his death in 430, the Vandal invasions had already reached North Africa and the Western Roman Empire was in terminal decay.

Augustine is often denigrated in our day as the theologian who bequeathed to Christianity its traditionally negative view of sex, but this view has to be questioned. Compared with other mainstream theologians of the Patristic period such as Tertullian and Jerome, he is noticeably positive, but he is open to the charge that in later life he was attempting to impose on others a discipline he had failed to achieve for himself. It is perhaps no bad thing that the most thorough reflection on sex and marriage in the early Church should have been achieved by a man who found following his own teaching difficult.

A concubine or a wife?

As a student in Carthage, Augustine was a conformist to the mores of his time. Taking a concubine was a relatively sober solution to his needs for sex and companionship, and this kind of second-class relationship was accepted practice for an ambitious man who had a career to build; an early marriage would have tied him to the limited prospects Thagaste could offer. After his conversion, he was initially dismissive of the woman and of the lust that had bound him to her, perhaps at heart angry with himself, but in mid-life when he was at Hippo he analysed his experience more carefully and felt able to admit his care for her. Apparently she did not subsequently marry and died a good Catholic. In his *Confessions* (398), a spiritual autobiography also written at Hippo, Augustine refers briefly to his concubine:

> In those years I had a mistress, to whom I was not joined in lawful marriage. She was a woman I had discovered in my wayward passion, void as it was of understanding, yet she was the only one; and I remained faithful to her and with her I discovered, by my own

experience, what a great difference there is between the restraint of the marriage bond contracted with a view to having children and the compact of a lustful love, where the children are born against the parents' will – although once they are born they compel our love.[31]

Augustine's personal relationships have a more than antiquarian interest because they relate closely to our present concern about the morality of cohabitation as an alternative to marriage. Although the Christian ethos initially tolerated concubinage for unmarried men, Roman law ruled that such women and the issue, if any, could not inherit, and it is perhaps surprising that four hundred years later even a rigorist like Ambrose could approve of the practice if it left a man free to make an advantageous marriage in later life. Three years after writing his *Confessions*, Augustine produced a long tract on the good of marriage, and here he reflects more carefully on what cohabition involves. It reads as if he had had some heart-searching about abandoning his former companion:

This problem often arises. If a man and a woman live together without being legitimately joined, not to have children, but because they could not observe continence; and if they have agreed between themselves to have relations with no one else, can this be called a marriage? Perhaps, but only if they had resolved to maintain until death the good faith which they had promised themselves, even though this union did not rest on a desire to have children . . . But if one or other of these conditions is lacking, I cannot see how this alliance can be called a marriage. Indeed, if a man takes a woman only for a time, until he finds another who better suits his rank and fortune, and if he marries this woman as being of the same class, this man would commit adultery in his heart, not towards the one he has married, but towards her with whom he had lived without being legitimately married. The same can be said for the woman . . . Nevertheless, if she was faithful to him, and if, after his marriage to another, she herself gave no thought to marriage, but abstained from all sexual relations, I would not dare to accuse her of adultery, even though she may have been guilty, in living with a man who was not her husband.[32]

The Good of Marriage

Apart from his own personal struggle towards mastering his sexual drives, Augustine spent his adult years deeply involved in the fierce debate about the nature of marriage and the sexual appetite. On one side, Ambrose and Jerome were staunch in their view that since these were irrational instincts, difficult if not impossible to control, it was part of the Christian package to be delivered from them. Only second-class Christians needed to marry, a concession that Paul had made as a remedy for fornication. On the other side, Julian of Eclanum insisted that celibacy and marriage were morally equal, and that since marriage was part of the original creation, it remained good if used properly. One test of the difference between these views was that the ascetics praised those who were married but sexually inactive with their partners, while the affirmers argued in the Jewish way that the delights of sex were one of God's gifts which one ought to share with one's married partner. Neither side, of course, approved of sex outside marriage or of divorce. Some years later Augustine set out his own considered views on marriage to distance himself from Jerome. His treatise *The Good of Marriage* gives his most balanced view, although later he was to qualify it with some less positive corrections.

In this treatise, he began to emphasize more strongly the companionate value of marriage, but he can never bring himself to commend marriage absolutely. In the new dispensation, it is to be replaced by friendship, and that need not surprise us for Augustine's own disposition was never to be a solitary. In his *Confessions*, he shows how much he values his male friends, and when he went back to Carthage he lived in a small religious community. He explains in the treatise why he thinks procreation is no longer the essential reason for marriage. Since God was making up the number of the elect from the baptized there was no need to breed children. In any case, as the empire dissolved and the Vandals reached even Carthage, the end was obviously near. More important, though, was his fixed idea that even if the sexual act was not intrinsically evil, it was almost invariably so in practice. Maybe this view reflected his own earlier experience, but he needed to find scriptural support for it. Like his fellow theologians, he spent a good deal of time interpreting the Genesis narratives, and since they were understood as accurate history, an intriguing question to be debated was whether or not Adam and Eve had sex before the Fall. If the answer was 'probably not,' as Augustine supposed, they were just good friends. If God had wanted there to be children in the paradise garden, he could have provided them in another way, or even arranged for Adam and Eve to breed without any sexual arousal. These hypotheses, he admitted, were unverifiable, but the result was that Satan's deceit led to the contagion of original sin being passed on to the whole human race. Augustine's opponents thought these speculations ridiculous, but as the following extracts show, he argued his case well.

Every human being is part of the human race, and human nature is a social reality and possesses a great and natural good, the power of friendship. For this reason, God wished to create all human beings from one, so that they would be held together in human society, not only by the similarity of race, but also by the bond of human relationship. Therefore, the first natural union of human society is the husband and wife. God did not create even these as separate individuals and join them together as if they were alien to each other, but he created the one from the other . . . The result is the bonding of society in children, who are the one honourable fruit, not of the union of male and female, but of sexual intercourse. For there could have been some kind of real and amiable union between the sexes even without sexual intercourse, a union in which the one rules and the other obeys. (1.1)

I do not believe that marriage is a good solely because of the procreation of children; there is also the natural association (*societas*) between the sexes. Otherwise we would no longer speak of a marriage between elderly people, especially if they had lost or never produced children. But now in a good marriage, even if it has lasted for many years and even if the youthful ardour between the male and the female has faded, the order of charity between husband and wife still thrives. The earlier they begin to refrain from sexual intercourse by mutual consent, the better they will be. This is not because they will eventually be unable to do what they wish, but because it is praiseworthy not to wish to do what they are able to do. (3.3)

Divorce

In a later section of *The Good of Marriage* Augustine turns to the question of divorce. He allows that in the Christian tradition, sexual infidelity by either spouse is a proper ground for it, but he rejects the argument that infertility always justifies it. He also insists that remarriage after the death of a spouse is not allowed. This leads him on to an exploration of the nature of the marriage bond, where his logic works as it were backwards. Since Christ forbade marriage after a divorce, calling it adultery, there must be some continuing vestigial bond between the couple even though they have gone their separate ways. Is their situation then akin to that of baptism, where the situation is that a repentant apostate can be readmitted to the fellowship of the Church without rebaptism? And further, in Paul's analogy of the marriage relationship between Christ and the Church, the great mystery, is there not a clue that conjugal oaths have a residual binding quality even if spouses quit their relationship by separation or adultery? Augustine thought so, but he did not attempt to define theologically or philosophically what that conjugal bond might be. He just sensed that God had intended marriage to be indissoluble.

> The unifying bond of marriage is so strong that, although it is created for the purpose of procreation, it may not be dissolved for the purpose of procreation. A man may be able to divorce a barren wife and marry someone who can bear his children, but in our times and according to Roman Law a man is not permitted to take a second wife, as long as he still has one wife who is alive. Certainly, when an adulterous wife or husband has been abandoned, it would be possible for many human beings to be born, if the woman or the man chose to marry again. But if this is not permitted, as the divine law seems to prescribe, who could fail to acknowledge the demands that the great strength of the conjugal bond makes for itself?
>
> I do not think it could be so powerful if there were not attached to it a kind of sacramental significance (*sacramentum*) of something greater than could arise from our feeble mortality, something that remains unshaken in order to punish those who abandon or wish to dissolve this bond. For even when there is a divorce, the nuptial alliance is not abolished, and the persons involved remain spouses even when they are separated. Furthermore they commit adultery if they have intercourse with anyone else after the divorce, and this applies both to the man and the woman.[33]

With this conclusion, Augustine sets the pattern of the Christian tradition of marital indissolubility, and strongly suggests that the nuptial bond is in some sense sacramental. Although he was by nature conservative, and reckoned he was saying no more than the divine law required, based on Christ's own teaching, he also succeeded in preserving for the Middle Ages a doctrine of marriage that the Church could work with as it became responsible for supervising the marriage regulations of Christendom. Had the extreme negativism of Ambrose and Jerome remained unchecked by Augustine, it would have been impossible for the Christian view of marriage to have been accepted by the population at large. Alongside this achievement we have to assess Augustine as a man. To understand him, we should turn away from his anxieties about sex and ask what kind of person he was. He needed sustaining relationships; his father counted for little, and his mother was dominant in her ambition for him, sadly dying before he became Bishop of Hippo. In his *Confessions*, he acknowledges his simple desire was to love and be loved.[34] He also valued friendship highly, but he was chiefly driven by his search for God, which becomes the major theme of his *Confessions*: 'You have made us for yourself, and our heart is restless until it rests in you' (Book 1, 1.5). Once he was able to accept that he was accepted by God, everything else seemed to fall into place.

Marriage in Christendom

Christendom established

This chapter offers an overview of Christian attitudes to marriage from the end of the Patristic period until the start of the Reformation, no less than a thousand years. Although concerned only with marriage and sex, it is impossible to provide anything more than the tightest précis of such an enormous swathe of Christian thought. But the plain fact is that whatever the political changes and chances of the Middle Ages, the Christian churches continued to teach the precepts hammered out in the Patristic age with very little modification, and the legacy of Augustine remained dominant. Until the Reformation, the view that celibacy was the more perfect way and marriage in some ways a second best was attested by the monastic life. In the western church, especially after the twelfth century, it was also attested by the rule that clergy should not marry. In both eastern and western churches, there was also the rule that bishops should be unmarried, examples such as that of Julian of Eclanum notwithstanding. However, the reality was that most people were married, and therefore the churches of Christendom had both to promulgate energetically their own doctrine and seek ways of gaining control of wedding ceremonies and of punishing sexual offences. As they gained jurisdiction, particularly through the burgeoning power of the papacy, it was inevitable that rules had to be defined in canons and continually revised, but it is not possible to trace that process in detail here. The later part of this chapter concentrates on the situation in England.

In the first millennium, the Christian faith turned pagan Europe into Christendom by a process which began, humanly speaking, with its official adoption by rulers, followed by a slow permeation among urban peoples, completed by seepage into the countryside. The conversion of Europe which began at the Milvian Bridge was only completed by the baptism of Grand Duke Jogaila of Lithuania in

1396.[1] In a similar way, Christian marriage followed the progress of the gospel, but just as the mass conversions and baptisms did not extinguish all pagan beliefs, neither did the ideals of marital life and sexual relations proclaimed by the Church extinguish alternative customs and practices.

The situation of the two empires was different. The Western Empire succumbed to the invasions and immigrations of a succession of Germanic and Frankish tribes, and this led to an ambiguous arrangement, because Alaric and some of his successors had already been converted to Christianity, albeit as Arians, before marching south. Clovis, king of the Franks, and eventual ruler of the vast Merovingian empire from the Pyrenees to Bavaria, whose wife Clothilde was a Catholic Christian, was himself baptized at Rheims *c.* 500. An informal accommodation of the marriage customs was the result, the immigrants observing Germanic rules, the Roman Christians keeping to their own system. The Germanic view of what made a legal marriage was different from the Roman and they did not adopt the patristic preference for virginity and celibacy. Instead of mere consent between the partners, they looked for evidence that the woman had been transferred into a new kinship unit. Whereas the Roman Christian tradition accepted as valid a marriage in which the partners remained continent, in the Germanic tradition an unconsummated marriage was void. Obviously there was some sense in both views. Only in the eighth century, in the time of Boniface, Charlemagne and Pope Leo I, was a serious attempt at harmonization made and the matter was still being debated in the twelfth century.

In the East, the Christian emperors, Constantine, Theodosius II and Justinian, gradually codified the old Roman law, in particular modifying the rules about marriage and divorce in the light of Christian teaching, but the political realities did not allow much implementation of the new codes. In the Orthodox tradition, the role of the priest in Christian marriage was established early, but in the West the general principle of Roman law continued: only consent between the parties with the approval of their families was needed. The Christian rule that a marriage should be effected by exchanging promises at the church porch, supervised and witnessed by a priest with the option of a nuptial mass, was not firmly established in the West until the thirteenth century, and by no means then universally followed. The church had to recognize the validity of customary marriage without clergy, which remained popular in rural communities, but less so in towns.[2]

Britain in Europe

For Britain, from the end of the Roman occupation until the conquest
by the Normans, there was a similar difference between Christian and
pagan attitudes to marriage. Although Roman Christianity in Britain
was sufficiently established for some churches to be built, the invasions
from Holland, North Germany and Scandinavia for a time virtually
extinguished organized Christianity in the east and south of Britain,
although it remained strong among the Celts. The revival led by
Dunstan, Oswald and Wulfstan, with their links with Rome, greatly
strengthened Anglo-Saxon Christianity, but it was threatened again
by the Viking attacks.[3]

In Anglo-Saxon Briton, tying the knot was usually a simple matter.
In an ordinary village community, the choice of partners would be
limited, everyone knew who was living with whom, but a joint public
statement of assent, the giving of a ring, the exchange of gifts and a
small celebration were thought seemly – the obvious setting being the
village pub. Often there was neither a church nor a priest in the village,
and if the marriage were to be blessed, that would mean a long journey to the nearest minster or cathedral, unless a local monk could be
invited. There were usually no written records of village weddings, but
the facts (and local memory) spoke for themselves. The rules against
consanguinity were made more extensive by Boniface,[4] who thought
the English were particularly lax in marrying close relatives and in
sexual morals generally.[5]

William of Normandy (1066) brought with him Lanfranc from the
Abbey of Bec to be Archbishop of Canterbury. William separated the
jurisdiction of the ecclesiastical courts from that of his own royal
courts. Under the previous Saxon system of Alfred, *c.* 890, the sheriff
and the bishop sat in court together, administering all kinds of law,
and settling matrimonial disputes. When the church courts took over
jurisdiction for marriage, church property and offences by the clergy,
the obvious benefit was the harmonizing of English marriage law with
that of the rest of Christendom. But the distinction between canon and
common law was not always clear, since property disputes remained
with the king's courts. This symbolized the conflict between the
authority of the Godly Prince in his own realm, and that claimed by
the far-away successor to Peter, to whom appeals about marriage
could be made.

In Plantagenet times, England was politically ruled by kings who were more French than British, of whom Henry II was the most important in respect to legislation. The confrontation between Henry and Becket, leading to Becket's murder, was all part of the endless seesaw of the power struggle between the European heads of state and the papacy. Particular irritants were the rights of the papacy to tax the citizens of national states, to appoint its own candidates to valuable clerical posts, and to determine the validity of marriage and give dispensation for divorce. Henry VIII was drawn into this labyrinth. Even more fundamentally, with the first steps towards the Renaissance, there were stirrings of discontent with some aspects of medieval Catholic theology. The seeds of the Reformation were being sown.[6]

Christian teaching about marriage in the first millennium

An unchanging tradition

It is difficult for us in our secular and pluralist society to appreciate how static and unchallenged the Christian traditional teaching about sex and marriage actually was in the Middle Ages. Several factors contributed to this stability. First, the European states were officially Christian and accepted the Church's claim that it had preserved the teaching of Christ. To disobey that teaching risked excommunication and divine wrath at a time when all human destiny was believed to be dependent on God's mercy and the successful invocation of the Blessed Virgin and the Saints. Second, the emphasis on celibacy for the clergy meant that few of the senior leaders of the Church had personal experience of the marriage relationship, unless clandestinely. (Prior to the twelfth century many of the lower-ranking clergy had wives and some clergy, of all ranks, had concubines. However, many of these may have been as much housekeepers as sexual partners. In general, the whole ambience remained sexually negative throughout the Middle Ages.) Third, the dominance of the monasteries continued, witnessing to the preferred way of curbing sexual drives. Officially, in principle, all Christians were either celibate or chaste within marriage, and if in fact the customs were different for both prince and pauper, absolution was readily available. Fourth, the teaching of Augustine had lodged in people's minds. It was not so much his actual writing, voluminous and brilliant though it was, but the sense that his exegesis of Scripture was correct that allowed his ideas to become entrenched in the medieval Christian tradition. By the sixth century, therefore,

Christian teaching about marriage and sexual morality was much as he had advocated.[7] Had his writings been lost, or other surviving documents given more prominence, the Christian tradition might have been better balanced. It was a world that all seems remote to us. As Peter Brown puts it in his epilogue:

> To modern persons, whatever their religious beliefs, the early Christian themes of sexual renunciation, of continence, celibacy and the virgin life have come to carry with them icy overtones. The very fact that modern Europe and America grew out of the Christian world that replaced the Roman Empire in the Middle Ages has ensured that, even today, these notions still crowd in upon us, as pale, forbidding presences. By studying their precise social and religious context, the scholar can give back to these ideas a little of the weight that they once carried in their own time. When such an offering is made, the chill shades must speak to us again, and perhaps more gently than we had thought they might, in the strange tongue of a long-lost Christianity. Whether they will say anything of help or comfort for our own times, [we] must decide for ourselves.[8]

The marriage of Julian of Eclanum

Even in Augustine's time Christian weddings were joyful occasions. In general terms, the Christian policy for marriage ceremonies was in favour of simplicity and against indulgence, and for most fourth-century Christians prayers and blessings were added to the normal civic and family ceremonies. But among the more prominent and literate Christian families, the Roman custom of having a marriage poem read was continued and used as an opportunity for setting out the Christian vision of marriage. The long poem of Paulinus for the wedding of Julian of Eclanum to Titia (*c.* 405) is an interesting example. Julian, a Christian humanist before his time, advocated sex between married people whenever they felt like it, a view to which Augustine took violent objection.[9] Julian was the son of a bishop, and later a bishop himself, but his marriage took place before his consecration. Paulinus, born in France of a wealthy family, and for a time Governor of Campania in Italy, was married to a Spanish lady, Therasia. After the death of their only son they adopted continence and he was ordained and became Bishop of Nola. He was a friend of Ambrose, Jerome and Augustine, so his poem for the marriage of Julian, who was to become their arch-enemy, adds spice to the occasion. It was in fact a substantial teaching sermon, not just a panegyric. This little-known poem by one married man to another about to be married, both spouses being children of married bishops (Titia was the daughter of Bishop Aemilius of Beneventum), deserves to be quoted as a counterbalance to the more familiar views of the Latin Fathers, who were all bachelors!

> Harmonious souls are being united in chaste love. A youth who is Christ's virgin, a maiden who is God's. Christ our God, lead to your reins these well-matched doves, and govern them under your easy yoke. For your yoke is easy, when a ready will receives it, and love makes light the burden of obedience . . . All vain and vulgar licence must depart these wedding rites, Juno, Cupid, Venus – the very essence of indulgence! . . . For the harmonious bond of marriage shares at once in the love of piety, the dignity of love and the peace of God . . . With his own lips God made this union holy, by the divine hand he established the human couple. He made the two abide in one flesh in order to create a love more indivisible . . . Let us celebrate with sober joys and quiet prayers, and let the name of Christ resound everywhere on the lips of pious people. Away with the crowds leaping in the decked out streets. Let no one strew the ground with flowers or cover the doorstep with garlands. There should be no mad procession in a Christian city. I will have no profane display to poison pious Christians . . . (153) At a wedding such as this, it is fitting that Mary, the mother of the Lord, be present, for she gave birth to God, while preserving her virginity. God himself built in this sacred virgin a pleasing temple with a secret window open to the sky . . . By this great mystery (*sacramentum*) the Church was wed to Christ and became at once the spouse and sister of the Lord.[10]

The poem concludes with several references to St Paul and the couple's parents. Perhaps a key phrase is the reference to marriage as an easy yoke, identifying marriage with Christ's service (Matt. 11.29–30).

The marriage legislation of the Christian emperors

Constantine was not free to impose a Christian form of marriage on his people, but he did issue a number of edicts reflecting Christian ideas. Marriage could be entered into by straightforward consent of the parties without legal formality, but the old rule that divorce was equally a matter of mutual consent (with return of dowries, etc.) was abrogated.[11] There had to be some kind of criminal or moral offence. During the reign of Theodosius II, a codification of Constantine's legislation was compiled (438), marking a further step in the Christianizing of the empire's laws, particularly in relation to divorce. The new rules applied equally to both the husband and the wife, and the interest of the children had to be considered. The wife could ask for a divorce if her husband committed capital crimes such as regicide, murder, kidnapping or cattle rustling, and for the more personal affront of his shaming her by bringing loose women into the home. He could divorce her if she stayed out all night, kept company with other men or attended the games or the theatre.[12]

Justinian was the Roman Emperor of the East, 527–65. He was married to Theodora, a lady of humble origins who had reputedly worked in circuses in her youth; both of them were Christian. Their best-known portrait is in the mosaic of San Vitale, Ravenna, where they appear a benign couple, but the evidence of their character is mixed. His military successes were matched by totalitarian violence and murder. Her campaign to suppress prostitution in Constantinople may be contrasted with allegations of her personal promiscuity.[13] Whatever the truth, they seemed a devoted couple, married for twenty-six years, and after her death Justinian did not remarry.

The Law Codes of Justinian

The Corpus Juris Civilis

Soon after becoming emperor, Justinian appointed a commission headed by Tribonian, the senior law officer (*quaestor*), to review and codify the existing laws of Rome, an immense collection of some two thousand precepts. The *Corpus Juris Civilis* would apply to all citizens, pagan and Christian alike, and since Justinian took his obligations as a Christian ruler seriously, the new law should not contain anything obviously contrary to Christian morals.

The Corpus, written in Latin in three parts, was completed in 533. The Code was the list of official statutes allowed to be quoted in court, of which a second edition has survived. It deals with Church law, private and criminal law, and official administration, five thousand enactments in all. The Digest, twice the length of the Code, was a compilation of the opinions of approved jurists over the past three hundred years. The Institutes were a simplified précis of the Code, intended to guide students through its main provisions. Revisions of the code, 'Novellas', continued to appear until the death of Tribonian in 545, but then stopped, although Justinian reigned for another twenty years.[14]

The rules for marriage in the Digest and Institutes

There are some fifty quotations from the Jurists in the Digest about marriage and sexual offences, chiefly from Ulpian, and these probably include some Christian interpolations. Thus, fornication and adultery are prohibited for men and women, except for men with prostitutes. A father has a duty to find a husband for his daughter, and a wife for his son, though the son may reject his father's choice. The class system is generally maintained, but a free man can marry a freed woman. A concubine is able to leave her free patron, and he can marry her, but she cannot leave him to marry another man of freed status 'because it is more honourable to be a concubine of a free man than the wife of a freed man'! The old custom of divorce by mutual consent is no longer allowed. Either the man or the woman could bring a petition to the magistrate, though this procedure was in practice only used if property was involved. A woman who is raped is not to be blamed but her assailant is to be executed. A father may kill his daughter and the man if he catches them in the act of adultery in his house, though, since his anger might blur his judgement of the facts, the case should be put before the magistrate, who could decide if the punishments of exile were appropriate. In a later Novella, Justinian noted that adulterous women were to be sent to convents for life, and their dowries were to be kept by their husbands. If she owned other property, two thirds went to her children and the remainder to the convent.

The legal requirements for a valid marriage are set out in the Institutes, Book X. Roman citizens may marry lawfully when the males have reached puberty, fourteen years, and the minimum age for females is twelve. Consent from their fathers must be obtained. The standard rules about consanguinity and incest are specified. Couples who unite themselves (cohabit) outside the rules of lawful marriage are not married, and any children of such unions are illegitimate (*spurii*) or without a father (*sine patre*), and are to be treated in the same way as the children of prostitutes. If the natural parents subsequently marry, such children can be brought within the *familia* by court order. Free women who are seduced into a form of marriage with slaves no longer lose their free status, though the slaves may be punished.

The lifelong nature of marriage

Justinian begins the Institutes with a note about justice and then defines the sources of Law:

> The precepts of the law are these: to live honestly, to injure no one, and to give every man his due. The study of law consists of two branches, public and private law. The former refers to the welfare of the Roman State; the latter to the advantage of the individual citizen. Private law has a threefold origin, being collected from the precepts of nature, from the law of nations and the civil Roman law. The law of nature is that which she has taught to all animals; a law not peculiar to the human race, but shared by all living creatures. Hence comes the union of male and female, which we call marriage, hence the procreation and rearing of children. (Inst. 1.1.1 Pref.)

The identification of the three sources of law (nature, nations generally and Rome) is a recognition that natural law is understood to be distinct from any human laws and should take precedence over them. This distinction will be emphasized in later Christian theology as a basis for the doctrine that marriage corresponds to the Natural Law, and as such is part of God's creation. There is no doubt that the Roman people held a high view of marriage and thought it should be lifelong and include the procreation of children, but it is equally clear that they had few qualms about ending by divorce a relationship that did not work out. So their assumption must have been either that Natural Law did not forbid divorce when the purposes of the marriage clearly failed, or that the function of Natural Law was to posit a general principle, while Civil Law had, perforce, to deal with human inadequacy. The text we have from the Institutes is: 'Marriage is a union between a man and a woman involving a single shared way of life.'[15]

This appears to be a slightly shortened form of the definition of marriage in the Digest, with the addition of a reference to divine and human law, attributed to Modestinus, a highly rated pupil of Ulpian, *c.* 240: 'Marriage is a joining together of man and woman sharing in all of life [or whole life] together in accord with divine and human law.'[16]

The key phrases here are *vitae continens* in the Institute text and *consortium omnis vitae* in the Digest, and their meaning is much discussed. They could mean either a common life in which everything is shared, or a lifelong relationship, or indeed both. Some scholars think that Modestinus meant to emphasize total sharing, and the life-long emphasis is a Christian interpolation from Justinian. Modern Christian marriage liturgies, influenced by the New Testament, usually include both meanings. Neither meaning was alien to the Roman legal tradition in the sixth century. The legislation about marriage is typical of the achievement of Justinian's Corpus, perhaps stating what ought to be done rather than what could be enforced by law at this time; it served as a bridge between old Rome and new Christendom. Some of its precepts faded away with the empire. Other precepts survived, and for lack of anything better were adopted into the state and Church laws of Europe. Being written in Latin, it was inevitable that the medieval lawyers and canonists, struggling to sort out the confusion of Celtic, Saxon, Frankish and Germanic laws, could turn with relief to the *Corpus Juris Civilis* and adopt and adapt it as their own.

Marital discipline in the Church

John Moschus

The political situation of the Eastern Empire after Justinian was somewhat unstable and his laws were only spasmodically applied. A sad example of what they could mean is given by John Moschus, a spiritual guide who was born in 550 and lived for a time at the monastery of Theodosius in Jerusalem and then travelled round many major monasteries in Egypt, Mt Sinai, Antioch, Cyprus and Rome. His *Spiritual Meadow* (*Pratum Spirituale*) has become recently well known because William Dalrymple used it as a guide to his own journey round the old sites of Byzantium.[17] Moschus mostly records anecdotes on monastic life, with occasional other moral tales. This one concerns the struggle of a widow to find a new husband to care for her and her children:

I, the wretched one, had a husband and two children by him, the one nine years old and the other five, when my husband died and I remained a widow. A soldier lived near to me and I wanted him to take me as his wife, so I sent some friends (women) to him. But the soldier said, 'I am not taking a wife who has children by another man'. Then, as I learned that he did not want to take me because of the children, and because I loved him, I, the wretched one, killed my two children and told him that now I did not have any. But when the soldier heard what I had done about the children, he said 'May the Lord God who lives in heaven above abide, I will not take her'. And fearing that this dreadful thing should become known and I should die, I fled.[18]

Although remarriage was forbidden by the Church, it often happened, and Byzantine law tried to protect the rights of children from previous marriages by requiring the step-father to adopt them. It may be the soldier knew this, and decided to keep clear. The widow's extreme action was condemned, of course, but Moschus will have had in mind the Church's duty to care for widows.

The Penitentials

The early church discipline of penitence for those who sinned grievously was exclusion from communion, as suffered by Theodosius. In its early form, largely focused on the problem of apostasy, restoration was only available once, but from the sixth century onwards a new system was introduced which was intended to provide an on-going procedure by which sinners could be reconciled on an 'as needed' basis. This was by means of a private confession to a priest or other spiritual guide who announced absolution and imposed a penance (punishment) to be worked through. The introduction of the private procedure led to the provision in the seventh century of detailed books of instructions for the confessors. The early Penitentials varied widely, and attempts were made to codify them in officially approved texts. Canon 25 of the Fourth Lateran Council (1215) made it obligatory for every Christian to make his confession to his parish priest at least once a year. The practice is still observed in many parts of the Roman Catholic Church and in some Anglo-Catholic parishes, but Reformation theology has preferred the view that the priest's role as an intermediary blurs the right of all penitents to receive God's forgiveness directly. The Catholic response has been that it is not safe for everyone to be their own absolver, but some Catholics now take the view that the general absolution given at the Mass is sufficient.

The Penitentials had much to say about sexual discipline between married couples. Remembering the old Jewish purity rules, they excluded intercourse when women were infertile, during menstruation, pregnancy, childbirth and lactation. Further, there was to be no sex on days of fasting and abstinence such as Advent and Lent, nor on the Feast days, Easter and Whitsun, and never on Sundays. Strict observance of these rules suggests that a healthy married couple who were meticulous in obeying all of them would only have some forty days a year when they could have sex, though it is very doubtful if there were many couples who were in fact that meticulous.[19] Surprisingly perhaps, some medieval theologians had little sense of delicacy about sexual acts. They gave explicit advice about the most effective forms of foreplay and love-making for married couples, suggesting that if the couple wanted to produce strong healthy children, they should learn together how to achieve simultaneous orgasm. This, they thought, was the best way of releasing a good supply of the necessary body fluids of both partners.

Councils, Synods and Popes

Virtually every Council of the Christian churches has had something to say about marriage and sex. Even the first, in Jerusalem (Acts 15.29), reiterated the Noachic command about fornication, and these subjects were still being seriously debated in the twentieth century at the Second Vatican Council, and at the Anglican Lambeth Conferences from 1948 to 1998. The beginning of the fourth century was a specially active time for Councils, for example, Elvira (312), Neo-Caesarea, Arles and Ancyra, the last three all beginning in 314.[20] These were local gatherings of bishops and senior presbyters, and not to be compared in authority with Nicaea or Chalcedon, and they show some diversity. Thus, Elvira forbids young Christian women to marry Jews, while Arles decided that if they married heathens they should be banned from communion for some time. Second marriages after the death of a spouse, or after being an innocent party in a divorce were usually discouraged, but it seems that the particular circumstances were taken into account. Clergy were expected not to marry or, if married, to put away their wives on ordination. If they committed adultery after ordination, they were laicized for life. The only sanction for these rules was excommunication by the local bishop, and the constant reiteration of these rules about marriage and celibacy suggests that they were not very effective.

With hindsight, it is possible to see the struggles of the medieval Church to establish a strict discipline about divorce and remarriage and yet recognize that there were situations where they should not be applied as less a blurring of principle and more a recognition that the problems of human relations can never be totally reduced to order. While it may usually be true that hard cases make bad law, circumstances may allow exceptions, as the Penitentials had recognized. The case of Lothair II, king of Lorraine, is an example of the difficulty, and also illustrates the somewhat chaotic hierarchy of appeals then available to those with time, money and persistence. At the end of the eighth century, the Emperor Charlemagne had been persuaded by his bishops to tighten up the observance of the traditional rule forbidding remarriage after divorce, though he himself had a somewhat chequered experience of marriage. He gave up his concubine to marry a Lombard princess, divorced her as barren a year later, had three more wives in succession who conveniently died, and then reverted to concubines as solace in his old age. Technically, he kept the rules; it proved much more difficult to determine if Lothair had.

In 858, Lothair wanted to divorce his barren wife, Theutberga, in order to marry his former concubine, Waldrada, who had borne him children who could, if he and Waldrada married, become the heirs he desperately needed. He accused his wife of adultery and of having been in childhood sodomized by her brother, who was now a bishop. Under pressure, Theutberga confessed to the second charge, privately to the Archbishop of Cologne and then publicly to a Synod of Bishops at Aachen. They felt unsure if they were able to award Lothair a divorce on this ground, and referred the decision to Hincmar, Archbishop of Rheims and a noted canonist. Hincmar produced a long thesis in reply and decided Lothair and Theutberga were still married, even though by now Lothair was living with Waldrada. Lothair then appealed to another Synod at Aachen, which declared his marriage void. Theutberga responded by a direct appeal to Pope Nicholas I, a man dedicated to emphasizing papal authority. His investigations led him to the conclusion that the marriage was still valid. In despair, both women went to convents, leaving Lothair with no heir; so his kingdom was split up when he died. The whole sad saga was in some ways a forerunner to the attempt by Henry VIII to get the Pope to give him a dispensation from his first marriage.[21]

The early patterns of Christian marriage

Although there are references to marriage ceremonies in the Patristic writings, the possibility of a specifically Christian way of getting married only appears from the fifth century onwards, and then by no means universally. For Diaspora Jewish converts, the familiar customs were followed, otherwise the Roman system obtained, with in both cases the formalities of betrothal and moving into the new home with celebrations. Marriage was now thought of as an event in which not only the families but also the Christian community might share, and they did this with a simple Eucharist at the new home, plus prayers for the couple led by the presbyter or bishop. This was the shape of Eclanum's marriage, and the simplicity enjoined by Paulinus echoes the advice of Plato in his *Laws*. In the East, the couple were crowned, possibly to honour the spouses, but also, some thought, as a sign of their victory over lust. In the West, the bride was veiled and the ring given as a symbol of transfer to her new family. Gradually the presbyter, as a trusted local official, became the chief witness, there being no written records. He could also check that there was no legal impediment to the marriage, such as bigamy or consanguinity. Marriage was now a public and social event.

The prayers offered either at the beginning or the end of the Eucharist acquired set patterns, and these show how the Old and New Testament typologies were becoming standard. The prayer from Tobit was popular and Sarah and Rachel were mentioned, following Jewish practice, and there were many local variations.[22] Charlemagne was keen to establish a standard liturgical form for the Eucharist throughout his Frankish empire, and asked the Pope, Hadrian I, to provide a copy of the text used in Rome. Hadrian's text, based on that of Pope Gregory I, includes an elaborate nuptial blessing, in effect a summary of Christian teaching about marriage:

O God, you who made all things out of nothing by the power of your goodness, at the beginning of the creation of the universe you established for man, made in the image of God, the inseparable assistance of women. Out of the man you gave to the woman the origin of her flesh, thereby teaching that what had been created out of one ought never to be separated. O God, you have consecrated the conjugal union with so excellent a mystery in order to signify the sacrament of Christ and the church in the bond of married persons.

O God, by your agency woman is united to man, and society is ordered from the beginning by the gift of that blessing, which is the only decree that was not removed either by the penalty of original sin or by the flood. Look with favour on this your handmaid who is to be joined in marital union, as she asks to be strengthened by your protection. May her yoke be one of love and peace; may she marry in Christ, as one who is faithful and chaste. May she always imitate the holy women. May she be loving to her husband like Rachel; wise, like Rebekah; faithful and long-lived, like Sarah.[23]

Canon Law

By the time of the Fourth Lateran Council, called by the reforming Pope Innocent III, Conciliar Resolutions and Papal Decretals were being incorporated into systematic collections of canon law, and enforced through ecclesiastical courts. The most famous of these collections, the *Concordia Discordantium Canonum*, known as the *Decretum*, was made by Gratian in 1139. It was studied closely by the canon lawyers in Bologna, Paris and Oxford, who now also had available Justinian's *Corpus*. Like all legal systems, as social life changed, such codes had to be continually revised and added to, and although the final appellate responsibility was retained by the Pope, the development of Canon Law and of the ecclesiastical courts where it was administered became a new element in church life. Whereas in the early church moral questions had been a matter for bishops and theologians, the churches of Christendom had become so immersed in such issues as the links between marriage, property and inheritance that a properly organised judicial system was necessary. Added to that were the discipline of clergy and the rights of parishioners *vis-à-vis* patrons, and a host of similar disputes. To abbreviate a long and complicated history, the Western Canon Law applied within the Roman Catholic Church has been continually revised, and the current edition, in Latin, dates from 1983.[24]

When King Henry VIII broke the links with Rome by the Act of Supremacy in 1534, he ordered a new set of canons to be prepared for the Church of England. That took some time and was finally completed for approval by the Convocations of York and Canterbury, and then by King James I, in 1604. These canons were an abbreviation of the old Roman Code, and for matters not included in the new code, the Catholic rules were still followed in the post-Reformation English ecclesiastical courts. It is convenient to look ahead at this point. New canons were produced in 1969, and small revisions continue. Much contemporary church legislation is dealt with by the General Synod of the Church of England and, after perusal by Parliament, is enacted by the queen and becomes, under the present rules of the Establishment, part of state law.[25]

Marriage in the later Middle Ages

The first Reformation

The so-called 'first Reformation', led by Pope Gregory VII at the start of the second millennium, reinvigorated the Western Church.[26] By the thirteenth century the well-nigh universal Christian culture was everywhere demonstrated in the topography of the European lands, dominated by the new and rebuilt abbeys and cathedrals. For example, any traveller to Chartres would see the great building looming above the fields from twenty miles away, and that was equally true of Cluny, Cologne, Lincoln and Durham. Christ was the king, aided by his saints, and medieval carving and glass declared the timeless truth of his ascendancy. Locally also, there would often be a small church built beside the manor house, served by a resident priest, though he might have more than one village in his cure. For a population in England of two and a quarter million there were now some ten thousand parishes, served by twenty-three thousand priests, assisted by twenty-five thousand monks. In towns, typically, a priest had some three hundred souls in his parish, and in the country he had some two hundred. As we have seen, the Fourth Lateran Council (1215) had made it obligatory for all Catholics to make an annual confession before Easter.[27] If he were assiduous, a parish priest might become the best informed person in the community. There were strict rules of penance for sexual offences, with recourse to the severity of the archdeacon's court and fines or even a spell in his prison for those who were recalcitrant. The Church thought it knew what its teaching was, and the work of the Councils and canon lawyers was directed to ensuring the rules were applied in various circumstances. They were not in the business of altering them.

Marriage at the church door

As Christianity permeated the rural scene through the parochial system, the clergy were instructed to supervise marriages, which now gained a more definite religious connotation and a more complex procedure. The parish priest became the chief witness on behalf of the church and the community. The process of marriage usually had two stages. First, when the families had agreed to the union, and financial arrangements if any had been settled, the marriage party went to the door of the church, where the priest met them and checked if there were any legal impediments such as bigamy or consanguinity. Then the ceremony of troth-plight (later called hand-fasting) took place before the witnesses. The formula was familiar: 'I take thee . . .' then there was a solemn joining of hands by the priest and the receiving of rings, and exchange of gifts. The priest's hope was that the newly-weds would then move into the church itself for a mass and nuptial blessing, but this did not always happen. Sometimes, if of age, the couple went off to bed and consummated the marriage instead. They would then wait until it was clear that the wife was pregnant. That proof of a fruitful marriage established, they would return to the church for the mass and blessing.[28] Legally, however, only the exchange of consent to be married between the spouses was necessary, and often this amounted to no more than a private agreement between the couple, without any witnesses. For such clandestine marriages, the convention was to accept that those who seemed to be living together as married people were in fact married, as it was undesirable to question the legitimacy of children or disturb an ongoing relationship for lack of public ceremony. The present-day custom of long-term cohabitation during which children are born would have been regarded in the Middle Ages as customary or common law marriage.[29] There were however some legal marriages which, even though they were blessed by a priest, were frowned upon – where the purpose was dynastic or financial. In Langland's fourteenth-century poem Piers Plowman, he observes: 'It is an oncomely couple bi Chryst, so me thinketh. To jyven a young wenche to an old feble, or wedden any widowe, for wealth of her goodis.'[30]

In many ways, the best guide to the Church's teaching about marriage was its liturgy, especially after printing made it widely available. Strenuous efforts were made by Church authorities to ensure all marriages took place at the church, and there was a proliferation of local rites, but eventually the dominant English pre-Reformation rite was Sarum (Salisbury, fourteenth century), much of which was preserved in Cranmer's Book of Common Prayer. In the Sarum rite, the man's vow is:

> I take thee to my wedded wife, to have and to hold, from this day forward, for better or for worse, for richer or poorer, in sickness and in health, till death us depart, if holy church it will ordain, and thereto I plight thee my troth.[31]

Policies and problems

Defining a Christian marriage

Once the medieval Church had firmly taken over the supervision of marriage it was necessary to sort out a coherent policy from a welter of different theological opinions about what made a valid marriage, and what grounds, if any, there could be for ending it. Opinions differed because it was genuinely difficult to find a way to preserve essential convictions from the past and yet encompass the good insights within the customs and morals of the large and mixed population they now worked amongst.[32] Reduced to its barest essentials the consensus between late medieval theologians and canon lawyers can be summarized as follows:

1) The celibate life in monasteries and convents was best of all, for those who had that vocation.
2) For everyone else, sexual intercourse was allowed only within marriage, which was instituted by God and intended to be lifelong.
3) Marriage came into being by the free consent of the man and woman, being of age, and not closely related, with the approval of their parents where available.
4) Christian marriage was to be supervised at the church door by the parish priest, who acted as the chief witness that there was free consent and no impediment through consanguinity, but other witnesses should also be present.
5) The priest should bless the couple either at the church, or at the bridal chamber. It was desirable but not essential that the exchange of vows should be followed by a Eucharist.
6) Consent to be married carried with it an agreement to consummate

the marriage sexually, and that act together with the blessing made the marriage sacramental and established the one-flesh bond.

The test is consent

The need for consent, inherited from Roman law, was an obvious principle. Among rich families, arranged marriages led to the betrothal of children; they were like pawns in a chess game, moved about or sacrificed in pursuit of financial or dynastic aims. To give them some protection, the canon lawyers distinguished promises for the future from that of actual commitment. If the agreement had been 'I *will* take thee . . .' in Canon Law the marriage was dissoluble, as the consent was *de futuro*, but when the agreement was 'I take thee . . .', that is here and now, *de praesenti*, it was valid and could not be annulled. This regulation marked a swing in emphasis from the traditional view of marriage as an institution arranged by families to a relationship agreement chosen by the partners to it. Promises for the future were similar to our practice of engagement. Betrothal ceased to be a separate event and now became the first part of the marriage ceremony at the church door.[33] Despite this good intent, and the rule against fornication, the traditional custom that private consent between the couple followed by sexual intercourse and cohabitation created a marriage was probably still widely observed, and continued to be until the eighteenth century.[34] The rule that free consent before witnesses was the essential requirement for a valid marriage provided a straightforward test of the couple's intentions and avoided the need to enquire about their sexual behaviour. But it was equally clear that the consent implied the future sharing of sexual intercourse between the partners.

Since the primary purpose of marriage was held to be procreation, set in the context of a shared life and agreed responsibility for the nurture of the children, mere consent to be married was not, doctrinally, sufficient; it should be followed by sexual consummation. The blessing of the bridal chamber assumed this; it was both a sign of God's approval and a wish that the couple would prove to be fertile. Out of respect for Joseph and Mary, celibate marriage was not frowned on, but since they had not really consented to marriage in its fullness, they were free to separate without breaking the rule against divorce, provided they then entered the religious life. However, there remained the difficult question of consent to marriage being followed by refusal to consummate by one of the partners. Was this a genuine marriage?

The story of Christina of Markyate's marriage is a well-documented example of this problem. Christina was the teenage daughter of a well-to-do burgess of Huntingdon, and a local nobleman, Burthred, asked to marry her, with her parents' approval. She wanted to remain celibate despite the endeavours of her parents and friends to get her married off. After some vigorous resistance she was finally persuaded to exchange vows and gifts with Burthred at the church door, and this was witnessed by the priest and the families, according to custom. She went to bed alone, without a nuptial blessing. Her family waited until she was supposedly asleep, and then let her husband into the bedroom. She was in fact fully awake, refused his embraces and lectured him on virginity and chastity. The marriage was not consummated. She said she wanted to enter a convent, and the parents appealed to the local bishop, who decided that, despite the consent, the lack of consummation made the marriage invalid. Christina eventually became prioress of Markyate convent.[35] Although technically the ground of his decision was non-consummation, it could be argued that consent obtained by parental pressure was false consent. In modern law, wilful refusal to consummate can make a marriage voidable, as can consent obtained by duress.[36]

Of course, then as now, many unmarried women found themselves pregnant. If marriage was already in prospect, there was no problem, and the priest would be glad to bless the union. But if marriage was not intended, usually because the putative father was reluctant or unidentified, the woman had to look to her family for support, or face ostracism and penury. There was therefore some pressure to get her married and legitimize the child, but this could be a hazardous solution. Full consent, in Christian understanding, implied commitment for life and the will to nurture children by the spouses, but if the reality was that after the ceremony the parents would go their separate ways, 'making it legal' for the child's sake could be something of a charade. There was no easy solution to this problem in the Middle Ages, though eventually defective intent could become a cause for annulling a marriage.

Marriage as a sacrament

If genuine consent between the partners is the basic test of a valid marriage, the question might be raised: Can they not equally consent to end it? The Roman answer, reiterated by Justinian, was that the consent was 'for life' and could not therefore be abandoned by agreement, though it could be for certain offences, such as adultery, which were in effect a unilateral declaration that the contract was repudiated. The medieval church accepted adultery as a ground for divorce, but, following St Paul and Augustine, came to the view that there was something sacramental about the marriage bond, which continued even after the couple went their separate ways. This sacramental quality was a stronger argument for the prohibition of remarriage than the pragmatic and humane considerations for the abandoned spouse and children, and it was based on the doctrine of the indissolubility of Christ's relationship to the Church. The marriage bond was a symbol or a paradigm of the mysterious union between Christ and his Church. Once consenting to marriage brought that bond into being, it could not be broken, however much the partners wished it to be. Unlike the other sacraments, originally only baptism and the Eucharist, but now including confirmation, ordination, penance and unction, the ministry of a priest or bishop was required, but the ministers of the sacrament of marriage were the couple themselves. In the Eastern Orthodox tradition, the priestly blessing was required to make the marriage sacramental, but that was not so in the West. The sexual consummation made the sacrament, and the priest acted only as chief witness. His blessing affirmed the marriage, but did not seal it sacramentally.[37] Intended to enhance the status of marriage and family life, this sacramental emphasis had much to commend it in principle, but was somewhat difficult to apply to the realities of vulnerable human relationships. The Orthodox Church, which allowed divorce and remarriage under certain conditions, took the view that little godly purpose was served by leaving two cats together tied by their tails. The Catholic Church found a partial solution by attributing some failed marriages to defects in initial intent, and the Reformation churches accepted divorce and remarriage albeit reluctantly.

The theological arguments for the sacramentality of marriage were strongly debated in the medieval Church and are well summed up by Schillebeeckx.

The difference between the patristic view of the indissolubility of marriage and the view which came into prominence in the twelfth and thirteenth centuries may be briefly summarised as follows. According to the church Fathers, marriage as a *sacramentum* in the older sense of a 'life commitment' or an 'oath of fidelity' was something that *might not* be dissolved, since it involved a personal commission to live married life in such a way that the bond of marriage was not broken. The indissolubility of marriage was a task which had to be realized personally. According to the later, scholastic concept of the *sacramentum*, on the other hand – a concept developed in the twelfth and thirteenth centuries especially from the ontological participation in the covenant between Christ and his church – marriage was seen as something that *could* not be dissolved. There was in marriage an objective bond which – once made – was exempt from any action or interference on the part of man. These two visions – the patristic view of marriage as a moral obligation and the scholastic view of marriage as an ontological bond – are not mutually exclusive, but rather mutually implicit. Both the patristic and the scholastic doctrines are firmly based on scripture.[38]

Courtly love

So far, the concept of romantic love has hardly appeared in this book. That is not because the phenomenon was only discovered in the Middle Ages, for it is obviously a timeless and universal human experience. Falling in love has always been the spur to entering a relationship, the arbiter of its quality and the justification for making and wrecking marriages. It has the power to make or mar a life, so it is not surprising that the ancient philosophers regarded it with caution. They saw it as either an irrational factor in human experience, controlled by amoral goddesses, or as a physical fire in the loins, to promote breeding or to be relieved with mistresses, prostitutes or slaves. Positively, from Homer onwards, affection, loyalty and companionship between men and women were highly valued, and Helen and Penelope loved their men and were loved by them, but the Platonists and Stoics were wary of passion, praising *philia*, and derogatory about *eros* in principle if not in practice. Even Catullus and Ovid appear to be somewhat mocking of the plight of the besotted man. For the early Christians, as we have seen, the sexual drive was understood as all too easily expressed in lust, hence the strict rules they made to resist it. The sudden explosion of the ideal of courtly love in the eleventh century therefore caught the Christian moralists unprepared.[39]

Courtly love was a serious challenge to the dour state of Christian attitudes to sexual longing. By definition dissociated from marriage, it could only be practised by those trained in courtesy. While the knight was away on the Crusades, his lady would be courted by other suitors, unattached knights and squires, or bored males in the castle community. Sometimes it would all be fantasy from afar, but chastity belts, perhaps seldom actually used, nevertheless symbolized the danger. Royal patronage of courtly love is attributed to Guillaume le Troubador, Duke of Anjou (1086–1127), and to his young relative, Eleanor of Aquitaine, who grew up at his court. She was first married to Louis VII of France, and bore him only two daughters, despite the Pope's advice that they should share the same bed. After this marriage was dissolved on grounds of consanguinity, she quickly married Henry II of England and France, with whom she had five sons and three daughters.[40]

Here is one of Guillaume's songs:

> I shall make a new song, before it blows, freezes or rains. My lady tests and tries me, wishing to see in what manner I love her. Despite her complaints, never will I untie myself from her. My fine lady, what will you gain if you distance me from your love? Do you really wish to be a nun? Make no mistake, such is my love that I fear to die from pain if hearing my plea, you do not change your mind. For that woman, I shake and tremble for I do love her with such passion. I do not believe that an equal love might be born from all of Adam's great lineage.[41]

Medieval love poetry of this period is often allegorical, reflecting in part the then standard interpretation of the biblical Song of Songs as an allegory of the love between Christ and his Church. Sometimes the poem was deliberately ironic, intended to expose for example the hypocrisy of monks and nuns, who were in theory married chastely to Christ, but spent much of their time living unchastely with each other. However, much timeless literature comes from this period, including the agonized love and secret marriage of Abelard and Heloise, the legend of Tristan and Iseult, Chaucer's *Canterbury Tales* and the collection of Latin and German poems known as *Carmina Burana*, which includes a reference to Eleanor.[42]

Perhaps the troubadours had all the best tunes, but there were counterattacks in favour of chastity, of which the fourteenth-century tale *Sir Gawain and the Green Knight* is a good example. The scene is set in Camelot. King Arthur and his knights are enjoying a New Year's

Eve dinner when a strange green figure appears and invites them to a challenge of two mortal combats, cutting off each other's heads in turn. Gawain accepts, and strikes the first blow, apparently deadly, but the Green Knight gathers up his head and goes off to await the next combat a year hence. Gawain sets off to search for the Green Knight and finds himself warmly welcomed at a beautiful castle where he makes a bargain with his host. The host will hunt animals in the forest while Gawain hunts for kisses in the castle. His host's wife kisses him, but he resists (only just) her invitation to make love. The point is that kissing is one thing, sexual intercourse another, and if he succumbs to her in that way, his integrity as a member of the Round Table will be lost. Gawain resists the temptation, and the lady gives him a golden girdle for protection at the second combat. The host of the castle turns out to be the Green Knight in another guise, and slightly wounds Gawain for keeping the girdle. Gawain then returns to Camelot, and all the knights start wearing girdles in honour of his achievement in preserving his chastity. The tale has been thought to explain the founding of the Order of the Garter. *Honi soit qui mal y pense*. Whatever the truth of that link, honour has been preserved all round.[43]

Thomas Aquinas

Responding to the Renaissance

If Augustine is the most powerful theologian to speak to us from the Patristic period, Thomas Aquinas (1225–74) takes his place as the medieval theologian whose teaching resonates to our day. In a review of how modern theologians face up to modernity, Professor David Ford has described Thomas Aquinas as 'for many a recurring point of reference'.[44] This is almost an understatement since Aquinas was by most standards the leading pre-Reformation Catholic theologian and is still regarded as the primary source for Catholic teaching about marriage, and clearly influenced the papal encyclical *Humanae vitae* (1968). He was the youngest son of Count Landolfo d'Aquino, who placed him aged five at the Benedictine Monastery of Monte Cassino. To the disappointment of his family he joined the relatively new Dominican order and was sent to their Priory at Paris University, becoming a Master of Theology in 1256, and Professor there in 1268. He died from a head injury while travelling to Lyon in 1274, aged 49.

His two great works were the *Summa Contra Gentiles*, a guide for his fellow Dominican friars in their controversies with Islam, and his *Summa Theologiae*, intended as an introduction to doctrine, though actually a long and erudite argument for its truths. In these, Thomas uses the Bible, Aristotle, Augustine and Gratian as his main sources, and he could be called a Christian humanist in the sense that, while taking the Bible and tradition seriously, he sets much store on human reason, seeking to demonstrate that rightly used there is no incompatibility. He is not so much putting old wine into new bottles as old wine into different old bottles, to link up traditional Christian teaching with classical humanism, now being rediscovered at the start of the Renaissance period.[45]

Thomas holds that the universe is governed by God's sovereignty, and this governance is expressed as Eternal Law, known in its fullness only to God. Natural Law is the part of God's Eternal Law that human reason can perceive. To these must be added Divine Law, known to Christians by revelation, and human law, enacted by states to correspond with Natural Law as far as possible. The belief that there is a Natural Law, available to all, was important for Stoicism, and for Justinian, who claimed the institution of marriage was governed by it. However, the word 'natural' is being used here in a philosophical and moral sense, and is distinct from the laws of nature as used to describe scientific rules and models of thought.[46] The style of argument Thomas uses is strange to us because he sets out first the contrary view which he will expose as false by explaining the objections to it, so that the true Christian view finally emerges. This method, typical of scholasticism, assumed a non-Christian readership, starting from where they are and leading them on to the Christian doctrine. In his *Summa Contra Gentiles*, he defends the Christian teaching of permanent monogamous marriage by first criticizing the standard argument in favour of fornication that it harms no one, then argues that monogamous marriage conforms to Natural Law, that divorce is contrary to that law, and then in parenthesis holds that sexual intercourse is not sinful.

His initial analysis of the amorality of fornication (modified by the later discussion) seems surprisingly modern.

Suppose there is a woman who is not married, or under the control of any man, either her father or another man. Now, if the man performs the sexual act with her, and she is willing, he does not injure her because she favours the action, and she has control over her own body. Nor does he injure any other person, because she is understood to be under no other person's control. So this does not seem to be a sin . . . Now to say that he injures God would not seem to be an adequate answer. For we do not offend God except by doing something contrary to our own good, as has been said. But this does not appear to be contrary to man's good. Hence, on this basis no injury seems to be done to God.[47]

He then turns to the proper use of semen. Its emission is not superfluous, such as sweat, but should be emitted for the purpose of generation, to which purpose the sexual act is directed. It is evident from this that every emission of semen in such a way that generation cannot follow is contrary to the good of man, except when by accident generation cannot result, as for instance if the woman happens to be sterile. But man's generative process would be frustrated unless it were followed by proper nutrition and upbringing of this offspring. A woman should not be expected to bring up the offspring by herself, even if she is rich enough to do so, therefore it is appropriate that a man remain together with a woman after the generative act, and not leave her immediately to fornicate with another man. Thomas finally links up his teaching with Ephesians and argues that it should be followed in state law:

> Since there is a natural prompting within the human species, to the end that the union of man and woman be undivided, it is necessary for this to be ordered by human law. But divine law supplies a supernatural reason, drawn from the symbolism of the inseparable union between Christ and the Church (Eph. 5.24–32). And thus, disorders connected with the act of generation are not only opposed to natural instinct, but are also transgressions of divine and human laws. Hence, a greater sin results from a disorder in this area than in regard to the use of food or other things of that kind.[48]

Thomas writes towards the end of the Middle Ages, marshalling the best arguments of his predecessors, and there is nothing new about his morality. We have seen it all before, for his work is an amalgam of classicism, Scripture, the rabbinic sources and Augustine. Christendom is shortly to be overtaken by the Reformation, and that will mean the Christian churches will eventually have three major patterns of thought about marriage, Eastern Orthodox, Western Catholic, and European Protestant, with Anglicanism attempting an uneasy synthesis of insights from all three.

8

The Reformers

The Reformation as a religious revival

Present-day ecumenical discussion between the Catholics, Anglicans and Lutherans tends to concentrate on the two theological issues that supposedly caused the split between the Western Catholic Church and the Reforming Protestants in the fifteenth and sixteenth centuries. We know that the Reformers asserted the sovereignty of the Bible against the claims of papal supremacy and insisted that the doctrine of justification by faith alone was the core truth of the gospel. However, crucial as these issues became, neither of them was the fundamental cause of the Reformation. At the heart of the protesting movement was the longing for a better quality religion, and this was felt equally by those who remained within the Catholic Church and by those who, albeit reluctantly, left it. The simple truth was that thinking European Christians at the end of the Middle Ages were genuinely and profoundly religious. As Karen Armstrong has put it: 'Instead of expressing their faith in external, collective ways, the people of Europe were beginning to explore the more interior consequences of religion.'[1]

They saw that the Church of Christendom had lost touch with its roots and fallen into a kind of Babylonian captivity to the ways of the world. Carnality of various kinds characterized its leadership, much of monasticism was benighted, the peasantry shivered from their deprivation and in fear of another great plague. Constantinople had fallen and Islam was at the gates of Vienna. It seemed as if the wrath of God hung over Europe, and since the Church was spiritually compromised, enthusiasm switched towards mysticism and support for alternative forms of Christian obedience.

The religious and political turmoil during the ninety-eight years between the birth of Erasmus in 1466 and the death of Calvin in 1564 split the previously united Western Catholic Church into four disparate Christian Confessions, replacing the hegemony of Christendom under the Pope with the conflicting interests of a profusion of small national states. The European rulers who embraced the Reformation gained the right to choose the religion of their subjects, on the principle *Cuius Regio eius religio* (the faith of the ruler is the faith of his people), and the eventual outcome was the division of the German states between the Lutheran North and the Catholic South. Each prince could make his own decision about marriage laws. Although Erasmus, Luther, Calvin and Cranmer aimed to improve standards in Christian life rather than achieve a structural disruption of the Church, they found themselves increasingly dependent on their political masters. Luther relied on the support of the Elector of Saxony, Calvin on the civil leaders in Geneva.

Apart from discontent with the ways of a worldly church, the other spur to reform was the wider knowledge of classical humanism. The advent of printing made the difference. There was nothing new in humanism, and Aquinas had shown two hundred years earlier how old learning could be assimilated and used. He was able to fit Aristotle and Augustine into his system, but his teaching was not widely circulated, and was regarded with suspicion even within his own Dominican Order. There was of course much about the old world which ought never to be revived, but the Reformers felt free to look afresh at both the Bible and the patristic writings. What the Church had said the sacred text meant could now be re-examined and different conclusions drawn.

A change of perception

The Reformers were together responsible for a decisive change in the Christian perception of marriage. They were faced by obvious evidence of a total mismatch between the medieval Church's teaching about sexuality and the realities of life among Christians. The Church taught that celibacy was best and marriage a concession for those who could not remain continent, while in practice neither those who were bound by the oath of chastity within the religious orders nor the secular clergy, from cardinals to parish priests, were obeying their own rules. They were rules of the mind but not of the heart. For the laity, marriage at the church door was the convention, observed by perhaps half the population, while the rest coupled by family or private agreement as they had always done. The ruling classes were a law unto themselves, and it would be hard to name a king or prince in

Christendom who was chaste in youth, married only once, and denied himself either concubines or adultery. Every royal entourage included a number of clergy, useful because they could read and write, but they were seldom in a position to protest, being often compromised themselves.

To explain the mismatch in sexual conduct between principle and practice in the traditional fashion, by putting all the blame on the Fall and human sinfulness, was a doctrine without hope, and the Reformers looked for a better solution. They had to hand new translations not only of the patristic writings but also of the Bible, and it soon became clear that to some extent the attitudes of Tertullian, Ambrose, Jerome and even the revered Augustine had put a spin on Scripture which ought to be questioned. The creation ordinances in Genesis could be read in another way – God did not intend a man or a woman to be lonely; they were meant to come together and to have children. These commands were given before the Fall, and were good in themselves, and although, like all human activity after the Fall, in some measure corrupted by sin, they remained the will of God for most people. This change of emphasis was not an accommodation to the ways of the world, as some traditionalists complained, but a recovery of the biblical truth about marriage and sexuality which had always been deeply embedded in Jewish theology. Perhaps for that reason it had been tacitly ignored, and supplanted by the patristic asceticism. Paradoxically, the Stoic view of life had proved to be far more generally followed by Christians, at least in theory, than ever it was by the Romans. But now it had to be made clear that marriage was ordained by God. The new attitude was firmly expressed in the prologue to Cranmer's first Prayer Book (1549). That it was 'ordained by God in Paradise' was a strong affirmation of marriage, not a concession to human frailty. What God 'ordained' was of high significance, important for humankind's salvation.

The Reformers set out to correct the patristic mistake by continually reasserting the goodness of marriage. They could not of course ban celibacy altogether, but they pushed it to the periphery of human experience. It could be a vocation (Calvin described it as a special grace to which God called some people), but otherwise it was said to be an evil imposition and a recipe for misery and frustration for people whose proper lifestyle was to be found in marriage. Luther, especially, devoted much pastoral care to the encouragement towards marriage of many priests, monks and nuns who had sought release from their confinement in the celibate state by leaving their communities. This reworking of the medieval theology of sex and marriage in somewhat more affirming ways was reflected in the new vernacular language of the liturgies. Erasmus did the spadework for the new approach. Like St Thomas Aquinas two centuries before, he took classicism seriously, but unlike Thomas he used its humanism to change the Christian tradition. He was the only one of the four to remain unmarried and within the Catholic Church. Both Luther and Calvin married in their mature years, somewhat hesitantly, though for different reasons. Cranmer married twice.

Erasmus

Erasmus (1466–1536) is remembered as the archetypal Christian humanist but he remained a Catholic and in his latter days fell out with Luther. He was a Dutchman, and admitted to having been born of an unlawful union.[2] Having obtained a dispensation from the Pope, Erasmus became an Augustinian friar at Gouda, and was ordained priest in 1492. He studied classics in Paris, and taught for brief periods at both Oxford and Cambridge, and then worked in Paris, Brussels and Freiburg, eventually retiring to Basle. His greatest achievements were a new translation of the Bible into Latin and a revised Greek text of the New Testament. Both books circulated widely and became essential sources for the later Reformers. Erasmus had been miserable as a monk, and may have had an unhappy sexual relationship in his youth, perhaps catching syphilis. Despite his familiarity with the views of Jerome and Augustine, and reflecting on his own life story, in one of his early epistles he sets out a positive view of marriage and a criticism of celibacy:

> Marriage was sanctioned by Christ at Cana. It is sanctioned by nature and condemned by heretics. It was instituted not by Moses or Solon, but by the Founder of the universe. For God said 'It is not good for man to be alone' and he created Eve, not out of mud, as in the case of Adam, but from his rib, that none should be closer and dearer than a wife. After the flood God told man 'to be fruitful and multiply'. Should not marriage be honoured above all the sacraments because it was the first to be instituted, and by God Himself. The other sacraments were established on earth, this one in paradise; the others as a remedy, this one as fellowship in felicity. The

others were ordained for fallen nature, but this one for nature unspoiled. If human laws are revered how much more the law of marriage which we receive from him who gave us life?[3]

Erasmus continues by suggesting that 'the excitation of Venus, which is necessary for marriage, is from nature and whatever is of nature is pure and holy. The most holy manner of life, pure and chaste, is marriage.' Although this dictum reflects some thoughts of Augustine and Aquinas, neither of them could have written as positively as this. Subsequently, although Luther and Calvin took the view that marriage was preferable to celibacy they never quite lost the suspicion that sex even in marriage belonged to the lower nature, not really good in itself but at least partly a remedy for sin.

While in Freiburg Erasmus learned of the attempts by Henry VIII to have his first marriage to Katherine of Aragon annulled by Pope Clement VII. Katherine argued that her brief marriage to Arthur, Henry's older brother, had never been consummated, but in any case Clement wished to maintain a good relationship with Charles V, the Holy Roman Emperor, who was Katherine's nephew. Clement refused the request and the upshot was Henry's break with Rome. Erasmus had met Katherine and sympathized with her predicament, sending her a long treatise in support:

Marriage is the most appropriate of all unions because based on nature, law and religion. It should be for life, and any marriage that is capable of being dissolved never was a marriage at all . . . It is not to be entered into lightly but soberly, advisedly.[4] Marriage should not be without the consent of parents, but they should not force the unwilling . . . As between the bride and groom, the church holds that marriage rests on consent. But does silence constitute consent? If a boy gives consent to one maid and then to another, shall he be held to the first? Better not to be too stringent in forcing him to carry through. If a girl will not receive a boy inflamed with wine unless he promises to marry her and he complies, do you call that consent? I will give you an example of genuine consent and marriage. A lame man married a blind woman that they might help each other in their infirmities. Never an unkind word passed between them. They had twelve sons, all healthy. I knew one of them, a priest in Britain. That's what I call a real marriage.[5]

Luther

Life and marriage

Martin Luther (1483–1546) was the son of a copper miner in Saxony. He was educated at Magdeburg, Eisenach and Erfurt University, and in 1505 entered the Augustinian order, being ordained priest in 1507. The next year he was appointed professor of moral theology and then professor of biblical exegesis at Wittenberg, where he continued to teach until his death. He is most famous for the 95 Theses on Indulgences he posted on the door of the castle church in Wittenberg in 1519, which led to a continued confrontation with the Papacy about primacy, the sale of indulgences and clerical celibacy. Luther discarded his monastic status in 1524, and the next year married Katherine von Bora, previously a Cistercian nun. Luther had for some time been encouraging other priests and monks who had opted to join his movement to become married, and he was clear that this was theologically right and that their original vow of celibacy was no longer binding. As part of his pastoral work he found homes for those who had left their religious communities, among whom was a small group of three nuns of noble birth, including Katherine. She said she would reject all suitors unless the great Doctor himself asked her. Luther hesitated for some time before he did; some of his friends had long encouraged him, but others thought he would lose credibility if he showed himself a mere mortal.

The marriage was a simple affair in three stages. First came the official betrothal at Luther's lodgings, witnessed only by five friends, followed by the 'copulation', which despite its name was the actual wedding ceremony, conducted by Luther's friend and associate teacher John Bugenhagen, who was a priest. This led on to the customary visit of the bride and groom to the marriage chamber, where Martin and Katherine lay briefly on the bed in front of the witnesses. The custom was by now entirely symbolic, not an act of physical consummation, and was followed by a wedding breakfast for this small group.[6] Two weeks later, the marriage feast proper was held, the interval allowing Luther time to tell his family and special friends that he was already married, the first they knew of it. Fifteen people attended. This hurried and secret event led to gossip that Martin and Katherine had been living together before the marriage, but their colleague Melanchthon declared that 'this was a plain lie'. Their first son, Johannes, was born a year later.[7] Domestic life suited Luther, and his work rate continued as usual. Katherine was a competent manager, though guests noted she had to spend some time each day tidying up his papers, typical of a scholar's household. They ran an open house, welcoming the young, the old and the homeless, with simple patterns of daily worship.

Luther's theology of marriage

Luther wrote and taught much about marriage, and perhaps his most concise statement comes from one of the sermons he preached on the Ten Commandments. He uses his exposition on the prohibition of adultery to define it as one kind of offence against a neighbour, and defends marriage as God's universal provision.

> Explicit injunction is here given against injury [to the neighbour] by the disgrace of his wife. Adultery is particularly mentioned, because among the Jewish people marriage was obligatory. Young people were advised to marry at the earliest age possible. Virginity was not particularly commended; harlots and libertines were never tolerated. There was no form of unchastity more common than that of breaking the marriage vow . . . We are to assist our neighbours to maintain their honour. In brief, the requirement of the commandment is chastity for oneself and the endeavour to secure it for the neighbour. But since particular attention is here called to the married state, let us carefully note how God especially honours and commends wedded life, since he confirms and protects it with a special command. Hence he requires us to honour, guard, and observe it as a divine and blessed estate. Significantly he established it as the first of all institutions, and with it in view, he did not create man and woman alike . . . God's purpose . . . was that they might be true to each other, beget children, and nourish and rear them to his glory. Therefore God blessed this institution above all others, and made everything on earth serve and spring from it, so that it might be well and amply provided for. It is not an exceptional estate, but the most universal and the noblest, pervading all Christendom, yea, extending through the whole world.[8]

Luther was at heart a generous, passionate man, quite different in disposition from the precise Erasmus and the austere Calvin. His original concern about indulgences came from his discovery that some members of his congregation had bought them as a guaranteed ticket to heaven, and he was always a pastor first and a polemical theologian second, as his personal letters show. Thus, he wrote reassuringly to some nuns who had left their community:

> Have you thoroughly understood that there are two grounds for abandoning convent life and Monastic vows? . . . The first exists when human laws and monastic works are imposed by force, are not assumed voluntarily, and become burdensome to conscience. Under such circumstances one should flee and let the convent and everything connected with it go . . . The other ground is the flesh. Although women are ashamed to acknowledge this, Scriptures and experience teach us that there is only one in several thousands to whom God gives the gift to live chastely in a state of virginity. A woman does not have complete mastery over herself. God so created her body that she should be with a man and bear and raise children. The words of Genesis ch. 1 clearly state this, and the members of her body clearly show that God himself formed her for this purpose. Just as eating, drinking, waking, and sleeping are appointed by God to be natural, so God also wills that it be natural for a man and a woman to live together in matrimony. This is enough, therefore, and no woman need be ashamed of that for which God has created and fashioned her, and if she feels she does not possess that high and rare gift, she may leave the convent and do that for which she is adapted by nature.[9]

Similarly, two months before his own marriage, Luther wrote to a former student of his, Wolfgang Reissenbusch, who was now the preceptor of St Anthony's monastery in Lichtenberg, and planning rather cautiously to take the step of marrying Anna Herzog, the daughter of a local tailor. Following this letter Wolfgang did marry her, and soon after the text of the letter was printed in Wittenberg. Luther clearly intended it to be a more general statement of his views.

> I have often spoken to you about it [marriage] and have observed that you are not only suited for and inclined towards marriage but are also forced and compelled to it by God himself, who created you therefor. I do not think you should be kept from it by the rule of your order, or by a vow . . . Whoever, therefore, considers himself a man and believes himself to be included in this general term should

hear what God, his Creator, here says and decrees for him: he does not wish man to be alone but desires that he should multiply, and so he makes him a helpmeet to be with him and help him so that he may not be alone. This is the Word of God, through whose power procreative seed is planted in a man's body and a natural, ardent desire for woman is kindled and kept alive. This cannot be restrained either by vows or by laws. For it is God's law and doing ... Our bodies are in great part the flesh of women, for by them we were conceived, developed, born, suckled, and nourished, and so it is quite impossible to keep entirely apart from them. This is in accord with the will of God.[10]

Many of Luther's most vigorous thoughts about marriage are recorded in his *Table Talk*, which was actually a collection of some nine hundred of his sayings, recalled by friends after his death and widely circulated to Lutheran churches. The book was banned for a time in Catholic states, and surviving copies contain some inconsistencies. However, in the sayings referring to marriage it is clear that Luther varied somewhat between understanding marriage as thoroughly good and necessary, and reckoning it as a dispensation for human frailty. Although he disliked divorce, he thought it inevitable after adultery, and proper after desertion. The innocent party should be free to remarry after a suitable interval, probably five years. The following extracts from the *Table Talk* are chosen to show the range of Luther's views. His humour sometimes shows.

Dr. Martin sighed and said: 'Good God, what a bother these matrimonial cases are to us. It takes great labour and effort to get couples together. Afterwards it requires even more pains to keep them together. The Fall of Adam so corrupted human nature that it is very fickle. It is as inconsistent as quicksilver. Everything is wonderful when a married couple sit down together or goes to bed. If they sometimes murmur at each other, this is to be taken as incidental to marriage. Adam and Eve must have scolded each other roundly during their nine hundred years together. Eve would have said: "You ate the apple!" And Adam would have replied, "But why did you give it to me!"' Afterwards the doctor added that man suffers martyrdom whose wife and maid do not know their way about in the kitchen. It is a calamity of the first order from which many evils follow.[11]

A preacher of the gospel, being regularly called, ought, above all things, first, to purify himself before he teaches others. Is he is able with a good conscience, to remain unmarried? Let him remain so; but if he cannot abstain living chastely, then let him take a wife; God has made that plaster for that sore.[12]

Maternity is a glorious thing, since all mankind have been conceived, born and nourished of women. All human laws should encourage the multiplication of families.[13]

The Elector of Saxony has a great number of ladies at his court, princesses, noble damsels, women of honour, women of the bedchamber and what not; but it does not follow that all these are his wives. As to Solomon's having entertained all these women as his wives, 'tis out of the question, impracticable.[14]

'Tis a grand thing for a married pair to live in perfect union, but the devil rarely permits this. When they are apart they cannot endure the separation, and when they are together, they cannot endure always seeing one another. 'Tis as the poet says *nec tecum vivere possum, nec sine te . . .* I have seen marriages where, at first, husband and wife seemed as though they would eat one another up: in six months they have separated in mutual disgust. 'Tis the devil inspires this evanescent ardour, in order to divert the parties from prayer.[15]

The hair is the finest ornament women have. Of old, virgins used to wear it loose, except when they were in mourning. I like women to let their hair fall down their backs; 'tis a most agreeable sight.[16]

St Ulrich, Bishop of Augsburg, related a fearful thing that befell at Rome. Pope Gregory, who confirmed celibacy, ordered a fish-pond at Rome, hard by a convent of nuns, to be cleared out. The waters being let off, there were found at the bottom, more than six thousand skulls of children that had been cast into the pond and drowned. Such were the fruits of enforced celibacy. Hereupon Pope Gregory abolished celibacy, but the popes who followed him re-established it.

After referring to a similar situation at a Convent in Austria, Luther concluded: 'How much better to let these people marry, than, by prohibition thereof, to cause the murder of so many innocent creatures.'[17]

Calvin

Life and marriage

Jean Calvin (1509–64) was born in Noyon in Picardy, where his father was an official at the cathedral. It was intended that he should become a priest, but it seems that lack of funds obliged him to train as a lawyer at Orleans where he became interested in Christian humanism. His shift towards Reformation thinking was gradual, and he moved to Basle where he wrote the first edition of his *Institutes of the Christian Religion* in 1536. Eventually, he settled in Geneva, providing for the city a new model of government on theocratic principles. Like Luther, he was hesitant about marriage:

> I, whom you see so hostile to celibacy, have never taken a wife, and I know not if I shall ever marry. If I did so, it would be in order to devote my time to the Lord, by being the more relieved from the worries of daily life.[18]

But his friends pressed him to take the step, and in 1540, while working in Strasbourg, he married Idelette de Bure, the widow of an Anabaptist, 'as elegant and sensitive a woman as the aristocratic tastes of the reformer would have required'.[19] Idelette brought with her two children from her previous marriage, and added a child by Calvin in 1542 who sadly died shortly after birth. She died in 1549.

Calvin's theology of marriage

Calvin's *Institutes* were his systematic presentation of Christian doctrine and he continually revised and enlarged them. The definitive version is that of 1559. While obviously starting from Scripture, with a particular mastery of the Old Testament, and influenced by Luther, Calvin's theology shows he was far more familiar with the works of the Church Fathers than Luther and Zwingli were. He quotes Chrysostom, Ambrose and Augustine frequently. In Book Two Calvin argues that the knowledge of God as the Redeemer was first disclosed to the Patriarchs, and the purpose of the Decalogue was to reveal God's moral law and show the corruption of the fallen nature of humankind. His commentary on the Seventh Commandment, against adultery, develops into a justification of marriage, expressed in a rather dour way, reminiscent of the third century:

> The purpose of the commandment is: because God loves modesty and purity, all uncleanness must be far from us. To sum up then: we should not become defiled with any filth or lustful intemperance of the flesh. To this corresponds the affirmative commandment that we chastely and continently regulate all parts of our life. But he expressly forbids fornication, to which all lust tends, in order through the foulness of fornication, which is grosser and more palpable, in so far as it brands the body also with its mark, to lead us to abominate all lust.
>
> Man has been created in this condition that he may not lead a solitary life, but may enjoy a helper joined to himself (cf. Genesis 2.18); then by the curse of sin he has been still more subjected to this necessity.
>
> Therefore, the Lord sufficiently provided for us in this matter when he established marriage, the fellowship of which, began on his authority, he also sanctified by his blessing. From this it is clear that any other union apart from marriage is accursed in his sight; and that the companionship of marriage has been ordained as a necessary remedy to keep us from plunging into unbridled lust.[20]

Calvin next considers celibacy, modesty and chastity. Celibacy is a special grace given only to a few:

> Let each man see what has been given to him. Virginity, I agree, is a virtue not to be despised. However it is denied to some and granted to others only for a time. Hence, those who are troubled with incontinence and cannot prevail in the struggle should turn to matrimony to help them preserve chastity in the degree of their calling . . . it is not given to every man to keep chastity in celibacy, even if he aspires to it with great zeal and effort; it is a special grace which the Lord bestows only on certain men, in order to hold them more ready for his work.[21]
>
> Now if married couples recognize that their association is blessed by the Lord, they are thereby admonished not to pollute it with

uncontrolled and dissolute lust. For even if the honourableness of matrimony covers the baseness of incontinence, it ought not for that reason to be a provocation thereto. Therefore let not married persons think that all things are permitted to them, but let each man have his own wife soberly, and each wife her own husband . . . For it is fitting that thus wedlock contracted in the Lord be recalled to measure and modesty so as to not wallow in extreme lewdness. Ambrose censures this wantonness with a severe but not undeserved judgement; he has called the man who has no regard for shame or honourableness in his marriage practices an adulterer towards his own wife.[22]

Much later in the *Institutes*, in Book Four, Calvin describes the external means or aids by which God invites us into the society of Christ, and holds us therein. Not surprisingly, in discussing Christian ministry, while allowing a distinction between clergy and laity, Calvin has much to say about the excesses of the Papacy and the episcopate. He then castigates the rule that clergy are not allowed to marry as a mistaken tyranny imposed by the church and contrary to Scripture:

In one thing they are extremely rigid and inexorable – in not permitting marriage to priests. But it is needless to speak of the extent to which fornication prevails among them unpunished; and how, relying upon their foul celibacy, they have become callous to all crimes. Yet this prohibition clearly shows what a plague all their traditions are. For it has not only deprived the church of good and fit pastors, but has also brought in a sink of iniquities and has cast many souls into the abyss of despair. Surely the forbidding of marriage to priests came about by an impious tyranny not only against God's word, but also against all equity. First, to forbid what the Lord left free was by no means lawful to men. Again, that the Lord expressly took care by his Word that this freedom should not be infringed upon is too clear to require a long proof. I pass over the fact that Paul in many passages wishes a bishop to be a man of one wife (1 Tim. 3.2; Titus 1.6). But what could be more forcefully said than when he declares by the Holy Spirit that in the Last Days there will be impious men who forbid marriage, and calls them not only impostors but demons (1 Tim. 4.1, 3).[23]

Marriage a sacrament

Despite the rather pragmatic justification of marriage as for purity and against loneliness, Calvin adds a more theological reason in favour based on Ephesians 5, but he remains firmly antagonistic to the Catholic teaching that marriage is a sacrament.

> Christ deems marriage of such honour that he wills it to be an image of his sacred union with the church (Eph. 5.23–4, 32). What more splendid commendation could be spoken of the dignity of marriage?[24] Paul, to show to married men with what singular love they ought to embrace their wives, sets forth Christ to them as a prototype. For as he poured out his compassion upon the church, which he had espoused to himself, thus he wishes everyman to feel towards his own wife . . . Truly indeed, this is a great mystery, that Christ allowed a rib to be removed from himself to form us; that is when he was strong he willed to be weak, in order that we might be strengthened by his strength; so that we ourselves should no longer live, but he should live in us (Gal. 2.20). The term 'sacrament' deceived them. But was it right that the whole church should suffer the punishment of their ignorance? Paul had said 'mystery'. The translator could have left this word as one not unfamiliar to Latin ears, or rendered it as 'secret'. He preferred to use the word 'sacrament' (Eph. 5.32, Vulgate) but in the same sense that the word 'mystery' had been used by St. Paul . . . But, having graced marriage with the title of sacrament, to call it afterwards uncleanness and pollution and carnal filth – what giddy levity is this? How absurd it is to bar priests from this sacrament! If they say they do not bar them from the sacrament, but only from the lust of copulation, they will not give me the slip. For they teach that copulation itself is a part of the sacrament, and that it alone is the figure of the union which we have with Christ, in conformity to nature; for man and woman are made one flesh only by carnal copulation.[25]

It is clear from the last part of this chapter of the *Institutes* that Calvin has wider concerns in mind than defending the right of Protestant pastors to marry. He is opposed to what he regards as the Church's takeover of matrimonial jurisdiction in general, which he believes, as Luther did, is more properly the concern of the godly state. Both Luther and Calvin regard marriage as a creation ordinance, and therefore think of the Church's attempt to define rules about the age of consent, consanguinity, restriction on marriage at certain liturgical seasons and the right to remarry after divorcing an adulterous wife as unfair interference with human rights. As he puts it, 'we need to extract ourselves from this mire of regulations, and I believe I have accomplished something in that I have partly pulled the lion's skin from these asses'. However, in practice in Geneva Calvin found it necessary to set up a panel of three lay people to adjudicate in matrimonial disputes between members of Protestant congregations.

Cranmer

Archbishop Thomas Cranmer (1489–1556) is chiefly remembered these days as the author of the Book of Common Prayer, and as the key ecclesiastical fixer for King Henry VIII's sequence of divorces and remarriages. His support for the king in his struggles with the Papacy was crucial to the emergence of the Church of England as a separate entity and for its pattern of Church and state relationships, which to a large extent survives in our current experience of an Established Church. It differed from the Lutheran and Calvinist models of government in retaining much of the Canon Law of the Western Church, and notably the threefold ministry of bishops, priests and deacons, the monarch replacing the Pope in making senior church appointments.

[The change in the appointment of senior clergy was not, in practice, that different as a result of the Reformation. As the historian J. R. Tanner pointed out, after the Statutes of Provision and Praemunire (1351–65), 'A common history of appointments [of English medieval bishops] was that the king nominated and the Pope provided the same person, the chapter duly elevating him.'[26] Ed.]

Cranmer was aged fourteen when he entered the newly founded Jesus College, Cambridge. He read classical literature and philosophy, taking his BA in 1511 and an MA in 1515, and was then elected to a College Fellowship. Four years later, tragedy intervened. Cranmer married Joan (surname uncertain), losing his college place thereby, but she died in childbirth within a year or two, and he was re-admitted to his Fellowship. Had Joan lived, Cranmer would not have been ordained (c. 1522). His academic career ended when he was talent-spotted by Cardinal Wolsey and invited to become a junior member of his diplomatic team in 1527. He was soon drawn into the difficult negotiations between Wolsey and the Papacy in the unsuccessful attempt to have the king's first marriage annulled, and when this failed and Wolsey was forced to resign, Cranmer became Henry's most important emissary to Rome.

In 1532 Cranmer was appointed Henry's ambassador to the emperor at Regensburg, and en route stayed for some time at Nuremburg with Andreas Osiander, a Lutheran New Testament and liturgical scholar. While there, he married a niece of Frau Osiander, called Margarete, apparently feeling free to ignore his priestly vow of celibacy on the ground that he was now living in a Lutheran state, where pastors were encouraged to marry. The marriage was somewhat disadvantaged by the need to keep it secret when the couple returned to England, though their friends knew of it. In 1539, in an attempt to keep England free from what he regarded as the Reformation contagion, Henry had Parliament impose the Religion Act of Six Articles, which included the prohibition of clerical marriage, with a threatened penalty of hanging. It was seldom enforced, but Cranmer as Archbishop thought it prudent to send Margarete back to Germany.[27] She returned to England when the Act was repealed in 1547. Among the charges laid against Cranmer at his trial was this illegal marriage, but Margarete continued to live in England after his execution, and fought several court battles to obtain a share in his estate for herself and their children.[28]

Reformation marriage services

The formal prayers of the Christian churches are often the best guides to the mainstream currents of their doctrine and this is certainly true of Christian beliefs about marriage. Comparison of the Reformation marriage services with the traditional Catholic rites shows a shift in emphasis while preserving the same basic elements. The Reformers retain the basic shape of a free consent in front of witnesses, set in the context of biblical teaching about marriage, and culminating with prayers and a blessing, but both Luther and Calvin firmly filter out what they regard as the mistaken accretions of medieval Catholicism, while the structure of Cranmer's marriage service of 1549 reflects a midway position between the traditional Catholic liturgies and the more radical work of the continental reformers.

Luther's Order of Marriage of 1534 follows a traditional pattern, but excludes an obligatory eucharist. It is preceded by the calling of banns, and the ceremony starts at the church door, with exchange of consent, the giving of rings and the joining of hands. The pastor declares the couple are married and recites the sentence, 'What God has joined together let no man separate' (Matt. 19.6), and then the couple move into the church and to the altar where a special lesson from Genesis (Gen. 18.21–4) is read over them. This is a significant part of the service, intended to place their marriage firmly within God's Word, followed by instruction on biblical passages including Ephesians 5 and Proverbs 18.22, 'He who finds a wife finds a good thing, and obtains favour from the LORD' (NRSV). The service concludes with formal prayers by the pastor, said with his hands stretched over them. Luther and Katherine were married like this. The words of consent would have been: 'Martin do you desire Katherine to your wedded wife?' and the pastor's declaration ended, 'I pronounce them joined in marriage, in the name of the Father . . .'

The concluding prayer of the service was like this:

> O God, who has created man and woman and has ordained them for the married state, has blessed them also with the fruits of the womb, and has typified therein the sacramental union of thy dear son, the Lord Jesus Christ, and the Church, his bride: we beseech thy boundless goodness and mercy that thou would not permit this thy creation to be disturbed or destroyed, but graciously preserve the same, through Jesus Christ our Lord.[29]

Calvin's marriage service, the Form of Prayers of 1542, has a simpler structure with less symbolism, beginning with biblical exegesis, then the exchange of consent and ending with prayers. It was usually conducted as an insertion into the normal non-eucharistic service, somewhat similar to modern baptism customs, and the words of consent are much more didactic:

> Do you, N, confess here before God and his holy congregation, that you have taken and do now take your wife and spouse N, here present, whom you promise to keep, loving and caring for her faithfully, as should a true and faithful husband his wife; living piously with her, keeping faith and loyalty with her in all things, according to the holy word of God, and his holy Gospel?[30]

Cranmer's marriage service

Cranmer had been working steadily at drafts of common prayer in English in the declining years of Henry VIII, and when the young Edward VI came to the throne in 1547, the king's Protestant mentors arranged for these drafts to be published. Several of the services were tried out in cathedrals and royal chapels and then considered by a group of bishops and theologians at a conference usually said to have been held at Windsor, but actually held downriver at Chertsey Abbey, from which it was possible to submit drafts to the king, at the time resident at Windsor. The new book was not referred to the Convocations but authorized by Parliament by the Act of Uniformity of 1549.

Cranmer's marriage service, entitled 'The Forme of Solemnizacion of Matrimonie', follows the traditional Sarum structure in general, translated into English. He knew Luther's service and Osiander's variations on it, and includes some phrases from them and from another German scholar, Hermann von Weid, but the whole is recast with his very special liturgical skill and mastery of language. He subtly changes traditional wording at some points to reflect Reformation doctrine while appearing to be retaining the old phrases unchanged. It has been suggested that 'Cranmer followed Luther in dismantling the sacramental status of marriage, but enough of the medieval super-structure remains to conceal theological revolution underneath liturgical evolution'.[31] One important innovation is that the whole ceremony takes place inside the church building. Instead of starting at the church door: 'the persons to be married shall come into the bodie of ye churche, with their friendes and neighbours', where the priest begins with the Preface:

> We are gathered together here in the syght of God, and in the face of his [sic] congregacion, to joyne together this man and this woman in holy matrimonie, which is an honorable estate instituted of God in paradise, in the time of mannes innocencie, signifying unto us the misticall union that is betwixte Christe and his Churche: whiche holy estate, Christe adorned and beutified with his presence, and first miracle that he wrought in Cana of Galile, and is commended of Sainct Paule to be honourable among all men; and therefore not to bee enterprised, nor take in hand unaduisedlye, lightlye, or wantonly, to satisfie mens carnal lustes and appetites, like brute beastes that haue no understanding: but reuerentely, discretely,

aduisedly, soberly and in the feare of God. Duely consideryng the causes for the whiche matrimonie was ordeined. One cause was the procreacion of children, to be brought up in the feare and nurture of the Lord, and prayse of God. Secondly, it was ordained for a remedie agaynst sinne, and to auoide fornicacion, that such persons as bee married, might live chastlie in matrimonie, and keep themselues undefiled membres of Christes bodye. Thirdelye for the mutuall societie, helpe and comfort, that the one ouyghte to haue of thother, both in prosperitie and aduersitie. Into the whiche holy estate these two persones present: come now to be joyned.[32]

This Preface emphasizes a positive attitude to marriage as a holy and honourable estate instituted in paradise, and Cranmer here agrees with Luther that only after the Fall did human sin spoil what was originally a good creative ordinance, so it is not as such an institution needing to be redeemed.[33] But now it serves as a remedy against sin for Christians. A distinction is made between the commitment the man makes to the woman to love, comfort, honour and keep her, while the woman promises to obey, serve, love, honour and keep him. Cranmer is careful to omit the inference of the old rite that the priest receives the bride at the exchange of hands; it is her family that gives her to the groom; the priest supervises the proper procedures, but does not act sacramentally in joining them. The couple are their own ministers in exchanging their vows, the man plighting his troth, while the woman gives hers, and then the man only gives a ring, putting it 'on the fourth finger of the left hand'.[34] The priest prays for the couple, reminding them of the faithful relationship between Isaac and Rebecca, and then makes the declaration: 'Those whome god hath joyned together : let no man put asundre' (Matt. 9.16).

This first stage of the ceremony ends with the priest's blessing of the couple, making the sign of the Cross, and the couple move into the quire while a Psalm is said or sung. The service concludes with a short litany, prayers for the couple and a final blessing. Cranmer requires a sermon to be delivered at this point, but provides, alternatively, a long biblically based homily, and directs the couple to receive Holy Communion the same day as their marriage.

The 1549 service was revised in 1552, but this version was only used briefly before Mary came to reign and the old liturgies were revived. Elizabeth restored the English Prayer Book and its final form was settled in 1662. It is still authorized for use, and remains popular.

The mild changes between 1549 and 1662 included the exclusion of the phrase in the closing prayers about the wives of the Patriarchs, 'amiable as Rachel, wise as Rebecca and faithful as Sarah', and the angelic blessing on Tobias. The blessings are reduced in status, now called prayers, and perhaps most significant, receiving communion is no longer required, only commended.

The Catholic Reformation

The Papacy and the Emperor Charles V, when not preoccupied with confronting Luther and Calvin, realized there was enough substance in the general criticisms of the Catholic Church to set in motion a process of internal reform. Central to this process was the Council of Trent (1545–63). Although sometimes given the status of the nineteenth Ecumenical Council as if it were a meeting of all the Catholic bishops in continuous session, it was in reality an intermittent sequence of meetings with varying membership over eighteen years. There were a number of issues where it seemed essential to find a common mind. Traditionalists from the Curia hoped to refute all the challenges of the Protestant Reformers, while the emperor and his supporters looked for freedom to read the Bible in the vernacular, for the virtual autonomy of bishops in their own dioceses and the right of clergy to be married. The debates vacillated over the years but the outcome was conservative on these issues, the traditionalist views were maintained, and the doctrinal and administrative control of the Pope was affirmed. Although some of the states in Southern Germany returned to Catholic loyalty, together with Hungary, Austria and Bohemia, the eventual outcome of the failure of the Catholics and Protestants to find enough common ground led to the tragedy of the thirty years war, only settled by the peace of Westphalia in 1648. The final decrees settled at Trent were given the status of canons and have been largely decisive for the Catholic Church ever since for matters they dealt with.

The Trent Canons declared that marriage was a special sacramental act created by the mutual consent of the partners. If it was also consummated physically it could not be dissolved, even in the case of adultery, though legal separation could be obtained. Separation did not, however, free the partners to remarry, and the indissolubility rule was a clear refutation of the view of the Reformers. The presence of a priest (or his representative) was required for a valid marriage, but his role was as chief witness to ensure that the appropriate legal requirements and free consent had been observed. From the time of Charlemagne onwards, a priest's presence had been ordered, with the purpose that he should pronounce a blessing, but the lack of it did not legally invalidate the marriage. So private consensual and clandestine marriage had continued, and the main purpose of the Trent decree about marriage, called Tametsi, was to ensure that all marriages were public events, properly witnessed. As Schillebeeckx has shown, the debate about this decree began with concern about publicity, and the early draft regulation suggested there should always be at least three lay witnesses. Only after fifteen sessions and much debate was it finally settled that a priest (or his representative) must be present.[35] The sacramental bond was created by the couple not the priest, but his blessing showed that the Church accepted that the bond had been validly made. It had to be duly recorded in the parish register.[36]

These Tridentine rules of course only applied to Catholic states, and had to be agreed with each government by concordat. The Protestant states went their own ways, and the eventual outcome for most of them was a dual system, a civil marriage required for all citizens, with church weddings by denominational rite as an optional extra. England was not bound by the Tridentine rules and for a good while was content that marriages should be solemnized only in parish churches.

The Church of England doctrine of marriage

After the excitements of the Reformation, the Church of England settled down with the doctrine of marriage expressed in Cranmer's service of 1549, as slightly amended in the text of the 1662 Book of Common Prayer. Because it was an amalgam of both classical and reform theology, the Caroline divines used it as a basis for their teaching. A good example is a pair of sermons by Jeremy Taylor entitled 'The Marriage Ring, or the Mysteriousness and Duties of Marriage'. Bishop Taylor (1613–67) was born in Cambridge and was for some time a Fellow of Gonville and Caius College. Appointed a Fellow of All Souls, Oxford by Archbishop Laud, he was briefly chaplain to King Charles I. Suspected of being a Romanist and Royalist, he went to Ireland, finally becoming Bishop of Dromore. Taylor's sermons, like those of Lancelot Andrewes, were typical of the learned discourses of the Caroline divines, very long, erudite, containing untranslated quotations from the classical Greek and Roman authors and assuming considerable acquaintance with the Christian Fathers, Clement, Tertullian, Jerome, etc. Such sermons were intended for publication. Taylor takes as his text Ephesians 5.32–3, and begins:

> The first blessing God gave to man was society, and that society was a marriage, and that marriage was confederate by God himself, and hallowed by a blessing; and at the same time, and for very many descending ages, not only by the instinct of nature, but by a super-added forwardness (God himself inspiring the desire), the world was most desirous of children, impatient of barrenness, accounting single life a curse, and a childless person hated by God. The world was rich and empty and able to provide for a more numerous posterity than it had.[37]

He then deals with the question of celibacy, which he understands as a temporary stage, and he suggests that the partnership of man and wife is more important than procreation:

> When the Messias was come, and the doctrine was published, and his ministers but few, and his disciples were to suffer persecution, and to be of an unsettled dwelling . . . and the state of marriage brought many inconveniences; it pleased God in this new creation to inspire into the hearts of his servants a disposition and strong desires to live a single life, lest the state of marriage should become an accidental impediment to the dissemination of the Gospel . . . But when the first necessities of the Gospel had been served, the state of marriage returned to its first blessing, for it was not good for man to be alone. Marriage is honourable in all men, so is not the single life, for in some it is a snare and a trouble in the flesh. Marriage was ordained by God, instituted in Paradise for the relief of a natural necessity; and the first blessing from the Lord; he gave to man not a friend, but a wife, that is, a friend and a wife too (for a good woman is in her soul the same that a man is, and she is a woman only in her body; that she may have the excellency of the one, and the useful-ness of the other, and become amiable in both): it is the seminary of the church, and brings forth sons and daughters unto God . . . Our Blessed Lord, though he was born of a maiden, yet she was veiled under the cover of marriage, and she was married to a widower; for Joseph the supposed father of our Lord had children by a former wife. The first miracle that Jesus ever did, was to do honour to a

wedding; marriage was in the world before sin, and it is in all ages of the world the greatest and most effective antidote against sin in which all the world had perished, if God had not made a remedy. And although sin hath soured marriage, and struck the man's head with cares, and the woman's bed with sorrows in the production of children; yet these are but the throes of life and glory.[38]

In the second part of this sermon, Taylor turns to the lot of married women, quoting Medea's speech from Euripides, and then suggests that the Genesis story has a different emphasis:

When Adam made that fond excuse for his folly in eating the forbidden fruit, he said 'the woman thou gavest to be *with* me, she gave me [the fruit]'. He says not 'The woman which thou gavest *to* me', no such thing; she is none of his goods, none of his possessions; not to be reckoned amongst his servants; God did not give her to him so; but 'the woman thou gavest to be with me' that is, to be my partner, the companion of my joys and sorrows, thou gavest her for use, not for dominion. The dominion of a man over his wife is no other than as the soul rules the body; for which it takes a mighty care, and uses it with a delicate tenderness, and cares for it in all contingencies.[39]

[Jeremy Taylor's positive view of marriage is often taken to reflect his own happy marriages. His first wife died and he remarried, having a number of children from both unions, several of whom died in infancy – which, sadly, was all too common at the time. Ed.]

9

From Elizabeth I to Elizabeth II

[As the Preface explains, this chapter has been constructed from a series of Bishop Coleman's notes, some substantial, some very incomplete. The sections up to, but not including those on the Lambeth Conferences are essentially Bishop Coleman's words, only slightly edited. The following sections, including the substantial note on 'gay marriage', are almost entirely the editor's words, but make use of Bishop Coleman's section headings, and in some cases very brief notes, which indicated the topics to be discussed. This applies until the section headed 'Modern liturgies'. From here to the end of the chapter the words are largely those of Bishop Coleman, and the two final comments entirely so.

Since the principal purpose of this book is to provide resource material for contemporary debates rather than to provide a series of answers to current problems, it was decided to present the notes for this part of the book in as coherent a manner as possible, rather than to produce a polished chapter, with a clear thread running through all of it. Ed.]

Introduction

The secular takeover and the parting of the ways

The four hundred years from the death of Elizabeth I to the start of the third millennium have seen a gradual parting of the ways between the traditional Christian attitude to marriage and the modern secular view of it. The churches still teach that marriage is a permanent union blessed by God, but in modern society the more widely held view is that marriage is a private and voluntary association between a man and woman who are equally free to end their commitment if the quality of their relationship deteriorates beyond an acceptable point.

Of course, to express the present situation in terms of these stark alternatives is too simple; most people's attitudes are not so clearly polarized. There is a good deal of residual if inchoate respect for the old tradition among non-Christians, and there are many Christians who have private qualifications about the Church's teaching, not least because their own experience or that of those close to them has made it seem no longer helpful or relevant.

It is not easy to identify the most important factors in the parting of the ways. The omnibus concepts often used to describe it are the Enlightenment or the advance of Secularism, and certainly these are useful explanations of the ways in which scientific and philosophical developments from the eighteenth century onwards have so changed our perspective of moral order and the status of Christian belief that the overarching hegemony of Christendom appears to have gone for ever. As the centuries passed, the churches were uneasily aware that the old world-view in the time of Elizabeth I, dominated in popular imagination by a stern and omnipotent God who called the shots, was fading. Gradually, this concept of God seemed to be a relic of the Old Testament, and the discontinuity between that and the character of Jesus revealed in the New Testament was often stressed. Mankind had come of age and the fear of God as the beginning of wisdom had been lost in the mists of time. One illustration of the difference can be seen in the reference in the Book of Common Prayer marriage service of 1662 to the bringing up of 'children in the fear of the Lord', compared with the *Common Worship* marriage service of 2000 that speaks of children 'growing to maturity in love'. Further, by the reign of Elizabeth II, for most people it was supposed that there was a free universe in relation to which, above, below or in the midst, there *might be* a benign and tolerant divinity who was able within his or her limited scope to assist the course of a human life or a nation in peril.

So in the early years of the third millennium, human society seems to be experiencing a growing sense of a single dominant perspective, loosely connected with the electronic culture, within which pluralism allows for a wide range of lifestyles and religious beliefs, all of which are to be respected but not allowed any kind of universal cohesive authority. Insofar as there are any universal rules for ordering life in our global village, they are expressed in the series of international declarations and covenants under the general heading of Human Rights. It can be said that the notional concept of human rights is, for a pluralist civilization, the logical development of Natural Law, but both are subject to blurred edges. Similarly in religion, while Judaism, Christianity and Islam have common roots, they also have marked differences in their attitudes to marriage and the status of women. It is sometimes in noting these differences that the modern secular world senses most sharply that the three monotheistic religions have certain clear incompatibilities. For a modern state therefore such rules as it makes about marriage, etc. will, while respecting diverse religious conviction, seek to regulate itself by a highest common factor. This leads to civil marriage, divorce, contraception and alternative partnerships and one-parent families all being recognized by the law, and supported as necessary with state funds.

The Christian reaction to the parting of the ways

Throughout the twentieth century the Christian churches of Europe had to come to terms with the hard fact that their long-held position as the arbiters of the meaning of marriage and sexual relationships was being gradually, but increasingly, eroded. Although – strictly speaking – history does not repeat itself, it does offer similarities for reflection. The present situation in which a pluralist secular society defines attitudes to sex and marriage for most people has some parallels with that which faced the early Christian church *vis-à-vis* the Roman empire in the second century AD. But it is by no means clear that the Christian churches are as yet confident that they will be able to regain lost ground, nor are they agreed about how to do it. A rough guide to the Christian response to secularism in the twentieth century might be described as an anxious pondering of the difficult question, 'Can there be a happy alliance between tradition and modernism?' Some Christians will answer: 'Yes, if we can identify afresh what is still essential in our traditional attitude to marriage, and then go on to filter out all that is transient and ephemeral in modernism.'

One obvious demonstration of the erosion of church influence was the series of government Acts that enabled and facilitated divorce for any couple who seriously wished to finish their marriage. Another was the recognition that contraceptive advice must be available for everyone who was likely to be or soon to become sexually active. Once upon a time the purchase of condoms had been furtive; now they had become openly available not only in chemists but in supermarkets, petrol stations and vending machines everywhere. Any notion of chastity had been replaced by pressure to practise safe sex. Thirdly, for most people, both serial marriage and open cohabitation had ceased to have any moral significance. Not having a sexual partner was more likely to raise the suspicion of something not quite right. Even gay people had to demonstrate their freedom. So in a society that had decided that the value of personal liberty and choice outweighed almost all other obligations, it was impossible for any government to continue to impose regulations that interfered with that personal liberty. Obviously, any government has the duty to control some aspects of its citizens' life for the common good and makes regulations to prevent serious dangers like drunken driving and to discourage relatively trivial ones like scattering litter. Some rules are positive in intention, such as all children having to go to school (or have adequate education at home); some measures are alleviative of hardship, such as the sickness benefit and the support of single mothers. Whereas the encouragement of stable marriage and difficult divorce was part of state policy until the 1950s, it is so no longer. The recent delay in implementing the Intention of the Family Act, 1999, that all potential divorcees should have obligatory consultation, demonstrates the inability of a government in the twenty-first century to impose restraint.

The same story is true of both the age and the context for sexual relationships. Officially the age of consent is sixteen, but it is widely disregarded and the notion that it is only within marriage is ludicrous to many modern people.

The response to all this by the churches has been characterized in three reactions: contradiction of the prevailing morality, competition, or co-operation within limits. All these need examination as all of them are intellectually and theologically respectable. However, it soon appears that the categories are not watertight.

Contradiction

Christian morality has always been distinct from the ways of the world, as is any religious faith which looks to revelation as its guiding principle. Judaism, Islam and Christianity differ in what they hold to be revealed but often maintain the same or similar moral principles (Islam is strictest on marriage and sex). Therefore – in terms of the reaction of 'contradiction' – when the prevailing morality is at odds, Christians simply go their own way. The strength of this position is its clarity,[1] its weakness is that it will only refer to the congregation of the faithful. More conservative Roman Catholics and evangelicals prefer this *humanae vitae* according to which those outside the company of the faithful simply suffer (here or hereafter), and this, it is believed, is their own fault.

Competition

This reaction suggests that the Christian way is simply better. However, the questions arise, 'Is it better because it is Christ-backed, given grace?' and 'Is it better because it conforms best to Natural Law and human rights?' Also, 'Can the advantages of the Christian way be evaluated by results?' To feel any justifiable confidence in this competitive response requires a kind of internal Christian dialogue to test the other side's strength and weaknesses and to assess as honestly as one can what history and experience show. Thus Luther and Calvin simply found the old (non-Christian) teaching leading to miserable results. They re-examined Scripture and found it did not justify the old teaching, but it did, rightly interpreted, show what the correct teaching was. It may be necessary to distinguish between the teaching precepts and the justification you give for them, e.g. were all the anti-bastard rules a matter of prudence, family name preservation and resistance to syncretism, or were they the true revelation of Jahweh in the Old Testament and of Jesus in the New? So check it out. But the result – in terms of this reaction – is always the expected result; we are right, though our mode of explanation may vary. Christian marriages are happier, longer, more durable, etc. just as church schools are better quality. Does the Christian way offer the Good Life in capital letters that anyone can recognize? Bishop John Robinson suggested that Christian love was a better way than any code-bound morality.[2]

Convergence

This reaction takes natural and revealed truth more equally. It takes God as saying something like, 'I have many things to teach you, and some of them come through Cyrus, rod of my anger. If you do not understand the need for sexual equality, if you do not comprehend your unloving forms of behaviour, if you do not understand the truths of all the new theologies, you are missing out on some of the truth. You can confidently swim in the wide river I have created.'[3]

In general, therefore, the reaction of convergence implies that there is some valuable information on both sides but neither is adequate by itself. This reaction encourages a creative dialogue between the Christian and the secular humanist, one that is open to the possibility that both might learn from the other.

The historical background to marriage issues in the twentieth century

After the Elizabethan settlement the situation, for a time, was relatively static, except for the development of civil marriage and divorce. The next period can be represented as a decline and fall but also, with at least equal truth, as a clash between different moralities about sexual and marital relationships with no synthesis between the churches and the secular thinkers. What follows is limited, for the most part, to England, with special emphasis on the Church of England experience.

The present reality is that the Christian churches find themselves in a position *vis-à-vis* marriage in some respects closer to that faced by the early church than to that of the long period of Christendom; they are offering an alternative to the standard practice of the community. Whereas from Justinian to Cranmer it was assumed, at least officially, that the church was entitled to enunciate how all citizens should be married, that privilege has been steadily eroded. The majority of weddings are now civil ceremonies conducted by a Registrar, and church weddings are seen as an alternative for those who have some connection with a church or are attracted to the traditional setting and ceremony. There is, at the same time, some residual sense or folk memory that a wedding blessed in church might be more durable, and some statistical evidence supports this. It remains true that everyone has a legal right to be married in the local church of the parish where they live, and the residence qualification can be satisfied by quite tenuous links, but for various reasons it is no longer the preferred option for many people. These reasons are considered later, but the consequence has been that marriage liturgies are no longer chiefly concerned to reassure couples that by marrying they escape the wrath of God for their sexual sinfulness and that their union will be blessed with healthy children. Instead the liturgy is a welcoming event, encouraging couples to place their already existing (in most cases) relationship of cohabitation, and quite often their (equally present) children in the safer and more durable context of God's blessing.

Europe

The leaders of the Reformation had hoped that by their emphasis on marriage they would be inaugurating a time of improved sexual morality, but this was not to be. The unexpected consequence of the attack on Rome was a gradual weakening of the belief in one universal and stable moral order. (But of course, the Reformation was not the only cause of this change. The Age of Reason encouraged the right to think for oneself and implicitly challenged the traditional role of the church as the teacher and guardian of what was right conduct.) As we have seen, in Christendom, the civil authorities usually allowed the Christian Church to be in charge of marriage and matrimonial problems, exercised within the rules of Canon Law and administered by the ecclesiastical courts. This tidiness was now threatened. Whereas up to the Reformation there were two systems, Catholic in the West, Orthodox in the East, from then the diversity increased. Luther and Calvin devised their own forms of service, and Cranmer followed. One married according to one's denomination, and as Luther himself had suggested, the formalities of marriage were for governments rather than churches to arrange. So there was a slow but decisive shift towards civic marriage.

In Europe much depended on the official religion of particular states; the South was mostly Catholic, and the Tametsi decree of the Council of Trent had to be followed, while in the Protestant North each ruling prince could make his own regulations within a general pattern. In France the situation changed during the French Revolution and the church was excluded from any political or legal role, but in the aftermath there was a concordat between Napoleon and the Papacy which restored some official scope to the church, but not its jurisdiction in marriage. From 1804 onwards, when the Code Napoleon was promulgated, civil marriage was obligatory, though a religious ceremony could be held on a separate occasion. In nineteenth-century Germany, the Chancellor, Bismarck, was pushing relentlessly towards a political union of the Principalities under the leadership of Prussia. In 1870 he was infuriated when the Pope, Pius IX, encouraged the First Vatican Council to declare the doctrine of papal infallibility and the duty of all nations to owe allegiance to the Holy See. Bismarck responded with a programme of cultural war against Catholicism, the *Kulturkampf*, which included the requirement of civil marriage for all, Catholics included, a reaffirmation that the Tametsi decree was not binding on Prussia and its allies. In more recent times the pattern has varied widely among nation states, some requiring universal civil marriage with an optional church ceremony, some allowing a choice between civil and church marriage of equal validity. The American system is a universal federal preliminary, followed by state rules and freedom to choose either a religious or civic ceremony.[4]

Marriage in England: seventeenth to nineteenth centuries

Mandatory church marriage

In England, throughout Stuart and early Georgian times there were more urgent matters to occupy parliamentary time than revising the marriage service. Cranmer's work was meant to be the norm, except in Cromwell's brief reign when the Book of Common Prayer was banned. Neither Catholics nor dissenters were allowed to have their own rites. But this did not mean all marriages took place in or at the door of a parish church. Since the fundamental rule for valid marriage was consent, exchanged in a variety of ways, followed by physical consummation, people who lived together and risked a penalty of cohabiting could escape by claiming that they had exchanged vows, clasped hands, etc., and were therefore married. It has been estimated that perhaps a third of the married couples in England in the sixteenth century had not had their union blessed by a priest. As Lawrence Stone has put it:

> It cannot be emphasized too strongly that according to ecclesiastical law, the spousals were as legally binding as the church wedding, though to many laity it was no more than a conditional contract. Any sort of exchange of promises before witnesses which was followed by cohabitation was regarded in law as a valid marriage.[5]

In the eighteenth century, changes in social patterns of life, concern for preserving family property and puritan influences brought pressure on the government to end the legal recognition of informal marriages. This was an urban rather than a rural problem. In country life, the rules for courting were well understood, and pairing off took place mostly in public; convention and peer pressure discouraged too much physical intimacy. The man who made a girl pregnant while courting her would be expected to marry her. While it was possible for a couple to exchange their vows entirely privately and still be counted as married, most people preferred to make a public declaration of their spousals with selected friends and family present as witnesses, unless there was family opposition. The couple would then go to bed or into a field or other convenient spot and consummate the marriage privately.[6]

In cities, however, and especially in London, there was an alternative method of obtaining an ostensibly church marriage. This was provided by irregular clergy, who conducted clandestine marriages as a private business from apartments within or near the Fleet prison, of which they may even have been prisoners themselves. Although technically legal, such marriages did not require family agreement, local witnesses or banns, and were therefore attractive to couples who wished to avoid publicity, for good or fraudulent reasons. Although the parochial clergy were deprived of their fees they might be complicit if they personally approved of the match but anticipated local protest if the wedding took place in their own churches. Apart from the activities of irregular clergy, the more general problems caused by informal marriage were uncertainty about children's legitimacy and right to inherit, the status of widows, and the risk that unmarried heiresses might be lured into temporary marriages whose actual purpose was to gain their estates. In Jane Austen's novel *Pride and Prejudice*, this is one of the sub-plots.

Parliament's solution was the Clandestine Marriages Act of 1753, usually called the Hardwicke Act, which made it obligatory for all marriages to take place within the Church of England system. Only marriages performed by an ordained Anglican clergyman in the church building after the calling of banns three times (or a licence from the bishop) were legally valid. At least one of the parties had to be resident in the parish where they married, and parental consent was required for those under twenty-one. The only exceptions made were for Quakers and Jews who could use their own Meeting Houses or Synagogues. Any Anglican priest who attempted to marry without using the Prayer Book service was liable to transportation, and altering the marriage registers was a capital offence. For obvious reasons the Hardwicke Act was not much opposed by the Church of England.

Implied in this legislation was the ending of the legal recognition that betrothal or informal consent created a marriage. In future, such agreements were to have no legal force and became like the modern system of engagement. The only remedy for a broken betrothal promise was to sue for a breach of promise of marriage, which provided some intriguing confrontations in court, but has now been abolished. The Hardwicke Act was given a tough passage in Parliament, because although it would solve some problems it would create others. It was argued that the poor would be disadvantaged as they could not afford church weddings, that a young woman who trusted the promise of marriage by a man she loved and admitted to her bed would now face abandonment if she became pregnant, and the actual effect would be to weaken religion and morality and encourage licentiousness.[7] In practice, however, the ordinary understanding that a promise to marry, especially if written down, imposed a real obligation was not changed just because the law said so. Conversely, some betrothed women found themselves in a more precarious situation as a result of the Act. If they became pregnant but remained unmarried they had their own personal rights and property, and could look for maintenance for the child; but if they married, they lost all these rights and were virtually dependent on the support of their husband. If, while betrothed, they had a regular paid employment, as many of them did, in domestic service, it was better to put the child out to fostering, and retain the job until or unless the natural father's own position was adequate to support a family.

It was not the main intention of the Hardwicke Act to give the Church of England a privileged position, and in fact its exclusive role was short-lived. It was obviously unfair to the other Christian churches, whose membership now numbered at least a tenth of the population, mostly Catholics and Methodists, but more fundamentally it was inconsistent with the principle that all citizens were entitled to equality before the law. The Marriage Act of 1836 corrected this inequality.[8] It allowed civil Registrars to register other places of worship for marriage (and, in 1889, for the minister thereof to act as Registrar of the marriage) and to provide for registry office weddings without any religious content at all. This dual system has continued virtually unchanged in England, but the range of 'approved premises' for civic weddings has been widened by the 1994 Marriage Act to include stately homes, hotels and reputedly Newcastle Football Club and the First Class Lounge at Ashford railway station.

After a slow initial take-up, civil weddings have gradually replaced church weddings as the most popular and it is usually assumed that this reflects the secularization of society. This is obviously true for couples who technically are entitled to be married in church but prefer the relatively informal procedure, or whose religious commitment is too unformed for participation in a church rite. But there are other contributory factors to this shift away from church weddings. In particular, the Catholic Church's refusal to marry divorcees and the Church of England's reluctance to do so has made many couples choose the alternatives of the Unitarian and Methodist Churches, who do not necessarily reject couples where one or both of them has a previous marriage partner still living, or the registry office. It is also clear that some government officials take the view that these days it would be more logical and administratively tidy for all weddings to be supervised by Registrars, even at a railway station, religious ceremonies being available for those who choose them, but with no legal effect. This universal civil marriage would also remove any of the difficulties about recognizing minor or quasi-religious sects that are bound to arise in a multi-faith society.

The Lambeth Conferences

Nearly all the thirteen Lambeth Conferences between 1867 and 1998 contain references to marriage both in the official resolutions and in Section Reports. While the need to maintain the Christian ideal of monogamous lifelong marriage is consistently agreed, the related topics considered show a shifting pattern of anxieties and uncertainties where the bishops have been asked to express a common mind. Thus in 1878 there is a recognition that local legislatures may impose rules for civil marriage, but the churches 'should maintain the sanctity of marriage, agreeable to the principles set forth in the Word of God, as the Church of Christ hath hitherto received the same'.

Some of the more important resolutions are listed below:

On divorce

This perennial subject was clearly faced in 1888 by Resolution 4 in the Section on 'The Ethical Standards of the Church':

(a) That, inasmuch as Our Lord's words expressly forbid Divorce, except in the case of fornication and adultery, the Christian Church cannot recognize Divorce in any other than the excepted case, or give any sanction to the marriage of any person who has been divorced contrary to this law, during the life of the other party.

(b) That under no circumstances ought the guilty party, in the case of divorce for fornication or adultery, to be regarded, during the lifetime of the innocent party, as a fit recipient of the blessing of the Church on marriage.

(c) That, recognizing the fact that there always has been a difference of opinion in the Church on the question whether Our Lord meant to forbid marriage to the innocent party in a divorce for adultery, the Conference recommends that the Clergy should not be instructed to refuse the Sacraments or other privileges of the Church to those who, under civil sanction, are thus married.[9]

Twenty years later, at the 1908 Conference, the issue of remarriage after divorce returned, and the same resolutions were reaffirmed with an addition discouraging a church blessing. The resolutions were approved by a very narrow majority, 87 to 84:

When an innocent person has, by means of a court of law, divorced a spouse for adultery, and desires to enter into another contract of marriage, it is undesirable that such a contract should receive the blessing of the Church.[10]

The disapproval of remarriage in church in 1908 is immediately preceded by the insistence that the sacraments should not necessarily be forbidden to 'the innocent party in a divorce' following a civil marriage. The issue is revisited in later conference reports, and important changes occur. In 1930, the case of a divorced and remarried person wishing to receive Holy Communion is to be referred to the bishop 'subject to provincial regulations'.[11] In 1948 there is another explicit change in the recommendations. The view that 'the leniency accorded to an "innocent party" should be denied to a person guilty of adultery who has repented of his or her sin' is firmly rejected, along with the assumption that the verdict of a civil court should always be binding on the church in matters of divorce.[12] There is also a new emphasis on the church's pastoral role in helping those who have remarried after divorce, and although there is still no indication (in 1948) of the approval of a remarriage in church, the realization that many of those involved are 'victims' paved the way for later, more liberal views on remarriage.[13]

Mixed marriages

We desire to warn members of our Communion against contracting
marriages with Roman Catholics under the conditions imposed by
modern Roman canon law, especially as these conditions involve a
marriage ceremony without any prayer or invocation of the divine
blessing, and also a promise to have their children brought up in a
religious system which they cannot themselves accept. (1908
Resolution 67)[14]

The 1978 conference sounds a more conciliatory note, following the
report of the Anglican–Roman Catholic Commission on 'The Theology of Marriage and its Application to Mixed Marriages' (1975).
There was agreement that such marriages could take place in either
church, and that in the case of children, it was sufficient that the
Roman Catholic parish priest had given written assurance that he had
put the Catholic partner 'in mind of his or her obligations'.[15] [There is
some evidence, however, that in the actual practice of mixed marriages, many tensions remained after 1978, and that the spirit of the
1975 report was not always followed.]

On polygamy

It is the opinion of this Conference that persons living in polygamy
be not admitted to baptism, but that they be accepted as candidates
and kept under Christian instruction until such time as they shall
be in a position to accept the law of Christ. [However, wives of
polygamists may be admitted to baptism if the local church so
decides.] (1888 Resolution 5)[16]

The topic is revisited in 1988. Here there is a stronger awareness of
the pastoral and moral problems that arise in certain countries, especially the problem of justice to women and children who have been in
polygamous relationships. After stressing the ideal of monogamy, it is
recommended that the polygamist himself, who wishes to join the
Anglican Church, may himself be baptized, along with his believing
wives and children, on certain conditions, including the consent of the
local Anglican community.[17]

On birth control

Here we can see an interesting and important development, notably in the teaching of the 1930 Conference. In 1908 the strict rules still apply:

> 41. The Conference regards with alarm the growing practice of the artificial restriction of the family, and earnestly calls upon all Christian people to discountenance the use of all artificial means of restriction as demoralizing to character and hostile to national welfare.
> 42. The Conference affirms that deliberate tampering with nascent life is repugnant to Christian morality.[18]

The 1920 Lambeth Conference reflects similar views, but there is a suggestion that because 'so-called prophylactics' are an invitation to vice, they should not be distributed 'before exposure to infection'. The implication is that the rules could be different for those who already have venereal disease, for whom treatment 'is an entirely different matter'. This could be read as a softening of the absolutist position. However, by the time of the 1930 Conference there is a sea change. Although this conference continued to argue that sexual intercourse outside marriage was a grievous sin (Section 18), in other ways it marked an important shift in Anglican teaching. Most importantly, the use of artificial methods of birth control, within marriage, was now considered to be permissible.

> Sex is a God-given factor in the life of mankind and its functions are therefore essentially noble and creative. Correspondingly great is the responsibility for the right use of it. We place this in the forefront of our report, for as it seems to us a new day has dawned, in which sex and sex matters are emerging from the mists of suspicion and even shame, in which for centuries they have been enveloped into the clear atmosphere of candour, honesty and truth . . . A veritable revolution has taken place in regard to the position of women, and this, in countries where for centuries she has been the victim of a hide-bound tradition.[19]

This view is still the official position of the Anglican Church. It was restated in the encyclical letter of the 1958 Lambeth Conference, with the claim that family planning 'in such ways as are mutually acceptable to husband and wife in Christian conscience, is a right and important factor in Christian family life'. According to one of her biographers, these words came in time to be of comfort to Marie Stopes (a prominent campaigner for birth control since her bestselling *Family Life* of 1918), who died later that year, aware of a growing acceptance of her once 'scandalous' views.[20]

On extra-marital sex

Although the conferences display a movement of liberalization with respect to birth control and a softening of attitudes to homosexuality (from denunciation to recommendations of sympathetic study), the view that extramarital sex is wrong is not changed. In line with earlier conferences, the report of the 1998 Conference includes the resolution (under 1.10):

> This Conference: . . . in view of the teaching of Scripture, upholds faithfulness in marriage between a man and a woman in lifelong union, and believes that abstinence is right for those who are not called to marriage.[21]

It is important to note that the official disavowal of all sexuality outside marriage, still affirmed in 1998, rightly or wrongly, has been challenged by an increasing number of Christians in recent decades. A good example of a new approach can be found in the 1963 report *Towards a Quaker View of Sex*.[22] In several places, this monograph refers to the work of the Anglican theologian, Dr Sherwin Bailey, in all but once case (p. 39) favourably. While there are strong statements about the sinfulness of sexual activity that does not respect the other person (36, 40, 44), on two grounds the old view of no sex outside marriage is questioned, and the responsibility of where intimacy should stop is placed with the individual (18). The first ground is that in a true faith 'there can be no ultimate contradiction between what it demands of us and what in practice works – works towards complete human fulfilment' (10). Obviously, this raises large questions about the measurement of 'fulfilment', but an important empirical emphasis is introduced to the debate which carries overtones of 'experience' in the Wesleyan Quadrilateral. The second ground is a denial that the difference between right and wrong can be made 'in terms of an external pattern of behaviour' (39).[23] The 1966 report to the British Council of Churches, *Sex and Morality*, shows a similar hesitation in advocating a complete ban (in terms of Christian morality) on all sexual acivity outside marriage.[24]

Church of England reports

Issues regarding sexuality and marriage which began to be obvious in the 1920s and 1930s were subject to greater scrutiny after the Second World War. This awareness led, in the case of the Church of England, to a series of weighty reports, now mostly forgotten but worth study. Often there is important data in the appendices.

Among these reports attention should be drawn to:

Putting Asunder, *1966*[25]

The principal subject of this report is the relationship of civil marriage law to the beliefs and discipline of the Church. The most important recommendation was that it would be appropriate to drop the old 'matrimonial offence' as a ground for divorce in favour of the criterion of 'breakdown of marriage'. In the main body of the report there is a thoughtful set of replies to the objections to such a change (33–4), which argue that the alleged disadvantages of the change are mistaken or exaggerated. While noting that this change might widen the ground for civil divorce, the clause (8,2) in the Matrimonial Causes Act 1965 is stressed which insists that no clergyman will be obliged to remarry divorced people, or be forced to allow them to be remarried within their jurisdiction (115–24). Another important topic concerns nullity. Reflecting on the 1955 Archbishop's Commission on Nullity, the report rejects the view that refusal to consummate a marriage should be a ground for nullity. Sexual impotence, or the hiding of important information that bears upon the agreement of a marriage contract, should be grounds for nullity, but refusal to consummate, in itself, was something that occurred *after* the marriage contract, and should therefore be grounds for divorce rather than nullity (124–5).

Marriage, Divorce and the Church, *1971*[26]

The most important element in this report is the plea to allow the remarriage in church of divorced Christians, whether they be the allegedly innocent or guilty parties, subject to certain conditions. Earlier in the report there is an account of the former, negative assessment of this view, going back to the 1908 Lambeth Conference (p. 7), and then the grounds for the proposed change are set out, with special reference to the persuasive arguments of Bishop Montefiore (pp. 71–2, 79–80). Further, it is claimed that such a change would not be at odds with either the Protestant or the Eastern Orthodox traditions, and would be in keeping with Scripture, bearing in mind its stress on forgiveness, a grace that can loose as well as bind, and that can 'create again' (pp. 72–3).

Marriage and the Church's Task, 1978[27]

This report arose out of the rejection by General Synod, in 1974, of the 1971 report *Marriage, Divorce and the Church* (also known as the 'Root Commission', after its chairman, Professor Howard Root). Another part of the context for this 1978 report was the passing of the Divorce Reform Act 1969, which came into operation in 1971, and which, adopting the recommendation of *Putting Asunder*, had abolished the concept of 'matrimonial offence'. The central part of the report is a review of the arguments for and against allowing the remarriage of divorced persons in church, and the majority view, adopted in the recommendations, is that the Church of England should revise its regulations in order to allow remarriage, within the lifetime of a former spouse, with the permission of the bishop (p. 110).

The majority rejected the view (approved by Schillebeeckx) that the dissolution of a marriage was neither *permissible* nor *possible* (53). Among the arguments was a desire to avoid the large-scale traffic in annulments which accompanied the rigorous rules, and which were frequently made use of both before and after the Reformation, and which are easily liable to abuse when a ground of defective 'intention' at the time of marriage is alleged.[28] In contrast, while Calvin continued to speak of the bond (*vinculum*) between man and wife, it was a bond which God had forged, and therefore God could dissolve (54). Additional arguments included (i) 'the faith that marriage is "for life" must also reckon with the fact that marriages can and do break down . . .'; (ii) the changing situation in which the church finds itself; and (iii) the fact that the church's invariable refusal to remarry 'leads many people to conclude that the Church regards the sin involved . . . as the one sin that can never be forgiven' (87–8).

The fourth appendix (138–9) comprises a useful discussion of New Testament passages relevant to the issues, including an account of different interpretations of what is meant by *porneia*. It is argued that Jesus did not seek to *change* the Deuteronomic law, but to interpret it. More significantly, it is argued that while the ethics of Jesus are 'radical, spontaneous, generous and free', the early Christians tended to regard his precepts as 'rules', and to treat them as 'laws'. It is in this context that an earlier, and important, section of the Report should be read:

> Jesus taught that marriage, according to God's will in creation, was lifelong, and that husband and wife were 'one'. What is not so clear is, first, the precise significance which this teaching has within the total context of Jesus' proclamation of the kingdom of God and his own ministry of challenge, forgiveness and renewal; and second, how the Church is to be faithful to the mind of Christ in developing a doctrine of marriage and a sound pastoral care for all those married people it comes into contact with, not least those whose marriages have broken down. (41)

An Honourable Estate, *1988*[29]

This was the report of a working party established by the Standing Committee of the General Synod of the Church of England, whose membership included Bishop Coleman. The focus was on what church policy should be 'in the context of changing contemporary attitudes and laws concerning marriage' (Preface).

The discussion begins with an insistence that marriage is a *human* rather than a Christian institution, although it can be given a specifically Christian meaning (7). Here there is an echo of a statement in *Marriage and the Church's Task*: 'It is more appropriate to speak of "a Christian doctrine of marriage" than of "a doctrine of Christian marriage"' (31). This does not take away from the suggestion that marriage is instituted by God, or that it is in some sense a 'mystical union', but marriage is rooted in a grace that is available to all human beings, as symbolized in the 'Noachian' covenant and commandments. It is a 'sacrament', but in a special sense, in that it is 'the only sacrament where the parties themselves are the ministers, the priest acting as prime witness to it' (10–15).[30]

Following a review of *Putting Asunder* the report then considers five options, ending with a strong endorsement of the fifth, which reads: 'To affirm the present position and to continue to make full use of the opportunities it offers to the church' (61). [Rejected were (i) giving the civil authority sole responsibility for marriages, (ii) the removal of the obligation of the Church of England to conduct marriages (for those qualified), (iii) the restriction of church marriages to those cases where at least one party was baptized,[31] and (iv) the introduction of universal, civil preliminaries.]

Issues in Human Sexuality, *1991*[32]

This comprises a statement by the House of Bishops of the General Synod of the Church of England, prepared by a small group in 1991. There is a positive statement of the Christian vision for human sexuality (p. 19), but with respect to the contentious issues of the time the statement was conservative. Outside marriage, 'full sexual relations, or behaviour that would normally and naturally lead to such relations, have no place in friendship or, indeed, in the life of the single person in general' (24, cf. 18). The same ideal is applied to homosexual relations, although – admitting the current controversy with respect to 'a loving and faithful homophile partnership, in intention lifelong' – the statement adds that while unable to commend such a life 'we do not reject those who sincerely believe it is God's call to them' (41). In the case of the ordained, however, this lifestyle is not to be accepted: 'Because of the distinctive nature of their calling, status and consecration, to allow such a claim on their part would be seen as placing that way of life in all respects on a par with heterosexual marriage as a reflection of God's purposes in creation'(45).

Two church reports from 2003

This section on church reports will end with a brief comment on two recent publications. *Being Human: A Christian Understanding of Personhood Illustrated with Reference to Power, Money, Sex and Time*[33] provides a valuable contribution to the topics discussed in this chapter. The value is in the exploration of the context in which the more specific issues need to be seen, in particular, an awareness of issues about human nature (1–2) and 'Listening to Scripture' (12–13). As I stress in the following section, we must not confuse 'literalist' arguments with genuine 'biblical arguments'. These themes lead to a deeper understanding of the 'relational' side of sexuality in the Bible.

The more recent *Some Issues in Human Sexuality: A Guide to the Debate*[34] is a discussion document from the House of Bishops' Group on Issues in Human Sexuality. Once again, this document is not so much a report on marriage as an exploration designed to achieve an understanding of human sexuality within the context of Christian theology. Thus the second chapter discusses the appropriate use of the Bible in sexual ethics, seeking an understanding that combines submission to a text that has real authority with a trust that God is at work within our honest and rational efforts at interpretation (e.g. pp. 42–4). This is followed by an overview of recent work in the theology of sexuality. Among areas that are indicated as in need of further reflection are those of bisexuality (ch. 6) and transsexualism (ch. 7). The final chapter discusses the question of how current controversies should be handled, and I will add the following comment.

In many areas of practical ethics we come to a point where it is clear that equally honest and intelligent people disagree. (It must be stressed that there are also many areas where they will tend to agree, for example, in the evil of female genital mutilation; but it is precisely in the areas that are often referred to as 'dilemmas' that understandable disagreement is found, because the shared principles referred to in the preface are in tension.) In the face of such 'rational' disagreement there are occasions when we can simply 'agree to disagree', but there are others when some *decision* has to be made, such as what the civil law should permit or what church policy will be. In such cases we need to move from questions of 'substantive justice' – where we know that disagreement will continue – to questions of 'procedural justice', in which we try to find a method for making, as fairly as possible, the decisions that have to be made. [Ed.]

An extended note on 'gay marriage'

[At this point in his draft, Bishop Coleman indicated that he intended to write a section on the subject of 'gay marriage'. Unfortunately, there is no material in the draft showing how he intended to approach this topic, but from several conversations with him, as well as from his other writings, the editor can outline the sort of position he is likely to have supported. However, it must be stressed that not only is all the wording of this section that of the editor, the underlying philosophy –

which is also that of the editor – is only what he *believes* Bishop Coleman's position to have been.][35]

There is, in the first place, a semantic problem with the notion of 'gay marriage' or 'lesbian marriage', given the etymological roots of 'marriage' through the French *mariage* to the Latin *maritus* and *marita* (husband and wife), and hence, as we saw in Chapter 7, Justinian's definition of marriage as 'a union between a man and a woman involving a single shared way of life'. In consequence, even if it is admitted – as it will be here – that there is a good case for the claim that same-sex couples ought to have the moral and legal right to make public commitments that (in some ways) correspond to traditional marriage, it does not follow that we should use the term 'marriage' for such public acts. However, it may follow that such couples should have the privileges and responsibilities that normally go with marriage in matters of inheritance, taxation, pension benefits, etc.[36]

This point soon becomes more than a matter of semantics when the public stake in the way in which children are raised is brought into the picture. Although many single parents and many non-traditional couples do a successful job in raising children, society may have good reasons for wishing to encourage a system in which children, typically, have two parents of different genders. There is empirical evidence (admittedly, still of a controversial nature) which suggests that this is, at least at the statistical level, a preferred way of child-rearing.

The upshot of this suggestion is that even if one supports the right of same-sex couples to enter into public contracts that are *analogous* to marriage, there is a strong argument for not using the term 'marriage' for these contracts. This point could be strengthened by reference to the frequency of public ceremonies for 'same-sex unions' that were not usually called 'marriages', not only in the ancient world, but – prior to the fourteenth century – even in the Christian world.[37]

The foregoing makes no reference to Christian doctrine, and at this point the obvious objections to any kind of formal union between members of the same sex, made on behalf of more conservative Christians (as well as Muslims and many others), need to be addressed. Behind these objections to a formal union lie more general objections to any homosexual practice, and therefore these objections need to be considered. After considering these objections it is likely that most people will hold one of four positions:

Position A (a typically 'liberal' position) holds that there is no sound argument against the morality of homosexual activity, provided it has equivalent rules for the protection of the vulnerable and the well-being of others to those that apply in heterosexual relations. In consequence, not only should same-sex unions of a formal nature be allowed, the church should be prepared to bless such unions.

Position B (a typical 'conservative' position) holds that there is something manifestly amiss in homosexual activity, and that the wrongness of it does not depend only upon religious revelation, and therefore that same-sex unions should not be given formal approval by the state. (Needless to say, this disapproval would not prevent some people from making formal acts of same-sex union, it would only prevent any legal recognition of them. It would also bar church blessings – at least officially.)

Position C (one of the compromises sometimes suggested) holds that there are serious grounds for doubting the morality of homosexual activity, but these grounds are not sufficient to demand that the state, as a secular power, prevent their formal recognition. This might be because the arguments are held to be too clearly theological and therefore not to carry weight for non-believers, or because the arguments, although not only theological, do not have enough force to show that homosexual activity is a serious enough offence to demand that the state withhold formal recognition of formal same-sex unions. For this position, however, official church blessings would be inappropriate.

Position D (the one that will be suggested at the end of this section), holds that while position A may have the best case, because of the arguments that will be discussed, in particular the one relating to tradition, we need to enter a period of profound reflection and dialogue (and for the Christian, of prayer), before making drastic changes.

To return to the objections, notably those underlying what I have called position B, the most familiar objection is biblical (although there are others, as I shall indicate later).[38] Here we may imagine the following dialogue, which gradually becomes more interesting and rational. Needless to say, the dialogue concerns the appropriateness, for a Christian, of homosexual *activity*, given the fact that sexual orientation, in many cases, is beyond anyone's control.[39]

CONSERVATIVE: The story of Sodom, in Genesis 19, indicates that homosexuality is against the divine law.
LIBERAL: But this story is about breaking laws of hospitality and about gang rape; it has nothing to say about loving, same-sex relationships.[40]
CONSERVATIVE: But then what about Leviticus 18 and 20 (part of

the 'Holiness Code') and other Old Testament passages concerning homosexuality, such as Deuteronomy 23.17?[41]

LIBERAL: Some of these passages certainly outlaw homosexuality,[42] but they are part of a whole range of Old Testament regulations that no modern conservative believes to be binding. Take, for example, the purification rules (involving animal sacrifice) following haemorrhage, in Leviticus 15.

CONSERVATIVE: But you are neglecting the vital distinction, clearly made for example at the Council of Jerusalem (Acts 15), between the ritual laws of the Old Testament, which no longer apply, and the moral laws (written in the hearts of all people, according to Romans 2) which apply for ever.

(Now, at last, the dialogue is beginning the enter the realms of a rational debate.)

LIBERAL: I agree with this distinction, but there are two problems with it. First, it is not always clear when an Old Testament rule is 'ritual' or 'moral', or indeed, whether there was a rigid distinction along these lines in the early days of Israel. Which, for example, is the sabbath rule – as part of the Decalogue it would seem to be purely moral, but as changed from Saturday to Sunday it might seem to be intimately related to ritual matters? What too of the rule that an animal involved in bestiality should be killed (Lev. 20.15)? Surely this is wrong – perhaps at all times, and certainly for us – but if the sexual rules of the Old Testament are 'moral' rather than 'ritual' then why does this rule not apply now? Moreover, commands like the killing of those who strike their parents (Ex. 21.15) are surely moral rather than ritual, but few conservatives now advocate them! What too of all the Old Testament laws about usury that are either ignored by most conservatives, or interpreted in ways that rob them of any practical force?

CONSERVATIVE: But all passages like these must be interpreted in the context of the whole of Scripture.

LIBERAL: I heartily agree, and that is why both of us – in our own ways – 'pick and choose' when it comes to individual verses of the Bible. This does not make the selection purely subjective because both of us are seeking to interpret earlier verses by the standards and principles of the later prophets, and of Jesus. I admit that I 'pick and choose', but I insist that you do also, and both of us have good reasons – based on a belief in a growing level of revelation – for doing so. Remember that Jesus said 'You shall no longer say "An eye for an eye and a tooth for a tooth . . ."', which was a direct reference to a commandment in the book of Exodus (Matt. 5.38; cf. Ex. 21.24).

Clearly, the debate could continue, and would certainly involve looking at the New Testament, where St Paul's prescriptions on homosexuality (in Romans, 1 Corinthians and 1 Timothy)[43] would be subject to the same kind of analysis. Paul himself sometimes distinguishes teaching that he claims to have directly from Christ from his own opinion (e. g. in 1 Cor. 7.12), and it is partly on this ground that many conservatives no longer feel bound by all of Paul's prescriptions – for example on the subject of women being silent in church (1 Cor. 14.34–5) – even though this prescription is not said, by Paul, to reflect his own opinion. As a result, in the case of Paul's outbursts against homosexuality there is inevitably, once again, a legitimate issue of interpretation concerning their relevance for today's society.

This imaginary dialogue indicates that what is often called the 'literalist' position on issues like gay sex is open to very serious objections, but it must be stressed that this does not settle the matter of Christian responses to gay and lesbian sex because of the obvious fact that an invalid argument does not necessarily mean a false conclusion. There are other issues to ponder before coming to a considered opinion on what a Christian response to homosexual activity should be. For example, there are: (i) questions of respect for tradition, an emphasis that is particularly strong in Orthodox objections to homosexual practice – especially in the light of the teaching that all human activities should be seen in the context of a discipline of practice that emphasizes the spiritual; (ii) questions relating to the alleged 'purposes' of sexual activity; (iii) questions relating to alleged physiological and health problems associated with some homosexual activities; (iv) empirical questions about how many people are genetically determined to have exclusively homosexual orientations – about which they have no choice whatsoever;[44] and (v) the significance of Jesus' teaching about the 'one-flesh' relationship of marriage (Mark 10) – which may have implications for homosexual activity, even though there are no direct references to it in the Gospels. This point needs to be put very forcibly. Not all biblical arguments are literalist arguments, and although there is a strong case for rejecting literalism, it is certainly possible to construct 'biblical arguments' (in many areas of both ethics and theology) that depend upon the appreciation of the biblical drama as a whole rather than on proof texts. Such arguments, however, nearly always go hand in hand with an appreciation that there can be legitimate disagreement.

I shall comment briefly on the first two of these five matters. Tradition is a notoriously difficult guide. It is at the same time a source of important values, since many practices (such as the Passover and the eucharist) enshrine enormous benefits which may only be discovered by entering into the traditions. At the same time traditions can be pernicious, as in the (Christian) traditions of anti-Semitism and the male domination of women. The consequence, I suggest, is that when an ancient tradition is seriously questioned on moral grounds, the church needs to enter a period of serious reflection and prayer. This is why, although I tend to take the 'liberal' position on this issue, I fully support Archbishop Rowan Williams' call for a time of reflection before drastic new steps are taken. A further ground for adopting this cautionary approach is a sensitivity to the position of those African and Asian church leaders who work in predominantly Muslim countries, and whose positions on sexual ethics could easily be misunderstood or misinterpreted.

On the subject of the 'purpose' of sexual activity, one has to be very careful not to assume that the biological purposes of sex (if these be known) settle the philosophical or theological questions. Even in the conservative papal encyclical *Humanae Vitae* (1968) there is granted to be more than one purpose of sex, that is to say, both procreation and (what we might term) the 'cementing' of the married relationship in loving expressions of union, or what Augustine, in his *The Good of Marriage*, called *societas*. The difference between the official Roman Catholic position and that of Anglicanism (as expressed in the Lambeth Conference of 1930) is that for the Vatican these purposes are in a kind of serial order, so that the first or primary purpose – that of procreation – must never be deliberately frustrated, even if conception is impossible, as among aged married couples. In contrast, for Anglicanism, either purpose may be sufficient in itself, and therefore artificial methods of birth control are not always wrong.

It might seem here that procreation is *the* biological purpose and the cementing of the marriage bond a non-biological purpose, but here one must tread carefully. In the first place, from a scientific perspective, we must be aware that scientists are usually nervous about using the word 'purpose', because it can suggest all kinds of things that do not fall within the domain of science. Nevertheless, allowing for this caution, it is reasonable to hold that procreation does not exhaust the value and function of sexual activity in the animal as well as the human world. Activities that promote 'bonding' can have value for the survival and flourishing of a species even when no procreation is possible.

Congruously, some Christians (as well as many secular thinkers) want to extend the two former purposes of sexual activity, arguing that there is an additional purposive value to some of them, namely that of fostering caring and committed relationships that are not necessarily those of marriage – and these might be either heterosexual or homosexual. Here, once again, one has to be careful about assertions that such a purpose could not be biological – in addition to the problem that human beings might either discover or create a 'purpose' for an activity which has no obvious connection with the biological survival of the species. In reference to homosexual activity, some conservatives ask, in a rhetorical way, 'Since when has x or y been an organ for sex?' The answer, from a strictly physiological point of view, is not certain. We now know that homosexual activity is common in the animal as well as the human world (a scientific fact that is often denied),[45] and it could be that some forms of homosexual activity do have a Darwinian purpose, that is in creating bonds and in relieving stress, and thereby contributing to survival. There is certainly some scientific evidence to back up this suggestion.[46] We don't know, but it is certain that all arguments based on the alleged 'purposes' of sexuality are fraught with difficulties, and that an element of caution is appropriate which does not fit the strident tones of many participants in the debate (a stridency found both among some conservatives and by many supporters of 'gay liberation').[47] With regard to the third suggestion regarding the 'purpose' of sexual activity, a related issue concerns the problem of applying to contemporary society, in which there is typically a ten- to twenty-year interval between puberty and marriage, sexual rules that developed in societies in which the interval was frequently none to three years.

Six additional points need to be stressed as a prelude to a more considered debate.

First, no Christian (or, I hold, serious-minded secular humanist) denies that there is a need for both moral and legal rules regarding sexual activity.[48] If people respond to their often incredibly powerful sexual drives without considerations of respect for the well-being of others, terrible damage will often be done. The issue is not whether or not we need moral and legal rules for the constraint of our sexual appetites (including measures to protect minors and other vulnerable people) – we do – but whether these rules should be different in the homosexual domain from those in the heterosexual.

Second, Christian 'liberals' who do not wish to condemn as sinful all cases of homosexual activity may, nevertheless, have good reason for being appalled at many aspects of the 'gay scene'. In part this may be because of a promiscuity that – even more than in the case of the heterosexual scene – commonly accepts a series of purely passing relationships that do not seriously consider the well-being of the other party; and in part because teenagers may be encouraged to believe that they can know their final sexual orientation – when in fact this cannot be known prior to one's twenties, and even then one can be mistaken.[49] This false presumption, needless to say, is a charter for the older exploiter.

Third, it is one thing to give the green light, in principle, to the ordination of gay or lesbian people who are in long-term, committed relationships; it is another thing to say that a parish church or a diocese should be forced to accept them *at this time*.[50] Although the church cannot be a pure democracy (because bishops and other elders have to preserve 'the faith that was once for all entrusted to the saints', Jude 3), it is increasingly recognized that there is a place for a democratic element, or (for example, in the Roman Catholic Church) a *consensus fidelium*. Forcing a reluctant parish to accept, say, a black pastor, against the wishes of a congregation, might or might not be good pastoral policy, but it would not be a good analogy for forcing a gay or lesbian priest on an unwilling congregation. The differences are, first, that (at least within the mainstream churches) there is no tradition to justify the exclusion of a black person, and second, there is no significant biblical argument for such an exclusion. On the other hand, while I have made it clear that I disagree with the literalist interpretation of the Holiness Code, the literalist position is not only sincerely held by many conservatives, it does represent an ancient tradition, and it does appeal to Scripture in an understandable way. At the very least, therefore, those within this tradition should have special respect paid to the nature of their pastoral oversight, not only during a period of communal reflection on a divisive issue, but afterwards as well.

Fourth, in all considerations of Christian ethics there is much to be said for the Wesleyan Quadrilateral, that is to say, looking at scripture, tradition, reason and experience as sources for reflection. Something has already been written of scripture and tradition in this matter. 'Reason', a notoriously difficult term on which I have recently written,[51] includes making appropriate distinctions and seeking a balanced judgement, frequently accepting that there are significant arguments on different sides of an issue. 'Experience' clearly overlaps with 'tradition', but the stress is on recent or contemporary experience (whereas 'tradition' tends to point to ancient and enduring experience), and in this case it would be remiss not to include among the considerations the witness of gay and lesbian Christians concerning the nature of the best kinds of same-sex unions. Bishop Coleman showed sensitivity to this dimension of the debate in his *Gay Christians*.[52]

Fifth, we must all beware one kind of dubious argument that is often found in letters to the newspapers on this subject. Here, the writer complains bitterly that the other side (whichever it be) is placing its own private judgement, or worse still, its own private agenda, over against the objective good, or the known and declared will of God. But in any serious debate we have to begin with the assumption that the other person is arguing in good faith, and in this case, the whole point is that there is a serious (and I hold, legitimate) disagreement as to what exactly is the objective good, or the will of God. What we have here, therefore, is not strictly speaking an 'argument' at all (except in the sense of an argument *ad hominem*), but a dogmatic claim that my side is right!

Finally, in the foregoing I have, except for the discussion of the third consideration, merged the issues of whether there is something intrinsically wrong in all active homosexual relations and of whether homosexual people should ever be ordained. Some Christians hold that the only issue is the former, on the grounds that there should be no difference between the moral rules that apply to the laity and those that apply to the clergy. Others support a different and 'higher' standard for the clergy. However, any argument based upon the need for a 'higher' standard has to be careful not the beg the key question, because of course many Christians see nothing wrong in committed, life-long homosexual unions – so that for them, talk of a 'higher' standard is, at best, patronizing. However, the situation is complex because some of those who oppose the ordination of homosexuals have *no* moral complaint to make about active, adult homosexuals in general, but believe that homosexual couples are nevertheless undesirable role-models for the young, and are therefore unsuitable candidates for either ordination or school-teaching because of the vulnerability of children who may be subject to sexual pressures that they are not yet able to handle, particularly if they are passing through a temporary phase of homosexual orientation.

Although this does express the opinion of many thoughtful people, I must confess myself unconvinced by the underlying argument. I do not think, in the long run, that children are usually well served by shielding them from issues that sooner or later must be faced, and those who live out their lives in loving relationships, albeit of different kinds, may provide a better range of role-model than any conservative selection. What I would suggest, is that all role-models discourage genital sexual activity – either heterosexual or homosexual – until children are mature enough to understand its extraordinary power, along with its potential for good or ill. One of the conservative elements in my generally liberal position is the conviction that this time is a lot later than is currently acknowledged. [Ed.]

Modern liturgies: revised marriage services

Church of England

Since the Canon Law of the Church of England is relatively modest in scope, and there is nothing in official Anglican founding documents similar to the comprehensive Confessions of the Reformed Churches, its official liturgies usually serve as a useful guide to its basic convictions, not least about marriage. The changes in the marriage service between Cranmer and the present Order in *Common Worship* reflect, albeit cautiously, how these convictions have changed.

The 1662 Book of Common Prayer service lasted unaltered for nearly three hundred years, and the alternative service proposed in 1928 made no changes in structure. The Preface, however, was rewritten to reflect a different attitude to sexuality. Out went any references to sin, fornication or beasts; marriage was now the opportunity for 'hallowing and ordering aright the natural instincts and affections implanted by God'. The oaths of commitment are made identical for the man and the woman and she is no longer expected to serve and obey; she is still to be 'a follower of holy and godly matrons', but these are not named. The man promises to share (not endow) his worldly goods with his wife. A Collect, Epistle and Gospel are provided in case of need, 'if there be a communion'. Although rejected by Parliament, the 1928 book was authorized by the Convocations, and in fact was widely used as a sensible modernization until replaced by the very similar Alternative Service Order, Series One, which is still authorized for a short term.

The next revision appeared in the *Alternative Service Book 1980*, a further cautious evolution; it has now been replaced by the marriage service from *Common Worship*, authorized from 2000 onwards and already widely used. Some years ago, a member of the Liturgical Commission was asked in Synod why it was taking so long to produce a new marriage service, and replied, 'When the Church has made up its mind what it now believes about marriage, we will prepare a service to match.' It is not clear that the Church of England has a common mind about marriage, but it may be that the function of a liturgy as a teaching medium is already beginning to provide a consensus. This service is among the least altered from its predecessors in the *Common Worship* collection, and retains the standard elements, consent, commitment and blessing in virtually the familiar form but, in the modern style, provides several alternative wordings. It does, however, present a clear theological shift towards making the marital relationship the central doctrine of Christian marriage. The old notion that marriage as a remedy against sin finally disappears, and emphasis is placed on the commitment of the couple's life together in the context of God's love and approval. The introduction, to be read by the congregation before the service starts, is:

A wedding is one of life's great moments, a time of solemn commitment as well as good wishes, feasting and joy. St John tells us how Jesus shared in such an occasion at Cana, and gave there a sign of new beginnings as he turned water into wine. Marriage is intended by God to be a creative relationship, as his blessing enables husband and wife to love and support each other in good times and in bad, and to share in the care and upbringing of children. For Christians, marriage is also an invitation to share life together in the spirit of Jesus Christ. It is based upon a solemn, public and life-long covenant between a man and a woman, declared and celebrated in the presence of God and before witnesses.

On their wedding day the bride and bridegroom face each other, make their promises and receive God's blessing. You are witnesses of the marriage, and express your support by your presence and your prayers. Your support does not end today: the couple will value continued encouragement in the days and years ahead of them.[53]

Apart from an extensive list of suitable readings for the ministry of the word, direct references to the Bible texts are sparse, limited to the mention of Cana in both the Pastoral Introduction and the Welcome. Jesus is said to have shared in the rejoicing, and blessed the celebration by his presence. Turning the water into wine is a sign of a new beginning for the couple. (This is a long hallowed, traditional interpretation, but it is probably not the main original purpose of the sign.) Although St Paul is not mentioned, Ephesians 5.21–33 is suggested as one of the epistles and the Ephesian mystery is alluded to: 'As the man and woman grow together in love and trust they shall be united with one another in heart, body and mind, as Christ is united with his bride, the Church.'[54]

The comparative lack of biblical quotation in the service presumably recognizes that few if any of those present would be familiar with scripture, and it is for the reading and sermon to fill this gap. The service is, however, permeated with biblical concepts of relationship and covenant, and a wide selection of suitable readings from the Old Testament, the Epistles and Gospels is provided. In contrast to the slightly coy reference to sex in the ASB as 'knowing each other in love and through the joy of their bodily union strengthening the union of their hearts and lives', the new service has: 'The gift of marriage brings husband and wife together in the delight and tenderness of sexual union and joyful commitment to the end of their lives.' Admittedly, the phrase 'knowing each other' comes from Genesis, and would now seem obscure to most people, and what is intended by the new wording is to hold together a positive statement about sex and a continuation of Church teaching that sex begins after marriage, but the phraseology is awkward.

Among the innovations, the blessing of the rings refers to the 'love which many waters cannot quench, neither the floods drown, that love which is patient and kind, enduring all things' (Song of Songs 8.7, and 1 Cor. 13). For the conclusion of the service, several forms of blessing are provided, the most interesting perhaps being apparently new, but reflecting elements from the Orthodox tradition.

Blessed are you, O Lord our God, for you have created joy and gladness, pleasure and delight, love, peace and fellowship. Pour out the abundance of your blessing, upon N and N in their new life together. Let their love for each other be a seal upon their hearts and a crown above their heads . . . Finally, in your mercy bring them to that banquet where your saints feast for ever in your heavenly home . . . [55]

A note attached to the *Common Worship* marriage service states that 'for communion members of the Church, it is appropriate that they receive communion soon after their marriage' or for the marriage to take place within the context of Holy Communion, and an alternative structure for this is provided. The traditional ceremony of the bride's family 'giving her away' is relegated to an option.

The Methodist Church

The Methodist marriage service is similar in structure, and includes the standard declarations and vows prescribed by law, but while at times reflecting ecumenical consultation, it maintains certain Methodist characteristics, notably perhaps in the opening welcome, strongly reminiscent of Calvin's service. In the introductory note, a marriage ceremony is defined as

a formal occasion when a solemn legal contract is made between a man and a woman. In a Christian context, it is also an act of worship in which marriage is celebrated as a gift of God and the joy of the couple is shared and their commitment to each other is witnessed by family and friends. The Marriage Service's themes of love, hope, faithfulness, sacrifice and trust are at the heart of the Christian Gospel.

The Preparation begins:

We meet together in the presence of God to witness the marriage of A and C, to ask God's blessing upon them, to support them with our prayers and to share their joy.[56]

This is followed by a series of paragraphs that emphasize that marriage is a gift of God by which the life of the couple and society will be enriched:

It is the will of God that, in marriage, husband and wife should experience a life-long unity of heart, body and mind; comfort and companionship; enrichment and encouragement; tenderness and trust. It is the will of God that marriage should be honoured as a way of life, in which we may know the security of love and care, and grow towards maturity. Through such marriage, children may be nurtured, family life strengthened, and human society enriched.

There is no scriptural text as such included in the Preparation, but six are specified in the Ministry of the Word, at least one of which must be read, from the Song of Songs, the Epistles, or the Gospels of Mark or John. Only among a list of additional readings are the Cana story and the mystical union of Ephesians 5 included. Similar provision to that in the Anglican rite is made for Holy Communion. The traditional ceremony of the father of the bride giving her away is clearly no longer regarded as politically correct, and the Anglican and Methodist services offer slightly different alternatives. For the Anglicans, a parent of the bride, a member of her family or friend may pass her hand to the minister; the Methodists prefer that both the man and the woman should be presented by a relative or friend. Unlike the Anglicans, the *Methodist Worship Book* also provides for the blessing of a marriage previously solemnized.[57] This assumes the couple have already exchanged their declarations and vows in a civil registry office.

The Roman Catholic Church

The Anglican service bears some characteristics of being suitable for a wide range of people who happen to be parishioners, rather than clearly for active members of a congregation; the Methodist service is somewhat more focused on the welcoming role of the local Christian family. The Catholic service markedly emphasizes the sacramental nature of the rite for baptized Catholics. Two rites are available to dioceses in England and Wales, within or outside of the Mass, and the relevant parts for the marriage are virtually the same. Within the Mass, the marriage rite starts after the Ministry of the Word with this collect: 'Father, you have made the bond of marriage a holy mystery, a symbol of Christ's love for his church . . .'

[For information on marriage rites in the Orthodox tradition see John Meyendorff, *Marriage: An Orthodox Perspective*, 3rd edn, New York: St Vladimir's Press, 2000. Ed.]

The evolving situation

From the death of Queen Elizabeth I in 1603 to the present day, the attitude of the Church of England to marriage has not changed, at least officially. The doctrine expressed in Cranmer's marriage service, only slightly modified in 1662, continues to set the standard, and is still supported by the current Canon B 30, as revised in 1964, except that the wording of the second cause reflects that of 1928 proposed prayer book.

> The Church of England affirms, according to our Lord's teaching, that marriage is in its nature a union permanent and lifelong, for better for worse till death them do part, of one man and one woman, to the exclusion of all others on either side, for the procreation and nurture of children, for the hallowing and right direction of the natural instincts and affections, and for the mutual society, help and comfort which the one ought to have of the other, both in prosperity and adversity.[58]

What has changed enormously in these 400 years is the attitude of most people to Christian marriage, at least in the form prescribed by the canon. The shorthand explanation for this is to claim that the change is the result of secularization – religion becoming an optional interest instead of an inescapable factor in human life. But actually English Canon Law continued much of the Catholic tradition, and the attempt by Henry VIII to provide new canons in the form of *Reformatio Legum Ecclesiasticarum* had been abandoned in 1571. A new collection of 141 canons was assembled in 1603 and received the approval of King James in 1606 and served until 1953. (The 1571 collection had *inter alia* provided for divorce after adultery, as with the continental reformers, but in 1603 the standard indissoluble rule returned. In Stuart times, the English had more on their minds than revising marriage services.)

In February 1984 the General Synod of the Church of England debated, not for the first or last time, the difficult question of whether or not those who had been divorced and had a partner still living could be married in church. The debate was inconclusive, and it was clear that the remarriage question was only one issue. The greater use of the registry office, the increasing divorce rate, and the questioning of the traditional morality that sex outside marriage was wrong made Synod members wonder if the right policy for the future should be a clearer distinction between two forms of marriage, secular and religious. Should the Church of England seek to withdraw from its obligation as the established church to conduct marriage services for all, irrespective of their religious convictions or lack of them? This was obviously a major question needing a period of reflection, and the Synod accepted a suggestion of the then Bishop of Chichester, Dr Eric Kemp, a noted scholar and expert on Canon Law, that the Synod Standing Committee should review the whole subject and report back. The Committee therefore set up a working party to advise them and their report was completed in 1988 and duly noted by Synod. Its main recommendation was that there should be no change in the existing pattern.

Christian teaching about marriage for the third millennium

Most recent Christian writing on marriage has focused on the quality of human relationships, and the newest liturgies reflect this priority (for example, compare the ASB and the 1999 Church of England version). But cohabitation, divorce by consent, and remarriage after divorce are still treated with reserve. The closing years of the twentieth century marked the development of the 'global village', enabled by instant electronic communication and tending to impose a universal Western culture. But individualism has a social cost, and the search is on to find an acceptable overview of morality, with a set of abiding values, to succeed older formulations of Natural Law, the old Christian tradition, and human rights. For Christian marriage, is it perhaps a case of trying to put old wine in new bottles?

The Reformation theologians reworked the medieval theology of sex and marriage in somewhat more affirming ways, and this was reflected in the new vernacular language liturgies.

The New Morality

The Second World War put serious thinking about moral philosophy into the deep freeze. The New Morality, especially since 1963, brought it back again.

Whereas between the wars existentialism and logical positivism seemed to be strong challenges to the old systems, the conflict against Fascism and later Communism reduced moral thinking to simplicities. Only bishops William Temple and George Bell challenged this unreflective period. However, it soon became evident that stable marriage was one of the casualties. The signs were that although marriage was increasingly popular in the 1950s and 1960s, there was a reduction in the number of marriages per head of the population, a decline in church marriages and an enormous increase in the divorce rate. (See the Lambeth report of 1948 and *Putting Asunder*.)

Ethics of character

[An unfinished, final section in Bishop Coleman's draft.] We may decide that we have been too much absorbed in the ethics of consequences, whereas a truer representation of the Christian contribution to moral problems is the ethics of character. (These terms are not what professional philosophers would use, but perhaps will serve.) Thus, when we apply the Christian doctrine of man and woman to each new generation of moral problems, we say that we will build up in you and me both the marks and dispositions of following the ethics of character. The temptation has always been to think in terms of consequences because this is easier, especially if we are speaking negatively, in terms of deterrence. Thus when faced with a proliferation of nuclear weapons, it was obvious that the consequence was mad mutual destruction, therefore we should reduce or even ban the bomb. In more individual terms, we have the basic instincts to preserve life and therefore even put up with organ transplants to achieve this short term, and our needs should apparently be enjoyed, even life. But excess of unrestricted feeding leads to gluttony which leads to ill health, etc.

When we turn to sex it is a good and necessary instinct and therefore we expect to enjoy it, and indeed the drive to have sex is very strong, after life and food and health, the strongest. But unmonitored there are problems. We used to point to the dangers of unplanned pregnancy and unwanted children; now we point to VD or AIDS. If you follow your instinct you may succeed in populating a village of hungry or unwanted people, or die of disease. So turn these ideas upside down by the ethic of character.

The character of the human race is not to be the kind of people who kill each other *en masse*; indeed, we might refuse to kill each other at all, not because of the risk that slaughter may be reciprocated, but because this is not our character.

Similarly we enjoy food and praise people who cook it attractively, but (if we are people of character) we do not eat to excess because our character is to feed the hungry by our self-restraint. Similarly, our instinct is to have sex often and to enjoy it, and we have a matching instinct to relate. It is not good to be alone – we need partners. Our character is to explore the multi-dimensional aspects of partnership and engagement and friendship with another person who is freely and equally committed, if possible, for life.

The offence of using a prostitute or having a one-night stand is that we do not take the other person seriously, nor expect them to take us seriously as a person. Sex is about breeding and desire but also about joining and entering a sustaining relationship, as Jack Dominian would say. We are called by God into sustaining relationships with him through Jesus and with each other by friendship and one-flesh activities. Sex is not a game of tennis.

The faithful spouses are people who have learned, often with difficulty, to take each other seriously, and that is why some marriages survive the occasional infidelity. The apparently cuckolded partner feels that the character is not limited to sex acts even if their drive is, seemingly, for the moment irresistible. So character means the capacity for forgiveness. The twentieth-century discoveries of the behavioural sciences therefore tell us how to be character-building people, not just sexual performers. Does the new marriage service look in this direction?

The institution of marriage

[A hand-written note by Bishop Coleman] This long history has shown that men and women have had and still have this capacity to love each other, to share a common life and to provide for the next generation, though the actual patterns of doing this have varied considerably. There is no particular evidence to suggest that the institution will not exist into the fourth millennium. But it is going through a mutation.

Notes

Chapter 1

1 Richard Coggins, *Introducing the Old Testament*, Oxford: Oxford University Press, 1990, p. 47. Resemblance does not necessarily imply copying.

2 Dan Cohn-Sherbok, *The Jewish Heritage*, Oxford: Blackwell, 1988, pp. 8–12 (for a brief historical survey).

3 Paula McNutt, *Reconstructing the Society of Ancient Israel*, Louisville, Ky: Westminster John Knox Press, 1999, pp. 94, 171. A thorough analysis of the social history of early Israel is too complex for consideration here.

4 Dale Patrick, *Old Testament Law*, London: SCM Press, 1986, p. 29.

5 For an eyewitness account of the excavations at Eshnunna and the original history of the City States, see Mary Chubb, *City in the Sand*, London: Libri, 1999, p. 44.

6 This code contains 282 precepts, 74 of which (127–95 and 209–14) deal with marriage and sexual offences.

7 W. Bayerlin et al. (eds.), trans. J. Bowden, *Near Eastern Texts relating to the Old Testament*, London: SCM Press, 1997, p. 166.

8 For introductory articles on the Pentateuch see *The New Jerusalem Bible*, ed. Henry Wansbrough, London: Darton, Longman and Todd, 1985 and *The Oxford Bible Commentary*, ed. J. Barton and J. Muddiman, Oxford: Oxford University Press, 2001, pp. 12–39 (by G. I. Davies).

9 R. E. Clements, *Deuteronomy*, Sheffield: JSOT Press, 1989, ch. 6.

10 J. B. Prichard (ed.), *The Ancient Near East Anthology*, vol. 1, Princeton: Princeton University Press, 1958, p. 135. The Laws of Eshnunna 27; cf. Hammurabi 128, p. 152.

11 H. W. F. Saggs, *Civilization before Greece and Rome*, London: Batsford, 1989, p. 161. Lipit-Ishtar Code 27.

12 J. B. Prichard (ed.), *The Ancient Near East Anthology*, vol. 2, Princeton: Princeton University Press, 1975, p. 72. Four witnesses are named. There was no coinage but silver bars were used, valued by weight. Fifty shekels weighed one mina, i.e. 600 grams, perhaps at this time a year's subsistence for a mother and child in a farming community.

13 *The Ancient Near East Anthology*, vol. 2, pp. 75–6. Five witnesses included the scribe.

14 *The Ancient Near East Anthology*, vol. 2, pp. 84–5.

15 See John Boswell, *The Marriage of Likeness*, London: Harper Collins, 1995, pp. 42–3.

16 *Civilization before Greece and Rome*, p. 162. Lipit-Ishtar Code 6–8. *The Ancient Near East Anthology*, vol. 2, p. 33.

17 *The Ancient Near East Anthology*, vol. 1, p. 138.

18 *The Ancient Near East Anthology*, vol. 1, p. 153. Hammurabi Code 138–40.

19 *The Ancient Near East Anthology*, vol. 1, p. 154. Hammurabi Code 148.

20 *Civilization before Greece and Rome*, p. 168. Hittite Code 31–3.

21 *The Ancient Near East Anthology*, vol. 1, pp. 153–4. Hammurabi Code 141–3.

22 Jeremiah 3.8.

23 *The Ancient Near East Anthology*, vol. 1, p. 152. Hammurabi Code 129, cf. Eshnunna 28, p. 135.

24 *The Ancient Near East Anthology*, vol. 1, pp. 152–3. Hammurabi Code 133–6, cf. Eshnunna 29, pp. 134–5.

25 *The Ancient Near East Anthology*, vol. 1, p. 152. Hammurabi Code 130–2.

26 *The Mishnah*, tr. H. Danby, Oxford: Oxford University Press, p. 246 (Ketuboth 1, 6).

27 *The Ancient Near East Anthology*, vol. 1, p. 162. Hammurabi Code 209–11.

28 David Daube, *Studies in Biblical Law*, Cambridge: Cambridge University Press, 1947, p. 148 (note 6). This distinguished Jewish and biblical scholar took the view that the Septuagint version best reflects the meaning of the Deuteronomic text.

29 *The Ancient Near East Anthology*, vol. 1, p. 155. Hammurabi Code 157.

30 The basis for the present-day lists excluding marriages on grounds of consanguinuity and affinity. *The Canons of the Church of England*, London: Church House Publishing, 5th edn, 1993, B 31.

31 *The Ancient Near East Anthology*, vol. 1, p. 161. Hammurabi Code 195.

32 *The Ancient Near East Anthology*, vol. 2, pp. 191–2.

33 *Near Eastern Texts relating to the Old Testament*, p. 16.

34 Barbara Watterson, *Women in Ancient Egypt*, Stroud: Alan Sutton, 1994.

35 Charles Freeman, *Egypt, Greece and Rome: Civilizations of the Ancient Mediterranean*, Oxford: Oxford University Press, 1966, pp. 46–7.

36 Jubilees 13.10–15.

37 The problem of God's providence in such a delicate matter was discussed by the rabbis in the second century AD.

38 G. von Rad, *Genesis*, London: SCM Press, 1972, pp. 356–7.

39 Athalya Brenner, *The Israelite Woman*, Sheffield: JSOT Press, 1985, ch. 9.

Chapter 2

1 R. Coggins, *Introducing the Old Testament*, Oxford: Oxford University Press, 1990, chs 1–3 and *The Oxford Annotated Bible*, ed. H. G. May and B. M. Metzger, New York: Oxford University Press, 1994, pp. xxxi–xxxii.

2 The order of the books of the Old Testament after the Pentateuch is different in the Septuagint and Vulgate from that of the Hebrew Bible.

3 G. von Rad, *Genesis*, London: SCM Press, 1972, p. 82.

4 Karen Armstrong, *In the Beginning*, London: HarperCollins, 1996, p. 23.

5 Attrib. J. Everard, but frequently quoted elsewhere in commentaries. Originally from Midrash, which is much more negative in tone.

6 Karl Barth, *Church Dogmatics,* III, 4, Edinburgh: T. and T. Clark, 1961, p. 117.

7 Cf. Psalms 22.19 and 40.13–17.

8 *The Septuagint Version of the Old Testament,* Greek and English, London: Bagster and Sons, 1906, p. 3. This is the Greek text, based on the fourth century Vaticanus MS, edited by Lancelot Brenton, with his English translation, first published by Bagster in 1844. Brenton's translation has 'a help suitable to him' for v. 18, and 'a help like to himself' for v. 20.

9 William Tyndale, *Old Testament,* modern-spelling edition, ed. D. Daniell, New Haven: Yale University Press, 1992, p. 17.

10 *The Jerome Biblical Commentary,* London: Chapman, 1968, vol. 1, p. 12.

11 By Jean Corbechon, *c.* 1415, where God joins the hands together. [See D. L. P. Byrne, *The Illustrations to the Early Manuscripts of Jean Corbechon's French translation of Bartholemaeus Anglicus' "De Proprietatibus Rerum" 1372–c. 1420,* Cambridge University PhD thesis, 1981, vol. 2, illustrations 75, 76, 107, 125, 142. Note that Corbechon was the translator, not the artist. Ed.] See also 'The Wedding' by the Jewish painter Chagall, 1917.

12 Cf. Plato, *Symposium,* 189 d–f.

13 Cf. Laban's greeting to Jacob, Genesis 29.14.

14 Hebrew has no word for 'body' in the sense that Paul uses *soma* to speak of a spiritual body over against the fleshly body, *sarx.*

15 *Marriage and the Church's Task,* London: Church Information Office, 1978, p. 144, Appendix 4, 'The New Testament Evidence'. For kinship in the Old Testament see Bruce J. Malina, *The New Testament World,* London: SCM Press, 1983, ch. 5.

16 The Hebrew word *yadha* (knew) can mean either acquaintance or sexual knowledge; here the latter is meant.

17 See Joseph Blenkinsopp, *Wisdom and Law in the Old Testament,* Oxford: Oxford University Press, 1983, pp. 102–3 for the link between the Decalogue and the prophets.

18 A. Phillips, *Ancient Israel's Criminal Law,* Oxford: Blackwell, 1970, pp. 110–11.

19 *Theological Dictionary of the Old Testament,* ed. G. J. Botterweck and H. Ringgren, rev. edn, Grand Rapids, Mi: Eerdmanns, 1977, vol. 1, pp. 99–100, under *Ahabh,* and *Theological Dictionary of the New Testament,* ed. G. Friedrich, Grand Rapids, Mi: Eerdmanns, 1968, vol. 6, pp. 579–80, under *porne.*

20 [The tale does however raise serious ethical questions, both about Rahab's apparent treachery to her own people and about truth telling. With regard to the latter, Augustine, in his *Contra Mendacium,* argues that Rahab is commended in the New Testament because of her faith *even though* she lied to her king. Her lie was not, he claimed, morally justifiable. Ed.]

21 Benny Morris, *Righteous Victims,* London: John Murray, 2000, p. 82. In the peace negotiations of 1919 Britain was awarded a mandate over Palestine under pressure from the Jewish delegates who, by the terms of the Balfour Agreement, had been promised a homeland. This was understood to be the original Israel from the time of King David, 'from Dan to Beersheba, from the

Jordan to the Sea'. The British Prime Minister, Lloyd George, unfamiliar with Old Testament geography, adopted the slogan. It was in fact a somewhat over-stated claim, as the Jewish negotiators knew.

22 The original ceremony of anointing was carried out by the High Priest (1 Kings 1.38–40). It is commemorated in Handel's popular coronation anthem 'Zadok the Priest'.

23 R. Coggins, *Old Testament*, pp. 66–7.

24 Micaiah is a famous example: 1 Kings 22.

25 Deuteronomy 28.15–68.

26 Adrian Thatcher, *Marriage and Modernity*, Sheffield: Sheffield Academic Press, 1999, p. 69.

27 Jeremiah 2, Ezekiel 16 and Isaiah 54.

28 P. McNutt, *Reconstructing the Society of Ancient Israel*, Louisville, Ky: Westminster John Knox Press, 1999, pp. 202–3.

29 The list is given in Ezra 10. Further racial cleansing, in Ashdod, is described in Nehemiah 13.23–7, where the sin of Solomon is recalled.

30 Proverbs 31.10–12 and v. 30, but see also the intervening verses.

Chapter 3

1 [In the *Apology*, when Socrates speaks of 'God', in the singular, he appears to refer to his inner voice, which he believed came from a divine source. How far he adopted the metaphysical views of the divine which Plato ascribed to him in the dialogues is a matter of conjecture. Although, in Plato, the Idea of the Good can properly be called the 'one, supreme Reality', the word 'God' (*theos*), in Plato, when used in the singular, was more likely to be applied to the Demiurge of the *Timaeus* (who is the active maker of this world), or to the World Soul. In Aristotle, the word, in the singular, indicated his 'first unmoved mover'. Ed.]

2 C. Freeman, *Egypt, Greece and Rome: Civilizations of the Ancient Mediterranean*, Oxford: Oxford University Press, 1996, pp. 87 onwards for a summary of Homer's life. For the *Iliad* and the *Odyssey*, standard translation in Penguin Classics.

3 Helen is linked with Faustus by Goethe and Marlowe. 'Was this the face that launched a thousand ships?'

4 *Iliad*, tr. E.V. Rieu, Harmondsworth: Penguin, 1950, p. 74.

5 Congreve, *The Mourning Bride*, Act 3, scene 10.

6 Euripides, *Medea*, 230–52.

7 Mary R. Lefkowitz, 'Influential Women' in *Images of Women in Antiquity*, ed. A. Cameron and A. Kuhrt, London: Croom Helm, 1983, pp. 49–64, discusses the place of women in Greek drama generally.

8 *The Oxford History of the Classical World: Greece and the Hellenistic World*, eds. J. Boardman, J. Griffin, O. Murray, Oxford: Oxford University Press, 1988, p. 209.

9 See Susan Walker, 'Women and Housing in Classical Greece' in *Images of Women in Antiquity*, ed. A. Cameron and A. Kuhrt, ch. 6.

10 *Appolodoros Against Neaira (Demosthenes 59)*, ed. and trans. C. Carey,

Warminster, Aris and Phillips, 1992. The orator was formerly thought to have been Demosthenes (384–322 BC).

11 H. D. F. Kitto, in *The Greeks*, London: Penguin, 1991 reprint, p. 206.

12 Paul's reference to the unknown god in his speech on the Areopagus is an early example (Acts 17.23).

13 Plato, *Symposium*. St Paul echoes this thought: 'this mortal body must put on immortality' (1 Cor. 15.53–4).

14 *Republic*, book 6.

15 Plato, *The Laws* (841), trans. T. J. Saunders, London: Penguin, book 8 part 14, p. 340.

16 Book 6. St Paul's discussion of rules of marriage for Christians in 1 Corinthians 7 may well have had Plato's advice in mind as well as rabbinic teaching.

17 The Roman Emperor Augustus imposed a similar rule in 14 BC.

18 Aristotle (Nicomachean) *Ethics*, 1160b–1161a, trans. J. A. K. Thomson, rev. H. Treddenick, London: Penguin 1976, p. 276.

19 *Ethics*, 1162a, p. 280.

20 *Ethics*, 1162a, pp. 280–1.

21 When children reached puberty their tutors were replaced by 'curators' whose main task was to monitor their property transactions until they reached maturity, i.e. 25 years.

22 U. E. Paoli, *Rome, its People, Life and Customs*, trans. R. D. Macnaghten, London: Longman, 1963. Not all marriages were as lavish as this; the only legal requirement was consent before witnesses.

23 British Law first allowed women to own property by the Married Women's Property Act of 1870.

24 J. F. Gardner, *Women in Roman Law and Society*, London: Croom Helm, 1986, for details of *Lex Julia de adulteriis*, 18 BC, and *Lex Julia Papia*, AD 9. See also Aline Rousselle, *Porneia*, tr. F. Pheasant, Oxford: Blackwell, 1988, which includes subsequent interpretation of these laws by the Roman jurists.

25 Cf. St Paul's advice to widows not to remarry unless they were young (1 Cor. 7.8, and 1 Tim. 5.3–16). Constantine later removed the taxes on celibate men and unmarried widows.

26 W. W. Fowler, *Social Life at Rome*, London: Macmillan, 1908. Also C. Freeman, *Egypt, Greece and Rome*, p. 379. The inscription has survived, but Lucretius Vespillo may not have been its author.

27 *Egypt, Greece and Rome*, p. 379. Pliny the Younger, AD 62–113, became Governor of Bithynia, Northern Turkey. His correspondence with the Emperor Trajan about the punishment of Christians is well known.

28 Tennyson visited Sirmio in his old age (1810) and wrote a short poem, 'Frater, Ave atque Vale', quoting Catullus, whom he called 'tenderest of Roman poets, nineteen hundred years ago'.

29 Gilbert Highet, *Poets in a Landscape*, London: Hamish Hamilton, 1957. Highet's translations of Ovid show his own wry humour at times, as in the line '*honi soit . . .*', which is in fact the motto of the British monarchy – in Norman French. It means 'dishonour to him who thinks ill of it'.

30 Aurelius's meditations have been a bestseller ever since.

31 R. Lane Fox, *Pagans and Christians*, New York: Viking, 1986, pp. 340–1,

thinks they had little effect on Rome, but A. Rousselle notes variety in different parts of the Empire (*Porneia,* pp. 101–2).

Chapter 4

1 Josephus, *Antiquities of the Jews*, is the best historical source.
2 NRSV, Introduction to the Apocrypha.
3 Bruce M. Metzger, *An Introduction to the Apocrypha*, New York: Oxford University Press, 1977, pp. 223–4.
4 This is followed by similar warnings against loose women, singing girls, prostitutes and dining with another man's wife (Ecclus. 9.3–9).
5 Ecclesiasticus 26; 36.24.
6 Rachel had died giving birth to Benjamin, so Bilhah may have been the substitute wife. A contrast is being drawn here with Joseph, who resisted Potiphar's wife.
7 J. H. Charlesworth (ed.), *The Old Testament Pseudepigrapha*, London: Darton, Longman and Todd, 1983, vol. 1, p. 335. (Sibylline Oracle, Bk 1. 22–37.)
8 *The Old Testament Pseudepigrapha*, p. 336. (Sibylline Oracle, Bk 1. 39–49.)
9 For example, in the book of Esther he adds the explanation that Haman is an Amalekite, hence his hatred of the Benjamite Mordecai. *Antiquities*, XI ch. 6.
10 Josephus, *Antiquities*, trans. W. Whiston, I, ch. 1. (There are many editions of Whiston's translation, first brought out in 1737.)
11 *Antiquities*, III, ch. 12.
12 *Midrash Rabbah. Genesis* (17,2), ed. H. Freedman and M. Simon, London: Soncino Press, 1939, p. 132.
13 *Midrash Rabbah. Genesis*, p. 133, and elsewhere.
14 *Midrash Rabbah. Genesis*, p. 141.
15 [I have been unable to find the exact reference for this quotation, but there is a variant in *Midrash Rabbah. Genesis*, p. 137. Ed.]
16 *Midrash Rabbah. Leviticus*, ed. H. Freedman and M. Simon, London: Soncino Press, 1939, p. 100 (on Lev. 8.1). The story is very popular in rabbinic literature, cf. *Midrash Rabbah. Genesis*, p. 617.
17 [I have been unable to track down the translation used by Bishop Coleman here, but the Hebrew text and a literal translation can be found in *The Metsudah Chamash/Rashi*, trans. Rabbi Avrohom Davis, Hoboken, N.J.: rev. edn, 1993, vol. 1, pp. 26–7. Ed.]
18 Geza Vermes, *An Introduction to the Complete Dead Sea Scrolls*, London: SCM Press, 1999, pp. 117f. Gerd Theissen, *A Theory of Primitive Christian Religion*, London: SCM Press, 1999, pp. 27f.
19 *An Introduction to the Dead Sea Scrolls*, pp. 162–3 and pp. 187–8. (Jesus commends celibacy to his first apostles for the sake of the kingdom. Matt. 19.2.)
20 Geza Vermes, *The Complete Dead Sea Scrolls in English*, London: Penguin, 1998, p. 130. Note that *An Introduction to the Complete Scrolls*, London: SCM Press, 1999, is a different book; they complement each other.
21 Tobit 8.19–21.

22 S. Safrai and M. Stern, eds, *The Jewish People in the First Century*, Amsterdam: Van Gorcum, 1976, vol. 2 pp. 752–3. Also E. Ferguson, *Backgrounds of Early Christianity*, Grand Rapids, Mi: Eerdmans, 1987, p. 55.

23 *Midrash Rabbah. Genesis*, 17.3, pp. 133–4. In another version Rabbi Jose finds his former wife being beaten by her second husband, who was poor. Jose pays to support them both.

24 The Mishnah collects together the best of the oral teaching of the rabbis for some four centuries before and after Christ, and is treated in Judaism as second only to the Torah in authority. It is a list of rules developed from the Bible, but not a commentary on scripture, and is quite distinct from Midrash. *The Mishnah*, trans. H. Danby, Oxford: Oxford University Press, 1933 and many reprints.

25 *Mishnah* (Gittin 9.10), p. 321.

26 G. von Rad, *Genesis*, London: SCM Press, 1972, p. 150. A. Phillips, *Ancient Israel's Criminal Law*, Oxford: Blackwell, 1970, pp. 110–11.

27 *Antiquities*, IV, ch. 8.

28 Matthew 19.3.

29 *The Jewish People in the First Century*, vol. 2, p. 791.

30 Based on Malachi 2.16 and quoted in the report *Marriage, Divorce and the Church*, London: SPCK, 1971, p. 80.

31 J. Neusner, *Judaism in the Beginning of Christianity*, London: SPCK, 1984, p. 32. See also Leonie J. Archer, 'The Role of Women in the Religion, Ritual and Cult of Graeco-Roman Palestine' in *Images of Women in Antiquity*, ed. A. Cameron and A. Kuhrt, London: Croom Helm, 1983, pp. 273–4. For a fresh look at the models of femininity in rabbinic interpretations of the Old Testament see Leila Bronner, *From Eve to Esther*, Louisville, Ky: Westminster John Knox Press, 1994. Prof. Bronner's father was a rabbi.

Chapter 5

1 Matthew 25.1–13.

2 John 2.1–11.

3 Mark 12.18–27 and parallels in Matthew 22.23–33 and Luke 20.27–40.

4 There was however much speculation in early non-canonical Christian writings about the relatives of Jesus, and some of the women mentioned in the Gospels may have been his aunts, cousins, etc. E. Hennecke, *The New Testament Apocrypha*, London: Lutterworth, 1963, vol. 1, pp. 418–32.

5 Mark 10.29 and parallels in Matthew and Luke.

6 After Luke 21.38.

7 Luke 6.37 cf. John 8.15. G. Thiessen, *A Theory of Primitive Christian Religion*, London: SCM Press, 1999, p. 30 takes this incident as an example of the radical demand of Jesus in going beyond the dictates of the law towards a recognition of the inadequacy of all human beings.

8 The Greek word *eunoukizo* means literally 'to castrate', and metaphorically, to choose celibacy.

9 A careful discussion of these texts can be found in *Marriage, Divorce and the*

Church, London: SPCK, 1971, appendix 1, by Bishop Hugh Montefiore, a New Testament scholar with Jewish antecedents. More recently, there is a useful review in Morna Hooker, *Commentary on the Gospel according to St Mark*, London: A. and C. Black, 1991, pp. 234–7. See also E. P. Sanders, *Jesus and Judaism*, London: SCM Press, 1985, pp. 256–7, or more briefly, his *Jewish Law from Jesus to Mishnah*, London: SCM Press, 1990, p. 5. For a recent and thorough examination of the exegetical problems involved see R. B. Hays, *The Moral Vision of the New Testament*, Edinburgh: T. and T. Clark, 1997, ch. 15. For the meaning of *porneia* see *Theological Dictionary of the New Testament*, ed. G. Friedrich, Grand Rapids, Mi: Eerdmans, 1968, vol. 6, pp. 579–80, or the comprehensive Aline Rousselle, *Porneia*, tr. F. Pheasant, Oxford: Blackwell, 1988.

10 For the circumcision issue see J. D. G. Dunn, *The Parting of the Ways*, London: SCM Press, 1991, pp. 124–5.

11 The list is given in *Midrash Rabbah. Genesis*, XVI.6, p. 131 – attributed to Rabbi Levi, who derived it as a commentary on Genesis 2.16, thereby dating it back to Adam. See also XXIV.5, p. 202.

12 Peder Borgen, *Early Christianity and Hellenistic Judaism*, Edinburgh: T. and T. Clark, 1996, pp. 233–4.

13 See also Galatians 5.1–6.

14 1 Thessalonians 4.3, 1 Corinthians 6.13, 2 Corinthians 12.21, Galatians 5.16–21.

15 Acts 5.34–9.

16 1 Corinthians 9.5.

17 As already noted, younger widows were advised to remarry (1 Tim. 5.3–14). The congregation could support only the older ones. The view that Paul was a widower is supported in the Anchor commentary (no. 32), *1 Corinthians*, by W. F. Orr and J. A. Walther, New York: Doubleday, 1976, p. 210, and pressed by Angela West in *Feminist Theology, A Reader*, ed. Anne Loades, London: SPCK, 1990, pp. 77–8.

18 The six letters to churches are, in supposed order of composition, 1 Thessalonians, 1 and 2 Corinthians, Galatians, Romans and Philippians, with one personal letter, to Philemon. Apart from Romans, Paul's letters to churches were written to those he had founded and with whom he still kept in touch.

19 Among many commentaries on 1 Corinthians are classics by J. Moffat (London: Hodder and Stoughton, 1938) and by C. K. Barrett (London: A. and C. Black, 1968). More recently, W. F. Orr and J. A. Walther (New York: Doubleday, 1976), R. B. Hays (Louisville, Ky: John Knox Press, 1997), R. F. Collins (Collegeville, Min: The Liturgical Press, 1999) and more specialist, D. G. Horrell, *The Social Ethos of the Corinthian Correspondence*, Edinburgh: T. and T. Clark, 1996.

20 Acts 18, 1 Corinthians 11.

21 Rowan Williams, 'Fobidden Fruit' in *Intimate Affairs*, ed. M. Percy, London: Darton, Longman and Todd, 1997, p. 27.

22 For a convincing attempt see R. B. Hays, *The Moral Vision*, p. 50.

23 John A. Ziesler, *Pauline Christianity*, Oxford: Oxford University Press, 1983, p. 11.

24 1 Corinthians 5.1–5. The NRSV 'living together' is the euphemism for the Greek *porneia*.

25 1 Corinthians 12.12–26 is the full development of this theme.

26 For a different appraisal of Paul's teaching on marriage and celibacy in 1 Corinthians 7 see E. S. Fiorenza, *In Memory of Her*, London: SCM Press, 1983, pp. 220–1.

27 R. B. Hays, *First Corinthians*, p. 186.

28 All the major Commentaries consider these verses. See also D. G. Horrell, *The Social Ethos of the Corinthian Correspondence*, p. 168 and J. Tomson, *Paul and the Jewish Law*, Minneapolis: Fortress Press, 1990, pp. 131–2 and the lively E. S. Fiorenza, *In Memory of Her*, p. 226 for much useful background detail.

29 The concept has been described as casting a new and brilliant light on married life. A. E. Harvey, *Companion to the New Testament*, Oxford: Oxford University Press, 1970, p. 628.

30 See NRSV note on v. 26 and on 1 Corinthians 6.11.

31 Fiorenza, *In Memory of Her*, p. 269, agrees.

32 See note in NRSV which offers alternative translations.

33 1 Corinthians 7.8, reiterated in 1 Timothy 5.3–16. See also Acts 6.1 and James 1.27.

34 Paul refers simply to joint heirs in Romans 8.17.

35 R. B. Hays, *The Moral Vision*, pp. 200–1.

36 1 Kings 3.3, 11.1.

37 Hosea's analogy between his marriage to the faithless Gomer and God's steadfast love for faithless Israel has already been noted in ch. 2.

38 The NRSV has the relatively unattractive 'Wondrously show your steadfast love, O saviour of those who seek refuge'.

39 Deuteronomy 6.50, NRSV.

40 The second love commandment is quoted from Leviticus 19.18, which, in the Septuagint, is the same word, *agapeseis*.

Chapter 6

1 Henry Chadwick, *The Early Church*, London: Penguin, 1987, pp. 42–3. For a concise analysis of the Christian impact on the closing centuries of the classical era see *The Oxford History of the Classical World: The Roman World*, ed. J. Boardman and others, Oxford: Oxford University Press, 1988 – the final chapter by H. Chadwick.

2 1 Corinthians 11.1, Ephesians 5.1.

3 Wayne Meeks, *The Moral World of the First Christians*, London: SPCK, 1987, pp. 41–2.

4 For the convergence of Stoic and Christian ideas about sex see J. A. Brundage, *Law, Sex and Christian Society in Medieval Europe*, Chicago: University of Chicago Press, 1987, pp. 18–21. [The reference which Brundage gives to Seneca (Letters, 124.2) seems to be wrong, but cf. Letter 97, 'On the Degeneracy of our Age'. Ed.]

5 Musonius Rufus, in Yale Classical Studies, vol. 10, ed. A. R. Bellinger, New Haven: Yale University Press, 1947, trans. (from the Greek) Cora E. Lutz,

pp. 89–93. See also D. G. Hunter (ed.), *Marriage in the Early Church*, Minneapolis: Fortress Press, 1992, p. 8.

6 [The author's term 'a bishop in Rome' is deliberate, since there is considerable controversy concerning whether or not there was a single bishop for the city at this time (later to be referred to as the Pope) or whether different house churches each had their own *episcopos*. Ed.]

7 The full texts of 1 Clement and Ignatius are in *Early Christian Fathers*, vol. 1 of the Library of Christian Classics, London: SCM Press, 1953. For a comparison between Paul and Clement on the place of women in Corinth see D. G. Horrell, *The Social Ethos of the Corinthian Correspondence*, Edinburgh: T. and T. Clark, 1996, pp. 263–4.

8 Gnosticism is a collective term for a variety of heresies that challenged Christian orthodoxy from the first century onwards. See H. Chadwick, *The Early Church*, pp. 34–5.

9 E. Schillebeeckx, *Marriage: Human Reality and Saving Ministry*, London: Sheed and Ward, 1965, vol. 2, pp. 244–5.

10 *Didache* 2.2; 5.1. *The Apostolic Fathers*, trans. J. B. Lightfoot, London: Macmillan, 1891.

11 *The Apostolic Fathers*, p. 423. Modern trans. by D. G. Hunter in *Marriage in the Early Church*, p. 29.

12 Peter Brown, *The Body and Society*, London: Faber and Faber, 1989, pp. 16–17.

13 1 Corinthians 15.50–8 is used as a standard lesson at Christian funerals.

14 J. Boswell, *The Marriage of Likeness*, London: HarperCollins, 1995, pp. 117–18.

15 *The Early Church*, p. 91.

16 Quoted in *Marriage in the Early Church*, pp. 33–4. For the complete text see Tertullian, *Treatises on Marriage*, trans. W. P. Le Saint, London: Longmans, Green and Co, 1951, *Ad Uxorem*, pp. 10–11.

17 cf. Plato, *Republic*, 329c.

18 Quoted in *Marriage in the Early Church*, Clement of Alexandria, *The Instructor*, book 2, pp. 44–5. See also *Christ the Educator*, trans. S. P. Wood, Washington, DC: Catholic University of America Press, 1953.

19 Quoted in *Marriage in the Early Church*, *Miscellanies*, book 2, pp. 44–9. See also Clement of Alexandria, *Stomateis I–III* (Miscellanies), trans. J. Ferguson, Washington, DC: Catholic University of America Press, 1991.

20 Book 3, par. 49. *Marriage in the Early Church*, p. 52.

21 E. Hennecke, *New Testament Apocrypha*, vol. 2, London: Lutterworth Press, 1965, pp. 370–3.

22 *New Testament Aprocrypha*, pp. 448–9, also *Marriage in the Early Church*, pp. 57–8.

23 *New Testament Apocrypha*, p. 354.

24 *Marriage in the Early Church*, pp. 64–5.

25 Ambrose, *On Virginity*, Bk. I, 7.35 tr. Boniface Ramsey, in his *Ambrose*, London: Routledge, 1997, p. 83.

26 Jerome's commentary on Matthew 19.10 in P. L. Reynolds, *Marriage in the Western Church*, Leiden: Brill, 1994, pp. 223–4.

27 Basil, *Letter to Amphilocius*, 199. *Marriage in the Early Church*, pp. 144–5.

28 'Almighty God, who hast given us grace at this time with one accord . . .'

29 John Chrysostom, *Homily 20 On Ephesians. Marriage in the Early Church*, pp. 77–81.

30 A good guide to Augustine is Peter Brown's *Augustine of Hippo*, London: Faber and Faber, rev. edn 2000. A brief account can be found in H. Chadwick, *Augustine*, Oxford: Oxford University Press, 1986. The quotation is from *Confessions*, VI, 23.

31 *Confessions* bk. 4, 2. Library of Christian Classics, London: SCM Press, 1955, vol. 7, p. 77.

32 [I have been unable to find the translation used here by Bishop Coleman, but the passage, with another translation, can be found in *De Bono Coniugali*, *c.* 401. *The Good of Marriage*, trans. C. T. Wilcox, Washington, DC: The Catholic University Press, 1955. ch. 5. Ed.]

33 Augustine, *De Bono Coniugali*, 7. *Marriage in the Early Church*, p. 109.

34 Augustine, *Confessions*, 2.2.

Chapter 7

1 Richard A. Fletcher, *The Conversion of Europe*, London: HarperCollins, 1997.

2 The Wife of Bath in Chaucer's *Canterbury Tales* was respectably married five times at the church door.

3 See Bede's *Ecclesiastical History*; also *The Anglo-Saxon Chronicle*, trans. and ed. Michael Swanton, London: Dent, 1996.

4 Born in Crediton *c.* 675 and later Archbishop of Fulda.

5 For marriage customs and the roles of men and women at the end of the Anglo-Saxon period see R. Lacey and D. Danziger, *The Year 1000*, London: Little, Brown, 1999, pp. 169–70.

6 Norman Davies, *Europe*, London: Pimlico, 1996, chs 5 and 6. J. Cannon (ed.) *Oxford Companion to British History*, 1997, pp. 32–3.

7 In the early Middle Ages it was widely predicted that Christ's return would occur at the end of 999, if not before.

8 Peter Brown, *The Body and Society*, London: Faber and Faber, 1989, p. 446.

9 Peter Brown, *Augustine of Hippo*, London, Faber and Faber, 2000, p. 393. Brown's full account of the controversy is in ch. 32.

10 Extracts from Paulinus, Carmen 25 (1–167), tr. D. G. Hunter, *Marriage in the Early Church*, Minneapolis: Fortress Press, 1992, pp. 128–9.

11 The rule 'consent makes marriage' is attributed to Ulpian, a third-century jurist, much quoted in Justinian's Digest.

12 P. L. Reynolds, *Marriage in the Western Church*, Leiden: Brill, 1994, pp. 49–50 (Digest 1.1.9).

13 Procopius of Caesarea, *The Secret History*, trans. G. A. Williamson, London: Folio Society, 1990, ch. 4.

14 The best brief guide to the preparation of the *Corpus Juris Civilis* is in C. F.

Kolbert's introduction to *The Digest of Roman Law*, Harmondsworth: Penguin, 1979.

15 *Nuptiae autem sive matrimonium est viri et mulieris coniunctio, individium conseutedinem, vitae continens. The Institutes of Justinian*, trans. J. A. C. Thomas, Cape Town: Juta, 1975, IX, 1.

16 *Nuptiae sunt coniunctio maris et feminae et consortium omnis vitae, divini et humani uris communicatio.* Digest 23.2.1 trans. P. L. Reynolds, *Marriage in the Western Church*, New York: E. J. Brill, 1994, pp. 8–9.

17 William Dalrymple, *From the Holy Mountain*, London: HarperCollins, 1997.

18 John Moschus, *Pratum Spirituale,* 76 in Judith Herrin's 'In Search of Byzantine Women: Three Avenues of Approach', in *Images of Women in Antiquity*, ed. A. Cameron and A. Kuhrt, London: Croom Helm, 1983, ch. 11, p. 173. This chapter also gives details of secular women's property and inheritance rules. See also John Moschus, *The Spiritual Meadow*, trans. J. Wortley, Kalamazoo, Mi: Cistercian Publications, 1992.

19 J. A. Brundage, *Law, Sex and Christian Society in Medieval Europe*, Chicago: University of Chicago Press, 1987, p. 163, has an amusing chart showing twenty-three disciplinary hurdles a married couple had to jump before responding to any randy feelings!

20 W. H. C. Frend, *A New Eusebius*, London: SPCK, 1987, pp. 290–1. The bishops of York, London and (probably) Lincoln were at Arles.

21 F. and J. Gies, *Marriage and the Family in the Middle Ages*, New York: Harper and Row, 1989, pp. 87–8.

22 K. W. Stevenson, *Nuptial Blessings*, London, SPCK, 1982, for a full account of marriage liturgies.

23 *Marriage in the Early Church*, pp. 152–3.

24 *Code of Canon Law*, Latin-English edn, Washington DC: Canon Law Society of America, 1983. Many countries now have their own secular systems for legal marriage, optional or obligatory, irrespective of church weddings.

25 See the outline of Canon Law in Mark Hill, *Ecclesiastical Law*, 2nd edn, Oxford: Oxford University Press, 2001. Full account in *The Canon Law of the Church of England*, London: SPCK, 1947.

26 Pope from 1073 to 1085. See J. N. D. Kelly, *Oxford Dictionary of Popes*, New York: Oxford University Press, 1986, pp. 154–5.

27 David Edwards, *Christian England*, London: Collins, 1981–4, vol. 1, pp. 157–8.

28 J. R. H. Moorman, *Church Life in England in the Thirteenth Century*, Cambridge: Cambridge University Press, 1945, pp. 85–6, 226–7.

29 The same custom still obtained in some parts of England in the twentieth century. The young people became engaged, and when the pregnancy occurred would come to the vicarage and fix a date for the marriage and the baptism.

30 *Church Life in England in the Thirteenth Century*, p. 85.

31 *Nuptial Blessings*, p. 44.

32 A full survey of the many views is in J. A. Brundage, *Law, Sex and Christian Society in Medieval Europe*, ch. 4.

33 *Church Life in England in the Thirteenth Century*, pp. 226–7. See also the

report *An Honourable Estate*, London: Church House Publishing, 1988, pp. 18–19.

34 Adrian Thatcher, *Marriage after Modernity*, Sheffield: Sheffield Academic Press, 1999, pp. 108–9.

35 R. and C. Brooke, *Popular Religion in the Middle Ages*, London: Thames and Hudson, 1984, pp. 110–11.

36 Matrimonial Causes Act, 1973.

37 Diarmaid MacCulloch, *Groundwork of Christian History*, London: Epworth Press, 1987, pp. 127–8.

38 E. Schillebeeckx, *Marriage: Human Reality and Saving Ministry*, London: Sheed and Ward, 1965, vol. 1, pp. 203–4, vol. 2, p. 167.

39 C. S. Lewis suggested that it would be impossible to explain romantic love to either Aristotle or St Paul. *The Allegory of Love*, London: Oxford University Press, 1936, ch. 1.

40 The Plantagenet era was complex. See Norman Davies, *The Isles*, London: Macmillan, 1999, pp. 333–4, and Alison Weir, *Eleanor of Aquitaine*, London: Jonathan Cape, 1999.

41 *The Isles*, p. 322.

42 A selection from *Carmina Burana* was set to music by Carl Orff in 1936.

43 J. R. R. Tolkien (ed.), *Sir Gawain and the Green Knight*, rev. edn by N. Davies and E. V. Gordon, Oxford: Clarendon Press, 1967.

44 *Church Times*, 18 May 2001.

45 Robin Gill, *A Textbook of Christian Ethics*, 2nd edn, Edinburgh: T. and T. Clark, 1995, p. 37.

46 The word 'nature' is nowadays ambiguous, sometimes meaning little more than instinctive desire, and tends to be replaced in terms of moral obligation by the concepts of human rights and duties. [For ancient and medieval philosophy, as well as for theology, the standard sense of the word 'natural' is given by Aristotle (*Politics* book 1), where the 'nature' of things is defined in terms of what they become when they achieve their potential. Thus humans are 'by nature' political animals, because we need a *polis* in order to realize fullness of being. A major reason for the decline of this sense of 'nature' is the loss of belief that we are born with certain capacities that God or Nature 'intends' us to realize if we are to be either fulfilled or truly happy. Ed.]

47 *A Textbook of Christian Ethics*, p. 483, based on *Summa Contra Gentiles*, trans. V. J. Bourke, London: University of Notre Dame Press edition of 1975, 3. 2. 122–3.

48 *A Textbook of Christian Ethics*, p. 489.

Chapter 8

1 Karen Armstrong, *A History of God*, London: Heinemann, 1993, p. 318.

2 The novel by Charles Reade, *The Cloister on the Hearth*, was supposedly based on Erasmus' own account of his origin as the son of a priest, but this is probably spurious. See R. H. Bainton, *Erasmus of Christendom*, London: Collins, 1970, p. 20.

3 *Erasmus of Christendom*, p. 70.

4 This expression is used in the Preface to Cranmer's first Prayer Book, and repeated in the Book of Common Prayer of 1662.

5 *Erasmus of Christendom*, pp. 274–5.

6 The visit to the bedchamber as a part of the marriage ceremony was discontinued for obvious reasons, and replaced by the blessing of the matrimonial home on a separate occasion.

7 Heinrich Bornkamm, *Luther in Mid-Career 1521–30*, trans. E. T. Bachmann, Philadelphia: Fortress Press, 1983, pp. 401–2.

8 M. Luther, *A Commentary on the Sixth Commandment*, quoted in *Ethics*, ed. Peter Singer, Oxford: Oxford University Press, pp. 104–5.

9 Luther, *Letters of Spiritual Counsel*, 6 August 1524, ed. and trans. T. G. Tappert, London: SCM Press, 1955, pp. 270–1.

10 *Letters of Spiritual Counsel*, 27 March 1525, pp. 272–3.

11 [This passage does not appear to be in the edition that Bishop Coleman cites elsewhere (the Hazlitt version of 1857) but variants can be found in another edition of the *Table Talk*, *Luther's Works*, vol. 54, Philadelphia: Fortress Press, 1967, e.g. p. 224. Ed.]

12 M. Luther, *Table Talk*, ed. W. Hazlitt, London: Bohn, 1857, p. 297.

13 *Table Talk*, p. 298.

14 *Table Talk*, p. 301.

15 *Table Talk*, p. 301.

16 *Table Talk*, p. 307.

17 *Table Talk*, pp. 307–8.

18 F. Wendel, *Calvin*, London: Collins, 1963, p. 65.

19 *Calvin*, p. 66.

20 J. Calvin, *Institutes of the Christian Religion*, ed. J. T. Mitchell, trans. F. L. Battles, vol. 1, London: SCM Press, 1961, II, ch. 8.41, vol. 1, p. 405.

21 *Institutes*, II, ch. 8.42–3, p. 406.

22 *Institutes*, II, ch. 8.44, pp. 407–8.

23 *Institutes*, IV, ch. 12.23, vol. 2, pp. 1249–50.

24 *Institutes*, IV, ch. 12.24, vol. 2, p. 1251.

25 *Institutes*, IV, ch. 19.35–6, vol. 2, pp. 1482–3.

26 *The Cambridge Medieval History*, vol. 7, J. R. Tanner and others (eds), Cambridge: Cambridge University Press, 1932, p. 451; cf. p. 277.

27 Diarmaid MacCulloch, *Thomas Cranmer*, New Haven: Yale University Press, 1966, p. 249. Thomas Cromwell also sent his wife abroad, and it shows something of the arbitrary and cruel power of the king that two of his principal officers could be treated thus.

28 *Thomas Cranmer*, p. 69.

29 Text of the Trau-Ordnung, 1534, in G. J. Cumming, *A History of Anglican Liturgy*, 2nd edn, London: Macmillan, 1982, pp. 275–6 or in K. W. Stevenson, *Nuptial Blessings*, London, SPCK, 1982, p. 127.

30 *Nuptial Blessings*, p. 131.

31 Stephen Lake, *Marriage, a Practical Guide*, London: Church House Publishing, 2000, p. 8.

32 *The First and Second Prayer Books of Edward the Sixth*, London: Dent, 1910 and reprints, p. 252.

33 1662 has 'instituted of God in the time of man's innocency' and 1928, 'instituted of God himself'. The ASB has 'marriage is a gift of God in creation'.

34 The man says he endows his wife with all his worldly goods, but this is a piety; it had no effect in law.

35 E. Schillebeeckx, *Marriage: Secular Reality and Saving Mystery*, London: Sheed and Ward, 1965, vol. 2, p. 167. J. A. Brundage, *Law, Sex and Christian Society in Medieval Europe*, Chicago: University of Chicago Press, 1987, pp. 562–3.

36 Present Catholic Canon Law is still the same and clearly states that the priest assists at the marriage, but he does not make it. If no priest is available, the ordinary may authorize a lay substitute. Code of Canon Law, ch. 5, Canons 1188–9.

37 Jeremy Taylor, *Whole Works*, ed. R. Heber, London: 1828, vol. 5, pp. 248–9.

38 *Whole Works*, vol. 5, pp. 249–53.

39 *Whole Works*, vol. 5, pp. 264–5. Emphases in the text.

Chapter 9

1 There is a problem here in that what is alleged to be the 'clear' moral teaching of the Bible, or of the Church's magisterium, is sometimes a matter of interpretation, and not all conservative Christians agree on this.

2 John A. Robinson, *Christian Freedom in Permissive Society*, London: SCM Press, 1970, ch. 11.

3 cf. Isaiah 44.28.

4 See *An Honourable Estate*, London: Church House Publishing, 1988, pp. 24–5. Bishop Coleman was a member of the group which produced this report.

5 L. Stone, *The Family, Sex and Marriage 1500–1800*, London: Penguin, 1979, p. 30.

6 See J. R. Gillis, *For Better, For Worse: British Marriages from 1600 to the Present*, Oxford: Oxford University Press, 1985, ch. 1.

7 *For Better, For Worse*, p. 142.

8 The Registration Act, passed in the same year, sought to establish a more efficient way of registering births, deaths and marriages.

9 *The Lambeth Conferences (1867–1948)*, London: SPCK, 1948, pp. 293–4.

10 *The Lambeth Conferences*, p. 295.

11 *The Lambeth Conferences*, p. 165.

12 *The Lambeth Conferences*, p. 101. Note that in this edition the pagination starts afresh with the 1948 conference and restarts yet again with the reports of committees.

13 *The Lambeth Conferences*, p. 99.

14 *The Lambeth Conferences*, p. 295.

15 *The Report of the Lambeth Conference 1978*, London: Church Information Office, 1978, pp. 50–1.

16 *The Lambeth Conferences*, p. 294.

17 *The Truth shall Make you Free. The Lambeth Conference 1988*, London: Church House Publishing, 1988, pp. 220–1. Polygamy is still an issue for

Christians in several parts of the world as Christian churches try to apply Christian norms of marriage to traditional societies. It is said that at Lambeth Conferences there was a tacit understanding that Western churches would not raise this issue too sharply – leaving churches time to make difficult adjustments – in return for an understanding that churches in the developing world would not be too aggressive in raising issues regarding homosexual behaviour, which was regarded differently by many Western churches. Any such tacit understanding was broken at the Lambeth Conference of 1998.

18 *The Lambeth Conferences*, p. 295. [Paragraph 43 shows cordial appreciation of medical men who oppose artificial birth control.]

19 *The Lambeth Conferences*, pp. 195–6.

20 Keith Briant, *Marie Stopes*, London: Hogarth, 1962, pp. 262–4.

21 *The Official Report of the Lambeth Conference 1998*, Harrisburg, Pen: Morehouse Publishing, 1999, p. 381.

22 London: Friends Home Service Committee, 1963.

23 This argument, quite clearly, will be challenged even by some of those who consider themselves to be 'liberals'. Human beings may have need of moral guidelines that cannot be rethought in every situation as it arises.

24 *Sex and Morality*, London: SCM Press, 1966, p. 55.

25 *Putting Asunder*, London: SPCK, 1966. A report appointed by the Archbishop of Canterbury in January 1964.

26 A report of a Commission appointed by the Archbishop of Canterbury to prepare a statement on the Christian Doctrine of Marriage, London: SPCK, 1971.

27 The report of the General Synod Marriage Commission, London: Church Information Office, 1978.

28 An appendix discusses the rules for nullity in the Roman Catholic Church (116–17). If it can be argued that either party did not truly intend to create a permanent and indissoluble union, then there can be a ground for nullity. cf. *Marriage, Divorce and the Church*, p. 63.

29 London: Church House Publishing, 1988.

30 On the 'sacrament' of marriage see also *Marriage and the Church's Task*, p. 49.

31 It is often believed that marriage law in the Church of England demands that at least one party be baptized, and The Canon Law Commission of 1947 drafted a canon to demand this. However, it is doubtful whether this would be a legal stipulation without the approval of Parliament. See *An Honourable Estate*, p. 78.

32 London: Church House Publishing, 1991.

33 London: Church House Publishing, 2003.

34 London: Church House Publishing, 2003.

35 Those familiar with Bishop Coleman's discussion in his *Gay Christians*, London: SCM Press, 1989, especially pp. 190–200, will notice that the position suggested here has moved from what he calls options B and C, towards one that might be said to include elements of B, C and D.

36 Those parts of pension or other rights that offset the special vulnerability and

lack of earnings that go with pregnancy (and perhaps early childcare) might be separated from those rights that do not.

37 John Boswell, *The Marriage of Likeness: Same-sex Unions in Pre-modern Europe*, London: HarperCollins, 1995 – a book referred to elsewhere by Bishop Coleman.

38 For a more adequate discussion of the relevant biblical passages see P. E. Coleman, *Christian Attitudes to Homosexuality*, London: SPCK, 1980 and *Gay Christians*; also Walter Moberly, 'The Use of Scripture in Contemporary Debate about Homosexuality', *Theology* August 2000. For a more conservative approach see Marion L. Soards, *Scripture and Homosexuality*, Louisville, Ky: Westminster John Knox Press, 1995. This author is open to the possibility of (active) homosexual people being members of the church, but is opposed to any suggestions of their ordination.

39 There may be a measure of control in the case of those people who are genetically disposed to be bisexual, in that a consistent practice may fortify one inclination rather than another.

40 cf. *Issues in Human Sexuality*, 1991, pp. 14–15.

41 For a survey of these passages see *Christian Attitudes to Homosexuality*, part B.

42 This liberal is not taking the 'way out' of claiming that only male prostitution or only pederasty were being condemned in the Bible. I think it much more likely that the Holiness Code, and St Paul, were opposed to all forms of active homosexual intercourse – although there is place for some debate on this matter. At the same time, some passages, including those in Deuteronomy, may only refer to temple prostitution and not to homosexual activity in general.

43 There is considerable doubt as to whether the third epistle was actually written by Paul.

44 Indications are that this figure may be around 4 per cent (Kinsey), although some surveys put the number as closer to 2 per cent (see A. F. Dixson, *Primate Sexuality*, Oxford: Oxford University Press, 1998, p. 164). The figure is probably lower in females. In addition, there is another (disputed) percentage that relates to those for whom there is a tendency to find homosexual activity more inviting than heterosexual activity, while both are physiologically possible. The actual number of those with homosexual orientations, needless to say, is often very different because of environmental factors. Whatever the figures be, they do not, of course, settle the moral questions, but they bear upon them on the grounds that the more certain it is that a significant number of people are genetically determined to be homosexual in orientation, the harder it is to insist that lifelong celibacy must be a standard rule for all these members of society.

45 *The Guardian*, 2 September 2003 (p. 3), reported the Archbishop in Nigeria as asserting that 'Even in the world of animals . . . we don't hear of such things.' In fact, homosexual activity is common among apes, monkeys, dogs and some species of birds. In contrast see *Towards a Quaker View of Sex*, p. 54.

46 See, for example, *Animal Behaviour Abstracts*, 'Cambridge Scientific

Abstracts', Maryland: June 2000, 28:2, p. 42, where 'relief of tension' is supported as a purpose of homosexual animal activity. On the frequency of homosexual activity in primates see A. F. Dixson, *Primate Sexuality*, pp. 159–64. This author points out that homosexual activity in animals does not necessarily imply homosexual orientation, which is a more controversial matter. See also F. De Waal, *Peacemaking Among Primates*, Cambridge, Ma: Harvard University Press, 1989, pp. 201–5.

47 Outside either a religious philosophy, or some other kind of metaphysical philosophy, questions about the 'purpose' of human or animal activities can only meaningfully be asked within a very limited context. Within biology, it is natural to use purposive language within what is sometimes called an 'internal teleology', for example, the heart has a 'purpose' in the sense of a function within the workings of a body. However, to ask for some 'external' purpose, with reference to God or (as in Aristotle) Nature, is to ask a question that many will refuse to entertain. With respect to 'gay liberation', I have heard the claim put forward that the 'purpose' of sex is simply 'fun'. However, not only is there a problem here about what is meant by 'purpose', if the *only* purpose of sex were fun, this would not rule out many kinds of exploitative sex, which all the more responsible supporters of gay and lesbian rights are most anxious to condemn.

48 These rules, of course, will not be identical, since it is the role of law only to enforce *some* moral rules, namely those most needed in the protection of others. Aquinas makes this distinction (*Summa Theologiae*, 1a 2ae, Q. 96, A. 2.).

49 Many teenagers, for example at single-sex schools, have exclusively same-sex urges until they mix in a wider circle. Some of them are convinced that they are purely homosexual by genetic disposition, only to find that they were mistaken. No one, in their teens, and possibly in their early twenties, can *know* whether or not this is the case. Even if their beliefs turn out to be right, they did not 'know' this in their teens. On this matter see *Towards a Quaker View of Sex*, p. 24.

50 The situation might change when both an adequate time has been given for reflection, and when (and if) a different consensus is reached.

51 Michael J. Langford, *A Liberal Theology for the Twenty-First Century: A Passion for Reason*, Aldershot: Ashgate 2001, chs 1 and 2.

52 *Gay Christians*, pp. 25–6.

53 From *Common Worship: Marriage*. London: Church House Publishing, 2001, p. iv.

54 *Common Worship*, p. 3.

55 *Common Worship*, p. 9

56 *The Methodist Worship Book*, Peterborough: Methodist Publishing House, 1999, pp. 367–9.

57 *The Methodist Worship Book*, pp. 385–6.

58 *Canons of the Church of England*, 6th edn, London: Church House Publishing, 2000. B 30, p. 51.

Further Reading

Ambrose, *On Virginity*, trans. Boniface Ramsey, in his *Ambrose*, London: Routledge, 1997.

Anglo-Saxon Chronicle (The), trans. and ed. Michael Swanton, London: Dent, 1996.

Apostolic Fathers (The), trans. J. B. Lightfoot, London: Macmillan, 1891.

Appolodoros Against Neaira, (Demosthenes 59), ed. and trans. C. Carey, Warminster: Aris and Phillips, 1992.

Archer, Leonie J., 'The Role of Women in the Religion, Ritual and Cult of Graeco-Roman Palestine', in *Images of Women in Antiquity*, ed. A. Cameron and A. Kuhrt, London: Croom Helm, 1983.

Aristotle, (Nicomachean) *Ethics*, trans. J. A. K. Thomson, rev. H. Treddenick, London: Penguin, 1976.

Armstrong, Karen, *A History of God*, London: Heinemann, 1993.

Armstrong, Karen, *In the Beginning*, London: HarperCollins, 1996.

Augustine, *Confessions*, Library of Christian Classics, London: SCM Press, vol. 7, 1955.

Augustine, *The Good of Marriage*, trans. C. T. Wilcox, Washington, DC: The Catholic University Press, 1955.

Bainton, R. H., *Erasmus of Christendom*, London: Collins, 1970.

Barrett, C. K., *Commentary on the First Epistle to the Corinthians*, London: A. and C. Black, 1968.

Barth, Karl, *Church Dogmatics,* Edinburgh: T. and T. Clark, 1961.

Bayerlin, W. et al. (eds), trans. J. Bowden, *Near Eastern Texts relating to the Old Testament*, London: SCM Press, 1997.

Bede (Beda), *The Ecclesiastical History of the English Nation*, London: Dent, 1910.

Being Human: A Christian Understanding of Personhood Illustrated with reference to Power, Money, Sex and Time, London: Church House Publishing, 2003.

Blenkinsopp, Joseph, *Wisdom and Law in the Old Testament*, Oxford: Oxford University Press, 1983.

Borgen, Peder, *Early Christianity and Hellenistic Judaism*, Edinburgh: T. and T. Clark, 1996.

Bornkamm, Heinrich, *Luther in Mid-Career 1521–30*, trans. E. T. Bachmann, Philadelphia: Fortress Press, 1983.

Boswell, John, *The Marriage of Likeness*, London: HarperCollins, 1995.

Brenner, Athalya, *The Israelite Woman*, Sheffield: JSOT Press, 1985.

Briant, Keith, *Marie Stopes*, London: Hogarth, 1962.

Bronner, Leila, *From Eve to Esther*, Louisville, Ky: Westminster John Knox Press, 1994.

Brooke, R. and C., *Popular Religion in the Middle Ages*, London: Thames and Hudson, 1984.

Brown, Peter, *Augustine of Hippo*, London: Faber and Faber, rev. edn, 2000.

Brown, Peter, *The Body and Society*, London: Faber and Faber, 1989.

Brundage, J. A., *Law, Sex and Christian Society in Medieval Europe*, Chicago: University of Chicago Press, 1987.

Byrne, D. L. P., *The Illustrations to the Early Manuscripts of Jean Corbechon's French translation of Bartholemaeus Anglicus' "De Proprietatibus Rerum" 1372–c. 1420*, Cambridge University PhD thesis, 1981.

Calvin, J., *Institutes of the Christian Religion*, ed. J. T. Mitchell, trans. F. L. Battles, 2 vols, London: SCM Press, 1961.

Cannon, J. A. (ed.), *Oxford Companion to British History*, Oxford: Oxford University Press, 1997.

Canon Law of the Church of England (The), London: SPCK, 1947.

Canons of the Church of England (The), 6th edn, London: Church House Publishing, 2000.

Chadwick, H., *Augustine*, Oxford: Oxford University Press, 1986.

Chadwick, H., *The Early Church*, London: Penguin, 1987.

Charlesworth, J. H. (ed.), *The Old Testament Pseudepigrapha*, London: Darton, Longman and Todd, vol. 1, 1983.

Christ the Educator, trans. S. P. Wood, Washington, DC: Catholic University of America Press, 1953.

Chubb, Mary, *City in the Sand*, London: Libri, 1999.

Clement of Alexandria, *Stomateis I–III* (Miscellanies), trans. J. Ferguson, Washington, DC: Catholic University of America Press, 1991.

Clements, R., E., *Deuteronomy*, Sheffield: JSOT Press, 1989.

Code of Canon Law, Latin-English edn, Washington DC: Canon Law Society of America, 1983.

Coggins, R., *Introducing the Old Testament*, Oxford: Oxford University Press, 1990.

Cohn-Sherbok, Dan, *The Jewish Heritage*, Oxford: Blackwell, 1988.

Coleman, P. E., *Christian Attitudes to Homosexuality*, London: SPCK, 1980.

Coleman, P. E., *Gay Christians*, London: SCM Press, 1989.

Collins, R. F., *First Corinthians*, Collegeville, Min: The Liturgical Press, 1999.

Common Worship: Marriage, London: Church House Publishing, 2001.

Cumming, G. J., *A History of Anglican Liturgy*, 2nd edn, London: Macmillan, 1982.

Dalrymple, William, *From the Holy Mountain*, London: HarperCollins, 1997.

Daube, David, *Studies in Biblical Law*, Cambridge: Cambridge University Press, 1947.

Davies, Norman, *Europe*, London: Pimlico, 1996.

Davies, Norman, *The Isles*, London: Macmillan, 1999.

De Waal, F., *Peacemaking Among Primates*, Cambridge, Ma: Harvard University Press, 1989.

Dixson, A. F., *Primate Sexuality*, Oxford: Oxford University Press, 1998.

Dunn, J. D. G., *The Parting of the Ways*, London: SCM Press, 1991.

Early Christian Fathers, vol. 1 of The Library of Christian Classics, London: SCM Press, 1953.

Edwards, David, *Christian England*, London: Collins, 1981–4.

Euripides, *Medea*.

Ferguson, E., *Backgrounds of Early Christianity*, Grand Rapids, Mi: Eerdmans, 1987.

Fiorenza, E. S., *In Memory of Her*, London: SCM Press, 1983.

First and Second Prayer Books of Edward the Sixth (The), London: Dent, 1910 and reprints.

Fletcher, Richard A., *The Conversion of Europe*, London: HarperCollins, 1997.

Fowler, W. W., *Social Life at Rome*, London: Macmillan, 1908.

Freeman, Charles, *Egypt, Greece and Rome: Civilizations of the Ancient Mediterranean*, Oxford: Oxford University Press, 1996.

Frend, W. H. C., *A New Eusebius*, London: SPCK, 1987.

Gardner, J. F., *Women in Roman Law and Society*, London: Croom Helm, 1986.

Gies, F. and J., *Marriage and the Family in the Middle Ages*, New York: Harper and Row, 1989.

Gill, Robin, *A Textbook of Christian Ethics*, 2nd edn, Edinburgh: T. and T. Clark, 1995.

Gillis, J. R., *For Better, For Worse: British Marriages from 1600 to the Present*, Oxford: Oxford University Press, 1985.

Harvey, A. E., *Companion to the New Testament*, Oxford: Oxford University Press, 1970.

Hays, R. B., *First Corinthians*, Louisville, Ky: John Knox Press, 1997.

Hays, R. B., *The Moral Vision of the New Testament*, Edinburgh: T. and T. Clark, 1997.

Hennecke, E., *The New Testament Apocrypha*, London: Lutterworth Press, vol. 1, 1963.

Hennecke, E., *New Testament Apocrypha*, London: Lutterworth Press, vol. 2, 1965.

Herrin, Judith, 'In Search of Byzantine Women: Three Avenues of Approach', in *Images of Women in Antiquity*, ed. A. Cameron and A. Kuhrt, London: Croom Helm, 1983.

Highet, Gilbert, *Poets in a Landscape*, London: Hamish Hamilton, 1957.

Hill, Mark, *Ecclesiastical Law*, 2nd edn, Oxford: Oxford University Press, 2001.

Homer, *Iliad*, trans. E. V. Rieu, Harmondsworth: Penguin, 1950.

Honourable Estate (An), London: Church House Publishing, 1988.

Hooker, M., *Commentary on the Gospel according to St Mark*, London: A. and C. Black, 1991.

Horrell, D. G., *The Social Ethos of the Corinthian Correspondence*, Edinburgh: T. and T. Clark, 1996.

Hunter, D. G. (ed.), *Marriage in the Early Church*, Minneapolis: Fortress Press, 1992.

Issues in Human Sexuality, London: Church House Publishing, 1991.

James Moffatt, *The First Epistle of Paul to the Corinthians*, London: Hodder and Stoughton, 1938.

Jerome Biblical Commentary (The), London: Chapman, 1968.

Josephus, F., *Antiquities of the Jews*, trans. W. Whiston, 1737 and later editions.

Justinian, *The Institutes*, trans. J. A. C. Thomas, Cape Town: Juta, 1975.

Kelly, J. N. D., *The Oxford Dictionary of Popes*, Oxford: Oxford University Press, 1986.

Kitto, H. D. F., *The Greeks*, London: Penguin, 1991.

Kolbert, C. F., Introduction to *The Digest of Roman Law*, Harmondsworth: Penguin, 1979.

Lacey, R. and Danziger, D., *The Year 1000*, London: Little, Brown, 1999.

Lake, Stephen, *Marriage, a Practical Guide*, London: Church House Publishing, 2000.

Lane Fox, Robin, *Pagans and Christians*, New York: Viking, 1986.

Langford, Michael J., *A Liberal Theology for the Twenty-First Century: A Passion for Reason*, Aldershot: Ashgate, 2001.

Lefkowitz, Mary R., 'Influential Women' in *Images of Women in Antiquity*, ed. A. Cameron and A. Kuhrt, London: Croom Helm, 1983.

Lewis, C. S., *The Allegory of Love*, London: Oxford University Press, 1936.

Luther, M., *A Commentary on the Sixth Commandment*, in *Ethics*, ed. Peter Singer, Oxford: Oxford University Press, 1994.

Luther, M., *Letters of Spiritual Counsel*, ed. and trans. T. G. Tappert, London: SCM Press, 1955.

Luther, M., *Table Talk*, ed. W. Hazlitt, London: Bohn, 1857.

MacCulloch, Diarmaid, *Groundwork of Christian History*, London: Epworth Press, 1987.

MacCulloch, Diarmaid, *Thomas Cranmer*, New Haven: Yale University Press, 1966.

McNutt, Paula, *Reconstructing the Society of Ancient Israel*, Louisville, Ky: Westminster John Knox Press, 1999.

Malina, Bruce J., *The New Testament World*, London: SCM Press, 1983.

Marriage and the Church's Task, The report of the General Synod Marriage Commission, London: Church Information Office, 1978.

Marriage, Divorce and the Church, A report of a Commission appointed by the Archbishop of Canterbury to prepare a statement on the Christian Doctrine of Marriage, London: SPCK, 1971.

Meeks, Wayne, *The Moral World of the First Christians*, London: SPCK, 1987.

Methodist Worship Book, Peterborough: Methodist Publishing House, 1999.

Metsudah Chamash/Rashi (The), trans. Rabbi Avrohom Davis, Hoboken, NJ: rev. edn, vol. 1, 1993.

Metzger, Bruce, *An Introduction to the Apocrypha*, New York: Oxford University Press, 1977.

Midrash Rabbah. Genesis, ed. H. Freedman and M. Simon, London: Soncino Press, 1939.

Midrash Rabbah. Leviticus, ed. H. Freedman and M. Simon, London: Soncino Press, 1939.

Mishnah (The), trans. H. Danby, Oxford: Oxford University Press, 1933.

Moberly, Walter, 'The Use of Scripture in Contemporary Debate about Homosexuality', *Theology* August 2000.

Moorman, J. R. H., *Church Life in England in the Thirteenth Century*, Cambridge: Cambridge University Press, 1945.

Morris, Benny, *Righteous Victims*, London: John Murray, 2000.

Moschus, John, *The Spiritual Meadow (Pratum Spirituale)*, trans. J. Wortley, Kalamazoo, Mi: Cistercian Publications, 1992.

Musonius Rufus, in Yale Classsical Studies, vol. 10, ed. A. R. Bellinger, trans. (from the Greek) Cora E. Lutz, New Haven: Yale University Press, 1947.

Neusner, J., *Judaism in the Beginning of Christianity*, London: SPCK, 1984.

New Jerusalem Bible (The), ed. Henry Wansbrough, London: Darton, Longman and Todd, 1985.

Official Report of the Lambeth Conference 1998 (The), Harrisburg, Pen: Morehouse Publishing, 1999.

Orr, W. F. and Walther, J. A., *1 Corinthians*, New York: Doubleday, 1976.

Oxford Annotated Bible (The), ed. H. G. May and B. M. Metzger, New York: Oxford University Press, 1994.

Oxford Bible Commentary (The), ed. J. Barton and J. Muddiman, Oxford: Oxford University Press, 2001.

Oxford History of the Classical World: Greece and the Hellenistic World (The), ed. J. Boardman, J. Griffin, O. Murray, Oxford: Oxford University Press, 1988.

Oxford History of the Classical World: The Roman World (The), ed. J. Boardman, Oxford: Oxford University Press, 1988.

Paoli, U. E., *Rome, its People, Life and Customs*, trans. R. D. Macnaghten, London: Longman, 1963.

Patrick, Dale, *Old Testament Law*, London: SCM Press, 1986.

Phillips, A., *Ancient Israel's Criminal Law*, Oxford: Blackwell, 1970.

Plato, *Symposium, Republic, Laws*.

Prichard, J. B. (ed.), *The Ancient Near East Anthology*, Princeton: Princeton University Press, vol. 1, 1958, vol. 2, 1975.

Procopius of Caesarea, *The Secret History*, trans. G. A. Williamson, London: Folio Society, 1990.

Putting Asunder, London: SPCK, 1966. A report appointed by the Archbishop of Canterbury in January, 1964.

Report of the Lambeth Conference 1978 (The), London: Church Information Office, 1978.

Reynolds, P. L., *Marriage in the Western Church*, Leiden: Brill, 1994.

Robinson, John A., *Christian Freedom in Permissive Society*, London: SCM Press, 1970.

Rousselle, Aline, *Porneia*, trans. F. Pheasant, Oxford: Blackwell, 1988.

Safrai, S., and Stern, M. (eds), *The Jewish People in the First Century*, Amsterdam: Van Gorcum, vol. 2, 1976.

Saggs, H. W. F. *Civilization before Greece and Rome*, London: Batsford, 1989.

Sanders, E. P., *Jesus and Judaism*, London: SCM Press, 1985.

Sanders, E. P., *Jewish Law from Jesus to Mishnah*, London: SCM Press, 1990.

Schillebeeckx, E., *Marriage: Human Reality and Saving Ministry*, London: Sheed and Ward, 1965.

Septuagint Version of the Old Testament (The), Greek and English, London: Bagster and Sons, 1906.

Sex and Morality, London: SCM Press, 1966.

Soards, Marion L., *Scripture and Homosexuality*, Louisville, Ky: Westminster John Knox Press, 1995.

Some Issues in Human Sexuality: A Guide to Debate, London: Church House Publishing, 2003.

Stevenson, K. W., *Nuptial Blessings*, London: SPCK, 1982.

Stone, L., *The Family, Sex and Marriage 1500–1800*, London: Penguin, 1979.

Taylor, Jeremy, *Whole Works*, ed. R. Heber, London, vol. 5, 1828.

Tertullian, *Treatises on Marriage and Remarriage*, trans. W. P. Le Saint, London: Longmans, Green; Westminster, Md: Newman Press, 1951.

Thatcher, Adrian, *Marriage and Modernity*, Sheffield: Sheffield Academic Press, 1999.

Theissen, G., *A Theory of Primitive Christian Religion*, London: SCM Press, 1999.

Theological Dictionary of the New Testament, ed. G. Friedrich, Grand Rapids, Mi: Eerdmans, vol. 6, 1968.

Theological Dictionary of the Old Testament, ed. G. J. Botterweck and H. Ringgren, rev. edn, Grand Rapids, Mi: Eerdmanns, vol. 1, 1977.

Thiessen, G., *A Theory of Primitive Christian Religion*, London: SCM Press, 1999.

Tolkien, J. R. R. (ed.), *Sir Gawain and the Green Knight*, rev. edn, N. Davies and E. V. Gordon, Oxford: Clarendon Press, 1967.

Tomson, J., *Paul and the Jewish Law*, Minneapolis: Fortress Press, 1990.

Towards a Quaker View of Sex, London: Friends Home Service Committee, 1963.

Truth shall Make you Free: The Lambeth Conference 1988 (The), London: Church House Publishing, 1988.

Tyndale, William, *Old Testament*, modern-spelling edn, ed. D. Daniell, New Haven: Yale University Press, 1992.

Vermes, Geza, *An Introduction to the Complete Dead Sea Scrolls*, London: SCM Press, 1999.

Vermes, Geza, *The Complete Dead Sea Scrolls in English*, London: Penguin, 1998.
von Rad, G., *Genesis*, London: SCM Press, 1972.

Walker, Susan, 'Women and Housing in Classical Greece' in *Images of Women in Antiquity*, ed. A. Cameron and A. Kuhrt, London: Croom Helm, 1983.
Watterson, Barbara, *Women in Ancient Egypt*, Stroud: Alan Sutton, 1994.
Weir, Alison, *Eleanor of Aquitaine*, London: Jonathan Cape, 1999.
Wendel, F., *Calvin*, London: Collins, 1963.
West, Angela, in *Feminist Theology: A Reader*, ed. Ann Loades, London: SPCK, 1990.
Williams, Rowan, 'Fobidden Fruit' in *Intimate Affairs*, ed. M. Percy, London: Darton, Longman and Todd, 1997.

Ziesler, John A., *Pauline Christianity*, Oxford: Oxford University Press, 1983.

Index of Names

Index of Subjects